THE ART OF INTELLIGENCE

Security and Professional Intelligence Education Series (SPIES)

Series Editor: Jan Goldman

In this post–September 11, 2001, era there has been rapid growth in the number of professional intelligence training and educational programs across the United States and abroad. Colleges and universities, as well as high schools, are developing programs and courses in homeland security, intelligence analysis, and law enforcement, in support of national security.

The Security and Professional Intelligence Education Series (SPIES) was first designed for individuals studying for careers in intelligence and to help improve the skills of those already in the profession; however, it was also developed to educate the public in how intelligence work is conducted and should be conducted in this important and vital profession.

1. *Communicating with Intelligence: Writing and Briefing in the Intelligence and National Security Communities*, by James S. Major. 2008.
2. *A Spy's Résumé: Confessions of a Maverick Intelligence Professional and Misadventure Capitalist*, by Marc Anthony Viola. 2008.
3. *An Introduction to Intelligence Research and Analysis*, by Jerome Clauser, revised and edited by Jan Goldman. 2008.
4. *Writing Classified and Unclassified Papers for National Security*, by James S. Major. 2009.
5. *Strategic Intelligence: A Handbook for Practitioners, Managers, and Users*, revised edition by Don McDowell. 2009.
6. *Partly Cloudy: Ethics in War, Espionage, Covert Action, and Interrogation*, by David L. Perry. 2009.
7. *Tokyo Rose/An American Patriot: A Dual Biography*, by Frederick P. Close. 2010.
8. *Ethics of Spying: A Reader for the Intelligence Professional*, edited by Jan Goldman. 2006.
9. *Ethics of Spying: A Reader for the Intelligence Professional*, Volume 2, edited by Jan Goldman. 2010.
10. *A Woman's War: The Professional and Personal Journey of the Navy's First African American Female Intelligence Officer*, by Gail Harris. 2010.
11. *Handbook of Scientific Methods of Inquiry for Intelligence Analysis*, by Hank Prunckun. 2010.
12. *Handbook of Warning Intelligence: Assessing the Threat to National Security*, by Cynthia Grabo. 2010.
13. *Keeping U.S. Intelligence Effective: The Need for a Revolution in Intelligence Affairs*, by William J. Lahneman. 2011.
14. *Words of Intelligence: An Intelligence Professional's Lexicon for Domestic and Foreign Threats, Second Edition*, by Jan Goldman. 2011.
15. *Counterintelligence Theory and Practice*, by Hank Prunckun. 2012.
16. *Balancing Liberty and Security: An Ethical Study of U.S. Foreign Intelligence Surveillance, 2001–2009*, by Michelle Louise Atkin. 2013.
17. *The Art of Intelligence: Simulations, Exercises, and Games*, edited by William J. Lahneman and Rubén Arcos. 2014.
18. *Communicating with Intelligence: Writing and Briefing in National Security*, by James S. Major. 2014.
19. *Scientific Methods of Inquiry for Intelligence Analysis, Second Edition*, by Hank Prunckun. 2014.
20. *Quantitative Intelligence Analysis: Applied Analytic Models, Simulations and Games*, by Edward Waltz. 2014.
21. *The Handbook of Warning Intelligence: Assessing the Threat to National Security—The Complete Declassified Edition*, by Cynthia Grabo, 2015.
22. *Intelligence and Information Policy for National Security: Key Terms and Concepts*, by Jan Goldman and Susan Maret
23. *Handbook of European Intelligence Cultures*, edited by Bob de Graaff and James M. Nyce, with Chelsea Locke
24. *Partly Cloudy: Ethics in War, Espionage, Covert Action, and Interrogation, Second Edition*, by David L. Perry
25. *Humanitarian Intelligence: A Practitioner's Guide to Crisis Analysis and Project Design*, by Andrej Zwitter
26. *Shattered Illusions: KGB Cold War Espionage in Canada*, by Donald G. Mahar
27. *Intelligence Engineering: Operating Beyond the Conventional*, by Adam D. M. Svendsen
28. *Reasoning for Intelligence Analysts: A Multidimensional Approach of Traits, Techniques, and Targets*, by Noel Hendrickson
29. *Counterintelligence Theory and Practice, Second edition*, by Hank Prunckun
30. *Methods of Inquiry for Intelligence Analysis, Third Edition* by Hank Prunckun
31. *The Art of Intelligence: More Simulations, Exercises, and Games*, edited by Rubén Arcos and William J. Lahneman

To view the books on our website, please visit
https://rowman.com/Action/SERIES/RL/SPIES
or scan the QR code.

THE ART OF INTELLIGENCE

MORE SIMULATIONS, EXERCISES, AND GAMES

EDITED BY

RUBÉN ARCOS
REY JUAN CARLOS UNIVERSITY

WILLIAM J. LAHNEMAN
EMBRY-RIDDLE AERONAUTICAL UNIVERSITY

ROWMAN & LITTLEFIELD
Lanham • Boulder • New York • London

Executive Editor: Traci Crowell
Assistant Editor: Deni Remsberg
Senior Marketing Manager: Karin Cholak

Credits and acknowledgments for material borrowed from other sources, and reproduced with permission, appear on the appropriate page within the text.

Published by Rowman & Littlefield
An imprint of The Rowman & Littlefield Publishing Group, Inc.
4501 Forbes Boulevard, Suite 200, Lanham, Maryland 20706
www.rowman.com
6 Tinworth Street, London SE11 5AL, United Kingdom

British Library Cataloguing in Publication Information Available

Library of Congress Cataloging-in-Publication Data
Names: Arcos Martín, Rubén, editor of compilation. | Lahneman, William J., 1952–, editor of compilation.
Title: The art of intelligence : more simulations, exercises, and games / edited by Rubén Arcos, Rey Juan Carlos University, William J. Lahneman, Embry-Riddle Aeronautical University.
Description: Lanham : ROWMAN & LITTLEFIELD, [2019] | Series: Security and Professional Intelligence Education series ; 31 | "This book is a follow-on work to The Art of Intelligence: Simulations, Exercises, and Games published in March 2014"—Introduction. | Includes bibliographical references.
Identifiers: LCCN 2019003655 (print) | LCCN 2019009133 (ebook) | ISBN 9781538123478 (electronic) | ISBN 9781538123454 (cloth : alk. paper) | ISBN 9781538123461 (paper : alk. paper)
Subjects: LCSH: Intelligence service. | Simulation games.
Classification: LCC JK468.I6 (ebook) | LCC JK468.I6 A87 2019 (print) | DDC 327.12076—dc23
LC record available at https://lccn.loc.gov/2019003655

♾™ The paper used in this publication meets the minimum requirements of American National Standard for Information Sciences—Permanence of Paper for Printed Library Materials, ANSI/NISO Z39.48–1992.

Printed in the United States of America

Contents

Foreword

The international intelligence community has been conducting national security exercises and simulations for many years. Wargaming is considered a vital element to scenario planning. Regardless of your mode for engagement, the goal is to construct alternative futures and to take them wherever they lead. These types of activities provide scenarios as the starting point for a coherent strategy in dealing with the possibility of the event, action, or decision if and when it happens. In the end, gaming, exercises, and simulations provide an opportunity to shape planning, validate capabilities, and highlight vulnerabilities.

The history of these types of activities, conducted not for recreational purposes but for national security, can be traced to the Polish town of Wroclaw, then known as Breslau, Prussia, when in 1811 Baron von Reisswitz invented a game that used a table model of real terrain with wooden blocks to represent military units. Since the terrorist attacks of September 11, 2001, local, state, and federal officials have used these activities to prepare for the previously unimaginable. In 2014 the first volume appeared in the Security Professional Intelligence Education Series. It was widely successful, and the next year we held the International Conference on Exercises, Gaming, and Simulations for Intelligence and National Security in Washington, DC.[1] The conference attendees included people from several countries representing government, industry, and academic institutions.

I hope you enjoy this book, whether you are interested in geopolitical conflict, international relations, intelligence operations, wargaming, or "just plain fascinated" with this subject. Nevertheless, this publication is an essential addition to the series by providing the tools that may allow us to anticipate and prepare for the future.

Dr. Jan Goldman
Founding Editor
Security Professional Intelligence Education Series (SPIES)
Rowman and Littlefield Publishing

Note

[1] The "International Conference on Exercises, Gaming, and Simulations for Intelligence and National Security" was held on March 24–25, 2015, at Georgetown University. A copy of the program can be found at https://paxsims.files.wordpress.com/2015/04/draft-program15-2.pdf.

Acknowledgments

We extend our grateful appreciation to the many individuals whose efforts contributed to making this second volume of intelligence simulations, exercises, and games a reality. Many thanks are due to our contributing authors, a group composed of an international cast of intelligence practitioners and scholars. We express special gratitude to our returning contributing authors who made the original 2014 volume possible and have now shared their new exercises, simulations, and games. We wish particularly to recognize, thank, and welcome our new contributors, whose work has added new dimensions to the growing body of experiential learning tools available for training and educating new critical thinkers in the nuances and pitfalls of intelligence analysis.

We wish to once again extend a special thank you to Jan Goldman, editor of the Security and Professional Intelligence Education Series (SPIES), for his continued support and enthusiasm for our project. We also wish to express our gratitude and thanks to Traci Crowell, our executive editor; Mary Malley, our assistant editor; and Charlotte Gosnell, our editorial assistant at Rowman and Littlefield, as well as Savitha Jayakumar, our project manager, for their dedicated efforts and patient guidance as we prepared the volume for publication.

We wish to specially acknowledge the scholars who gave their valuable time to provide their expert reviews of the early draft of the volume: Jan Goldman, Southern New Hampshire University; Loch Kingsford Johnson, University of Georgia; Gordon R. Middleton, Patrick Henry College; Johan Modee, Malmo University; and Damien Van Puyvelde, University of Glasgow. Your valuable insights greatly improved the final draft.

We are extremely grateful to the readers of our first volume who incorporated our various simulations, exercise, and games into their courses. Your enthusiastic support has contributed to the continuing expansion of experiential learning techniques in intelligence education.

The views contained in this volume are those of the respective authors alone. Any other persons thanked above are not responsible for its content and should not be blamed for any defects that might be present. The views expressed in this volume do not represent the views, attitudes, or policies of the authors' parent institutions, or any agency or component of their respective national governments.

Introduction

Rubén Arcos and William J. Lahneman

This book is a follow-on work to *The Art of Intelligence: Simulations, Exercises, and Games* published in March 2014. This book contains more exercises, games, and simulations to enhance the learning experience for students in intelligence courses. It presents 13 new and original simulations and games covering many aspects of the intelligence profession: intelligence analysis and production, strategic foresight, deception, war gaming techniques, competitive intelligence, and more. Additionally, chapter 1 includes new research on the educational value of experiential learning that provides a solid background for instructors to use these interactive learning devices.

Similar to the earlier book, we believe this will be a valuable resource for instructors and students from the fields of intelligence studies, homeland security, international relations, international business, and any field that requires analyzing information for decision-making support. The book has an international focus in terms of both its contributing authors and its intended audience: teachers of undergraduate and graduate courses in intelligence, intelligence analysis, business intelligence, and various kinds of national security policy courses. Courses in these subjects are taught not only at universities but also at government facilities and business enterprises, wherever the need for training in analytic principles and tradecraft is required.

Intelligence simulations, games, and exercises are presented in ready-to-run formats that will minimize the time needed for instructor preparation.

The book includes a companion website https://textbooks.rowman.com/art-of-intelligence-2 with the necessary materials for running the simulations, exercises, and games.

1

Experiencing the Art of Intelligence

Using Simulations/Gaming for Teaching Intelligence and Developing Analysis and Production Skills

William J. Lahneman and Rubén Arcos

This chapter[1] discusses the use of simulations, exercises, and games to enhance student learning in intelligence courses at universities to prepare students for careers in intelligence organizations and every profession that prizes critical thinking and writing capabilities. Our goal is to expand the number of instructors who use interactive learning methods in their courses. We are enthusiastic supporters of these learning activities because we believe that they enhance student learning of difficult concepts that are critically important for every intelligence analyst to understand and that lectures alone often fail to instill.

We have used simulations, exercises, and games in our undergraduate and graduate intelligence courses for over a decade in both Spain and the United States. Along the way, we became aware that we are members of a larger community of scholars around the world who design and use active learning techniques in their courses. In 2014, we published *The Art of Intelligence: Simulations, Exercises, and Games*, an edited volume of ready-to-run class-room simulations with submissions from scholars and practitioners from the United States, Spain, Portugal, Romania, Sweden, and the UK. These educators had independently constructed simulations, exercises, and games to enhance their students' learning of intelligence collection, analysis, and production processes.

The chapter begins by describing simulations and locates them within the larger category of active (or experiential) learning methodologies. Next it surveys the literature on simulations, exercises, and games, highlighting the strong empirical evidence that their use improves student learning. The chapter then addresses reasons why these techniques are essential teaching elements in today's classrooms. This section draws upon the nature of human cognition, social psychology, and studies about current trends in student expectations from their teachers.

Before starting to explore the value of simulations, exercises, and games for improving student learning, it is important to address a common misconception. These active learning techniques almost never teach students *exactly how* to perform competently some important intelligence skill, although some four-month term, semester or yearlong exercises can achieve such a result. Rather, the shorter simulations provide a shorthand method to expose students to important major intelligence concepts and give them firsthand opportunities to test known concepts and reflect upon and reformulate ideas based on the feedback provided by concrete experience (Kolb 1984, 21–22). These experiences give them a visceral and therefore lifelong appreciation of important intelligence knowledge, skills, and abilities.

We believe that active learning techniques are so important for intelligence education largely because intelligence is both an art and a science, notwithstanding views that locate it exclusively in one area or the other. Simulations, exercises, and games help primarily with the "art" aspects of intelligence analysis by requiring students to experience and grapple with some of the subtler aspects of the intelligence process in a way that lectures cannot accomplish. Active learning also is fun when properly conducted, which casts a positive aura over the learning experience, and it has been found to enhance learning.

Overview of Interactive Learning

Classroom simulations, exercises, and games that employ small groups of students acting as teams to carry out some process or to play the role of an actor of some kind are a form of *interactive learning*. Interactive learning, in turn, is a subset of *active or experiential learning*. Other examples of experiential learning are any assignments that require students to take an active role in their learning process, such as a requirement for students to maintain reflective journals about what they have learned; group activities during a lecture; student-developed examination questions; student knowledge surveys at beginning and end of a course; and frequent writing assignments to overcome procrastination (Nilson 2013, x–xv). The common thread among these activities is that they require students to perform some activity that causes them to experience the subtleties involved in some aspect of the intelligence profession. The underlying assumption is that students learn some things better by doing something (or approximating doing something) than by listening to a teacher explain it. Although the terms are not used, examples of "inactive" or "passive" learning processes would be listening to lectures, watching videos, and writing assignments that only require description. Inactive learning methods are essential to any course of instruction that requires students to learn specific content, which includes all university courses to one degree or another. Accordingly, lectures will remain an essential feature of post-secondary education.

The types of simulations, exercises, and games used in intelligence courses are *inquiry-based interactive learning processes*. As the name implies, these classroom activities task students with actively participating with their peers to discover the answer to some question. When the type of inquiry involves attempting to solve a problem, the process is also known as "problem-based learning (PBL)." Usually the questions posed deal with "fuzzy problems," meaning that there is no single correct answer but rather a range of possibilities that might be "true." More formally,

> A "fuzzy" problem is embedded in a realistic, troublesome situation and complex enough to defy a clearly correct solution. While multiple solutions exist and some may be better than others, they all exact trade-offs—maximizing some values while undermining others—and present risk and uncertainty. Experts confront and attempt to solve these kinds of problems, which require expert skills and experience to develop feasible, cost-effective alternative solutions and to project all the likely, foreseeable consequences of choosing one over the others.
>
> (Nilson 2013, 48)

Intelligence analysts deal with fuzzy problems every day. Any technique that helps them learn how to deal with such problems should be employed in the classroom. Lecturing, class discussions, reading assignments, professional/personal stories, and historical case studies on intelligence and intelligence analysis undoubtedly constitute a set of useful teaching methods and techniques for the education of future intelligence professionals. Nevertheless, most disciplines and academic fields *additionally* employ laboratories, simulations, internships, and practical exercises when the learning objective is to develop the required skills to successfully practice a professional discipline. Are there reasonable concerns that can justify not approaching education and training in intelligence analysis in the same way other professions and disciplines produce their future practitioners?

Virtually all science courses either incorporate laboratory sessions or require related lab courses so that students get the opportunity to conduct experiments that reinforce learning by requiring them to demonstrate concepts taught in lectures. Engineering courses follow the same pattern and often add the further step of a group project that designs and builds some artifact requiring the use of concepts taught in class. Nursing and medical students are required to spend time in affiliated hospitals, clinics, and other healthcare venues to reinforce what they learn in class and demonstrate competence at the core activities of their future professions. Fine arts majors make artistic artifacts (paintings, sculptures, jewelry, etc.) as part of their educational programs, and dramatic arts majors practice what they have been taught in class by participating in musical, dance, theater, and other live performances, by creating videos, and through other appropriate manifestations of their future professions. Kinesiology majors participate in athletics. The list goes on. In fact, many US intelligence agencies utilize simulations to train and educate their workforce.

Some areas of the liberal arts and social sciences appear to be among the relatively few academic disciplines that do not require frequent, mandatory active learning exercises as part of their core curricula. One exception is the emphasis that many programs give to student internships. While these are a form of active learning, they often do not correlate highly or systematically with desired learning objectives.

Being exposed to the challenge of solving a problem by using the defining knowledge and competences of a given discipline challenges the student/trainee in ways that inactive learning techniques alone cannot achieve. The use of active learning techniques challenges prospective intelligence professionals to learn by exercising previously learned concepts, frameworks, and tools in simulated "real-world" scenarios, leading them to gradually become more technically skillful and effective. By using active learning techniques, instructors put the focus on "how to do," while passive learning techniques stress "what is."

The design of effective simulations and games to provide education and develop specific abilities and skills in intelligence studies and intelligence analysis programs requires theoretical knowledge on these methods, their strengths and problems as well as careful planning and structure. Fortunately, there is an extensive body of literature in this area.

Experiential/Active Learning Methods

Detailed Description

Experiential education has been described as "a complex relational process that involves balancing attention to the learner and to the subject matter while also balancing reflection on the deep meaning of ideas with the skill of applying them" (Kolb et al. 2014, 229). By developing their Educator Role Profile model and applying it to a sample of educators (n = 222), Kolb et al. reported that educators tend, to a certain degree, "to teach the way they learn," which means that those educators with concrete learning styles tend to employ more learner-centered (active learning) methods and prefer a facilitator role, while those educators with abstract learning styles tend to use more subject-centered techniques and prefer to adopt the expert and evaluator roles (Kolb et al. 2014, 229). The experiential learning model developed by Kolb (1973) conceives of learning as a four-step cycle process where (1) immediate concrete experience constitutes the basis for (2) observation and reflection that are (3) used by the individual "to build an idea, generalization, or "theory" from which new implications for action can be deduced"; and (4) the implications and hypothesis then serve as orientation guides in acting to generate new experiences (Kolb 1973, 652–673; Kolb and Fry 1975, 33–57; Kolb 1981, 232–255; Kolb 1984).

From this experiential perspective, learning is defined as "the process whereby knowledge is created through the transformation of experience" (Kolb 1984, 38). The Educator Profile Role model describes four roles that educators can take—facilitator, subject expert, standard-setter/evaluator, and coach (see table 1.1 and figure 1.1)—and the corresponding instructional practices associated with each of those roles.

| TABLE 1.1 | Kolb's Educator Profile Role Model | | | |

Educator Role	Help learners	Goals	Learning style (Nine-style learning cycle) See figure 1.1	Instructional practices
Facilitator	To deal with personal experience and reflect on it	Empathy and understanding of others	Experiencing, imagining, reflecting	Class discussions, personal examples, brainstorming
Subject expert	To organize and connect their reflection to the knowledge base of the subject matter	Analytic and conceptual abilities	Reflecting, analyzing, thinking	Lecturing, reading texts, written assignments
Standard-setter/ evaluator	To master the application of knowledge and skill to meet performance requirements	Problem-solving skills	Thinking, deciding, acting	Laboratories, graded assignments
Coach	To apply knowledge to achieve their goals	Ability to work productively with others	Acting, initiating, experiencing	Role-playing, simulations, field projects

Source: Adapted from Kolb et al. (2014)

Focus on Simulation/Gaming

Simulation/gaming is mainly a learning approach to education and training. It is formed by a diverse set of methodologies and techniques where participants actively engage in the learning process and perform actions as required by the instructors and facilitators of learning. By the means of having direct experiences previously designed by educators/trainers or researchers, and posteriorly reflecting on those experiences, participants acquire knowledge and develop hard and soft skills.

Additionally, from a research viewpoint, simulation is a research technique used by social and behavioral scientists that builds an operating model (not necessarily of normative nature) representing, either physically or symbolically, aspects of social or psychological processes (Dawson 1962, 1–15).

Over 55 years ago, Richard Dawson summarized these key functions of simulations: (1) teaching students about the behavior of complex social systems; (2) training participants on how to play different operating roles in the real system by playing comparable roles in simulated models, and thus, getting a practical feeling of what they would experience in the real situation and potential outcomes derived from their actions; and (3) to experiment and explore phenomena

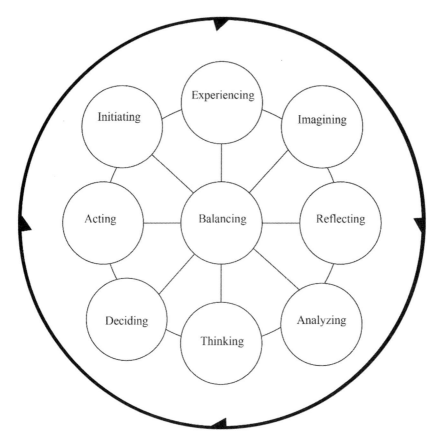

FIGURE 1.1 Kolb's Nine-Style Experiential Learning Cycle and Matching Educator Roles

Source: Adapted from Kolb et al. (2014)

and to investigate about the behavior of individual and group processes (Dawson 1962, 1–15).

From an educational perspective, David Crookall and Warren Thorngate (2008) identify three major categories of simulation/gaming depending on their purpose and the educator's assumptions about how learning works: (1) knowledge-to-action; (2) action-to-knowledge; and (3) integrating-action-knowledge. In the first type, simulations are used instrumentally to enable participants to apply their previous knowledge to practical situations. In the action-to-knowledge approach, events are "designed, run, and debriefed primarily to enable or encourage participants to generate understanding, learn new skills, and gain new knowledge from participants' concrete experience" (Dawson 1962, 1–15). The last type seeks to enable participants to "make connections between their actions and the related knowledge" (Dawson 1962, 1–15).

Regarding the terminology associated with the simulation field and the set of different techniques used, the early literature of the field distinguishes between simulations (the general term), gaming, "a particular type of simulation involving the use of human decision-makers in the simulation of a real-life situation which concerns conflicting interests" (Guetzkow 1962, 189), and Monte Carlo techniques. Dawson (1962, 8–12) identifies the following types of simulations:

- Simulations involving human actors: individuals act and interact within the simulated system; includes human machine simulations and gaming.
- Games: including war games, business/management gaming, political/IR gaming.
- Human-machine simulations: interaction between human decision makers and machines occurs in the simulation.
- Pure-machine simulations: machines are the sole actors involved.
- Real-time simulations: simulation in which the time length of actions in the simulated systems equals the length of the real system simulated.
- Monte Carlo method: data of probabilistic nature is introduced into a model.

Assessing the Effectiveness of Active Learning

Like other academic fields, the field of intelligence and intelligence studies needs to define a set of goals or objectives for its educational processes. Bloom's Taxonomy of Educational Objectives (1956) and subsequent revisions to this work provide a general framework to "curriculum builders" and teachers/instructors/trainers to (1) help them specify objectives with regard to their field of study or discipline and (2) assist them in planning learning methodologies, techniques, and experiences as well as evaluation tools to meet those objectives. Bloom's taxonomy includes three main parts: the cognitive domain, the affective domain, and the psychomotor domain. *The Handbook I: Cognitive Domain* was published in 1956 and received greater attention than *Handbook II: The Affective Domain* (Krathwohl, Bloom, and Masia, 1964). As Bloom pointed out, their work was not about

> attempting to classify the instructional methods used by teachers, the ways in which teachers relate themselves to students, or the different kinds of instructional materials they use. We are not attempting to classify the particular subject matter or content. What we are classifying is the intended behavior of students—the ways in which individuals are to act, think, or feel as the result of participating in some unit of instruction.
>
> (Bloom 1956, 12)

Accordingly, the cognitive domain includes as major classes those objectives that deal with remembering knowledge and with developing intellectual abilities and skills: comprehension, application, analysis, synthesis, and evaluation. Bloom used as an operational definition of abilities and skills that

> The individual can find appropriate information and techniques in his previous experience to bring to bear on new problems and situations. This requires some analysis or understanding of the new situation; it requires a background of knowledge or methods which can be readily utilized; and it also requires some facility in discerning the appropriate relations between previous experience and the new situation.
>
> (Bloom 1956, 38)

On the other hand, the affective domain includes "objectives which describe changes in interest, attitudes, and values, and the development of appreciations and adequate adjustment" (Bloom 1956, 7).

The academic literature on active learning effectiveness assessment reflects the interest by simulations scholars to justify this teaching approach when faced with the questioning posed by those scholars who support the validity of traditional lectures, discussions, and case studies (Gosen and Washbush 2004, 272). For example, Geithner and Menzel reported that results from their evaluation of "C2," a role-play business simulation game designed for developing project management hard and soft skills, indicate that it "contributed to the development of soft skills and helped to increase knowledge in project management" (Geithner and Menzel 2016, 250–251). Similarly, Ranchhod et al. (2014, 75–90) designed an Educational Value Generation Model (experience generation, conceptual understanding, skills developments, and affective evaluation) to measure the outcomes of Markstrat, a popular marketing management simulation game, as perceived by students. A dated synthesis of findings on this issue maintained that "the available evidence suggests that simulations games are at least as effective as other methods in facilitating subject matter learning and are more effective aids to *retention*" (Bredemeier and Greenblat 1981, 322, emphasis added). Gosen and Washbush, reviewing the scholarship on effectiveness assessment, came to the conclusion that "the empirical research reviewed supports the notion that experiential learning is effective. However, the studies showing these results reflect a long-standing trend of not meeting the highest of research design and measurement standards" (Gosen and Washbush 2004, 270). Nevertheless, other studies hold that even with this problem, "when it comes to assessment (i.e., providing evidence that an activity is achieving its intended goals), the community of simulation gaming is ahead of the curve" (Chin, Dukes, and Gamson 2009, 565).

With regard to the affective domain, Bredemeier and Greenblat found that the impressionistic and testimonial assessment reviewed in their study showed that

> in course evaluations, students frequently mention the simulation-gaming experience as outstanding, report high satisfaction with the course, express appreciation of knowledge gained about simulation-gaming as an instructional technique, and perceive the experience as having stimulated their motivation and interest.
>
> (Bredemeier and Greenblat 1981, 325)

Even agreeing that this testimonial evidence should be questioned as a valid effectiveness assessment technique, they also provide signals on the effectiveness of simulations and games in the affective domain and motivation.

Why Experiential Learning Enhances Student Learning

The literature details two main reasons why active learning methods improve student learning. First, student learning is enhanced if they enjoy the learning process.

In terms of learning content, students are more likely to remember material in which they have made an emotional investment. This is why many teachers try to help students care about what they are learning by using simulations, role playing, journal writing, and relating what students are learning to real world experiences.

(Barkley 2010, 35)

Of course, emotions can be good or bad. Research shows that students learn best when a learning process is positive. "A positive learning climate . . . leads to endorphins in the blood, which in turn give feelings of euphoria and stimulates the frontal lobes" (Barkley 2010, 35). Note that this is a physiological as well as a psychological explanation of why active learning techniques improve student learning.

Second, research shows that it has become increasingly challenging to keep students engaged and interested in the educational process, and active learning techniques help in this regard. "Studies have demonstrated that many graduate and undergraduate students believe that learning was something that was happening to them, and the faculty's job was to make it happen. These learners were not at all intentional, independent, or self-directed" (Nilson 2013, 2). Many younger undergraduate students also were found to display the same attitude. Researchers noted that students assumed little or no responsibility for their own learning, but rather blamed their own poor performance on the poor quality of their instructors.

Furthermore, they admit to having little or no interest in learning, certainly not for learning's sake. They find many of the topics that they are being taught irrelevant. Reinforcing their avoidance of responsibility for their learning is their widespread belief that learning should not require effort. Effort didn't seem necessary in elementary and high school, where many of them received credit just for showing up, so why should learning require so much time and hard work now?

(Nilson 2013, 2)

Another source makes essentially the same observation in more neutral language:

How would you characterize today's college students? Empowered, confident, self-motivated learners? That is not how I would describe mine. The ones in my class are hopeful but generally anxious and tentative. They want all classes to be easy but expect that most will be hard. They wish their major (whatever it might be) did not require math, science, or English courses. A good number will not speak in class until called on. Most like, want, indeed need teachers who tell them exactly what to do. Education is something done unto them. It frequently involves stress, anxiety, and other forms of discomfort.

(Weimer 2002, 23)

The use of active learning, as the name states, can overcome these inherent biases of students toward a passive approach to learning. When viewed through this lens, active learning is still a good technique to use *even if* it does not teach any additional content because it helps students to take responsibility for some portion of their learning process. Acceptance of such responsibility, in turn, helps students to improve their meta-cognition.

Being aware of oneself as a learner and constantly monitoring the effectiveness of one's learning involves metacognition, a term used by cognitive psychologists to describe the "executive function" of the brain. . . . Metacognitive strategies require activity on the part of learners, not for grading purposes, but for the pedagogical purpose of actively monitoring and controlling their own learning processes.

(Barkley 2013, 30–31)

Many experts consider this metacognitive ability to be at the core of what they call critical thinking. How many times have intelligence educators heard intelligence community (IC) managers and analysts state the importance of analysts being able to "think about thinking while they are thinking," that is, questioning how they know what they know and monitoring whether they are falling prey to some cognitive bias that degrades the quality of an analysis as they are performing that analysis.

To the degree that the foregoing description of student attitudes toward post-secondary education has merit, the use of active learning techniques becomes essential if universities are to cultivate self-regulating critical thinkers and lifelong learners.

Debriefing Simulations

It is critically important that instructors conduct a thorough debrief of simulations and exercises. Just because students enjoy them and willingly participate in active learning processes does not mean that learning objectives are obvious to students and that they automatically assimilate them into long-term memory as lifelong lessons. Accordingly, instructors must allow adequate time for meaningful discussions during debriefs.

Conclusion

This introductory chapter has described various types of experiential, or active, learning methods and has surveyed the literature on how and why the use of these methods enhances student learning. Active learning techniques are particularly useful in fields like intelligence education, which aims to produce effective practicing professionals. Simulations, exercises, and games allow students to practice certain aspects of their future profession in basic but extremely informative ways. Instructors can also introduce more complex and advanced exercises in the course curriculum to make learners practice specific skills, like writing finished intelligence products using open source information. They improve students' critical thinking skills by requiring them to exercise these skills in challenging scenarios. In addition, active learning methods are invaluable in helping students to understand subtle concepts such as denial and deception, the need to verify raw intelligence against multiple sources, the inevitability of intelligence gaps and their effects, the legal constraints faced by intelligence organizations in democratic states, and what intelligence ethics means in practice. Lectures expose students to these concepts but are less likely than experiential learning methods to transform them into deeply understood, important lifelong knowledge. The use of active learning techniques also raises student interest in intelligence as a career choice and helps them better appreciate the challenging environment in which they plan to work one day. It is very unlikely that students can learn how to produce an intelligence assessment and understand the difficulties and problems involved in making judgments about the likely or unlikely future developments of current events *only* by reading declassified products or by carefully listening to the instructors' lessons in the classroom. Rather, exposing students to the simulated challenge of how to do and present analyses and assessments lets them experience firsthand what it is like, how they felt while they were doing it, and what the main steps were. It also helps them to reflect on the principal lessons learned and integrate their experience with the lessons and standards given by instructors.

Most fields that are focused on producing practicing professionals incorporate experiential learning methods into their curricula. Intelligence studies programs should not be an exception.

Note

[1] The material in this chapter was previously published in William J. Lahneman and Rubén Arcos (2017), "Experiencing the Art of Intelligence: Using Simulations/Gaming for Teaching Intelligence and Developing Analysis and Production Skills," *Intelligence and National Security*, 32, no. 7, 972–985. At https://www.tandfonline.com/doi/full/10.1080/02684527.2017.132885 1. Reprinted by permission of Taylor and Francis, Ltd.

References

Barkley, Elizabeth F. *Student Engagement Techniques: A Handbook for College Faculty*. San Francisco: Jossey-Bass, 2010.

Bloom, Benjamin S., ed., et al. *Taxonomy of Educational Objectives: The Classification of Educational Goals/Handbook I: The Cognitive Domain*. London: Longmans, Green and Co., 1956.

Bredemeier, Mary E. and Cathy Stein Greenblat. "The Educational Effectiveness of Simulation Games: A Synthesis of Findings." *Simulation & Gaming* 12, no. 3 (1981): 307–332.

Chin, Jeffrey, Richard Dukes, and William Gamson. "Assessment in Simulation and Gaming: A Review of the Last 40 Years." *Simulation & Gaming* 40, no. 4 (2009): 553–568.

Crookall, David and Warren Thorngate. "Editorial: Acting, Knowing, Learning, Simulation, Gaming." *Simulation & Gaming* 40, no. 1 (2009): 8–26.

Dawson, Richard E. "Simulation in the Social Sciences." In *Simulation in Social Science: Readings*, edited by Harold Guetzkow, 1–15. Englewood Cliffs, NJ: Prentice-Hall, 1962.

Geithner, Silke and Daniela Menzel. "Effectiveness of Learning through Experience and Reflection in a Project Management Simulation." *Simulation & Gaming* 47, no. 2 (2016): 228–256.

Gosen, Jerry and John Washbush. "A Review of Scholarship on Assessing Experiential Learning Effectiveness." *Simulation & Gaming* 35, no. 2 (2004): 270–293.

Guetzkow, Harold, ed. *Simulation in Social Science: Readings*. Englewood Cliffs, NJ: Prentice-Hall, 1962.

Kolb, Alice Y., David A. Kolb, Angela Pasarelli, and Garima Sharma. "On Becoming an Experiential Educator: The Educator Role Profile." *Simulation & Gaming* 45, no. 2 (2014): 204–234.

Kolb, David A. *Experiential Learning: Experience as the Source of Learning and Development.* Upper Saddle River, NJ: Prentice-Hall, 1984.

Kolb, David A. "Learning Styles and Disciplinary Differences." In *The Modern American College: Responding to the New Realities of Diverse Students and a Changing Society,* edited by Arthur W. Chickering, 232–255. San Francisco: Jossey-Bass, 1981.

Kolb, David A. "On Management and the Learning Process." Alfred Sloan School of Management Working Paper, No. 652–73. Cambridge: MIT, 1973. Retrieved from https://ia802205.us.archive.org/5/items/onmanagementlear00kolb/onmanage mentlear00kolb.pdf

Kolb, David A. and Ronald Fry. "Toward an Applied Theory of Experiential Learning." In *Theories of Group Processes,* edited by Cary L. Cooper, 33–57. London: Wiley, 1975.

Krathwohl, David R., Benjamin S. Bloom, and Betram B. Masia. *Taxonomy of Educational Objectives: The Classification of Educational Goals/Handbook II: Affective Domain.* New York: David McKay, 1964.

Lahneman, William J. and Rubén Arcos, eds. *The Art of Intelligence: Simulations, Exercises, and Games.* Lanham, MD: Rowman & Littlefield Publishers, 2014.

Nilson, Linda B. *Creating Self-Regulated Learners: Strategies to Strengthen Students' Self-Awareness and Learning Skills.* Sterling, VA: Stylus, 2013.

Ranchhod, Ashok, Călin Gurăub, Euripides Loukisc, and Rohit Trivedi. "Evaluating the Educational Effectiveness of Simulation Games: A Value Generation Model." *Information Sciences* 264, no. 20 (2014): 75–90.

Singleton-Jackson, J. A., D. L. Jackson, and J. Reinhardt. "Students as Consumers of Knowledge: Are They Buying What We're Selling?" *Innovative Higher Education* 35, no. 4 (2010): 343–358.

Twenge, J. M. *Generation Me: Why Today's Young Americans Are More Confident, Assertive, Entitled, and More Miserable Than Ever Before.* New York: Free Press, 2007.

Weimer, Maryellen. *Learner-Centered Teaching: Five Key Changes to Practice.* San Francisco: Jossey-Bass, 2002.

2

Open Source Intelligence Portfolio

Challenging and Developing Intelligence Production and Communication Skills through Simulations

Rubén Arcos

S imilar to journalism professionals, intelligence analysts have to develop data and information research, analysis and interpretation, and writing skills to be able to produce finished intelligence. Graduate students in journalism receive education on journalism theory and practice at colleges and universities and develop competences on how to do research using open literature and human sources like public officials and experts. Reporters are trained in how to plan and conduct interviews of sources of information. They are trained and educated on the differences between information and opinion articles, how to provide a consistent structure to each kind of article, the major differences in writing style for news and opinion writing, and how to write headlines and leads. A key strategy for developing these skills is to design practical exercises in which students are requested to write articles on ongoing newsworthy issues in the classroom that meet specific requirements highlighted by the instructors, including a maximum number of words or characters with spaces; interpretative or opinion headlines, internal structure, and use of images; and under the time pressure associated with meeting deadlines.

The simulation exercise described in this chapter addressed the need for developing intelligence production and writing skills. Instructors at higher education institutions that offer courses in intelligence studies or intelligence analysis may use this simulation exercise with their students. The simulation exercise may also be used in continuing education courses aimed at practitioners in government or business.

The simulation exercise looks at different sources of inspiration or models for designing the portfolio of open source intelligence products that the participants will have to produce. These models include declassified and unclassified intelligence reports, best practices identified in the relevant intelligence literature or existing intelligence standards, commercial open source publications like *Jane's Intelligence Review*, and analysis and interpretive articles in major newspapers or periodic publications.

Open source information, as defined by the Intelligence Community Directive (ICD) 301, is "publicly available information that anyone can lawfully obtain by request, purchase, or observation," open source intelligence being the intelligence "produced from publicly available information that is collected, exploited, and disseminated in a timely manner to an appropriate audience for the purpose of addressing a specific intelligence requirement" (ODNI 2006, 8).

The simulation exercise also considers the impact of digital communication in journalism and open source publications and suggests the need for developing storytelling skills through the use of web-based services to enrich classic textual reports with interactive video, audio, maps, and links.

The design of the simulation is mainly based on the experience accumulated as instructor of the course on journalism of analysis and opinion with undergraduate students of journalism[1] and with graduate students of intelligence analysis programs.[2] It also draws upon the experience as a freelance contributor for *Jane's Intelligence Review*.

Basic Data

Learning/training objectives: To develop competencies in producing intelligence reports. To strengthen the knowledge acquired in intelligence analysis and production and to develop writing skills through in-class practice.

Simulation exercise objectives: To produce a set of intelligence products and submit them in a timely manner.

Target audience: Students of intelligence analysis and intelligence studies programs; students of international relations and related disciplines interested in the field of intelligence.

Playing time: Most open source pieces can be produced in sessions of two hours, while the estimated time for producing the longer assessments will require the combination of two similar sessions or equivalent time, as well as the previous preparation and research work of the participants.

Debriefing format: Instructors can facilitate a short debriefing session once the time assigned for each written piece is finished to elicit impressions from participants and reflect on the nature of each assignments.

Feedback: It is highly recommended that instructors provide preliminary feedback to participants when they are working on the assignments and provide a final feedback on the finished pieces produced by the participants.

Debriefing time: Twenty minutes per finished product. A longer debriefing session can be facilitated once all the finished products have been delivered.

Number of players required: Neither a minimum nor a maximum number of participants is required. A maximum of 30 participants is recommended per facilitator.

Participation materials included: Products' internal structure descriptions, examples, and guidelines. Facilitators who may want to produce the digital publication with the open source pieces can access the design and layout file for the Open Source Simulation Intelligence Brief at the companion website: https://textbooks.rowman.com/art-of-intelligence-2.

Materials/equipment required: A computer with an Internet connection for each participant and for the instructor; a word processor and web browser; a learning management system for assigning and submitting the written pieces.

Background

Journalistic genres guide news producers and consumers on the aims and structure of textual content and the degree of subjectivity that is considered allowed or expected for each genre (Patterson 1998; Hjarvard 2010; see also table 2.1). Journalism genres can be categorized depending of the degree of presence of the journalist in the text (written, oral, or audiovisual) into news, news plus interpretation, interpretation, and opinion (Grijelmo 2014, 28). The presence of the journalist is very high in the genres of opinion journalism and low in news genres (ibid.). As stated in the *New York Times* manual of style (2015), in reference to newspapers, the term "news" should be reserved for "the factual reporting and analysis by the news staff," reserving editorial and opinion for the opinion section (Siegal and Connolly 2015, 107). Wyatt and Badger proposed a different journalism taxonomy consisting on five modes of composition: description, narration, exposition, argumentation, and criticism (1993).

Benson and Hallin, in a comparative study of the US and French national newspapers in the 1960s and 1990s, developed a classification of newspaper stories based on four journalistic functions: "reporting current facts or statements, giving background information, giving interpretation and giving opinion" (Benson and Hallin, 2007, 32). Current facts reporting is considered to be statements without adjectives or adverbs: news stripped of speculation or judgments. Similarly, background information is a news story that adds a temporal base to current facts by considering previous related events. Interpretation is considered as a kind of empirical statement that "goes beyond current facts, setting or historical context to speculate on such things as significance, outcomes and motives,"

TABLE 2.1	Hjarvard-Patterson Framework of Journalistic Roles and Forms of Journalism		
	Detached	**Interpretative**	**Partial**
Passive	Disseminator: reports facts and events	Observer: Explains events and actions	Supporter: selectively partisan reporting of facts and events
Active	Watchdog: critical and investigative reporting	Commentator: Evaluation and prediction of actions and events	Advocate: criticism and advocacy

Source: Adapted from Hjarvard (2010, 32)

while the last category, opinion, consists of "the exercise of judgment, either normative (what is good or bad) or empirical (what is true or false)" (ibid.). Based on this categorization, Esser and Humbricht differentiate between:

> "news items" (stories offering concise descriptions of events or—if longer—additional background information and broader circumstances), "information mixed with interpretation" (stories offering explanation, investigation or speculation about the motivations, tactics, and consequences of political events), "information mixed with opinion" (stories offering peripheral commentary, opinionated perspectives, or subjective viewpoints despite not being marked as commentary), and "commentary" (editorials, leaders, opinion columns).
>
> (Esser and Humbricht 2014, 239–240)

According to Brant Houston, "interpretive journalism goes beyond the basics facts of an even or topic to provide context, analysis, and possible consequences," and reporters "are expected to have expertise about a subject and to look for motives and influences to explain what they are reporting" (Houston 2015, 301). For Thomas Patterson, descriptive journalism positions the journalist in the role of an observer, while in interpretative journalism the practitioner is also required to be an analyst (Patterson, 2000, 250). And, similar to analysis in the field of intelligence, the analyses of events in interpretative journalism can be good or badly informed by the sources and contents reported by them. As Salgado and Strömbäck have noted, "These interpretations and analyses can be well informed as well as uninformed, critical as well as uncritical, and providing context as well as distractions" (Salgado and Strömbäck 2012, 147).

Esser and Umbricht use the notion of hard-news paradigm as the dominant shared mindset among members of the journalism community, which is characterized by the use of the inverted pyramid paragraph, balanced reporting, stressing verifiable facts, source attribution, a detached point of view, and a demarcation of functions between news and editorial (Esser and Umbricht, 2014: 230). According to these authors, the paradigm came under attack during the 1960s and 1970s with the rise of calls for blending "the hard-news paradigm with analytic and interpretative elements," and resulting in a mixed approach that "retains from the hard-news paradigm a distance from political commitment but complements it with reflexive knowledge and critical expertise of the journalist" (ibid: 232). Writing on the need for interpretation in journalism and its growth, Curtis MacDougall, in his pioneering work on interpretative reporting, stated that:

> The successful journalist of the future is going to have to be more than a thoroughly trained journeyman if he is going to climb the ladder of success. He must be capable of more than routine coverage and to interpret as well as report what is going on.
>
> (MacDougall 1968, 13)

As for the meaning of "interpretation," an array of illustrative expressions can be found on MacDougall's work, including: "Make sense out of the facts," "put factual news in perspective," "point up the significance of current events," and "expand the horizon of the news" (ibid., 17). For Wyatt and Badger, exposition is the form of composition "that operates mainly through logical and explanatory devices to provide a heightened perspective on or understanding of its subject" (1993, 7).

What does interpretative journalism look like? An example of interpretation mixed with information, providing background, explanation, implications, and perspective to the readers can be found on the following excerpts from an article published by the *Wall Street Journal* on December 22, 2016, with the headline "Multibillion-Dollar Jet Deals with Iran Will Test Trump Policy":

> European plane maker Airbus Group SE joined Boeing Co. in completing a multibillion-dollar plane deal with Iran's state air carrier, creating another big test case for how the incoming Trump administration responds to the West's accelerating economic opening with the Islamic Republic.
>
> Airbus, the world's No. 2 plane maker after Boeing, said Thursday it had completed an agreement—first announced in broad strokes in January—to sell 100 planes to Iran Air. The contract is valued at more than $18 billion based on list price, which doesn't include sometimes-big discounts. Airbus said it would start delivering planes early next year.
>
> The agreement comes close on the heels of Boeing's deal to sell Iran 80 jets for $16.6 billion, based on list price. The two contracts are far and away the most valuable commercial agreements between Western firms and Iran since the completion of a nuclear pact between the U.S. and other world powers and Tehran. In exchange for Iran curbing its nuclear program, the international community agreed to lift many of the sanctions that have isolated Iran economically for years.
>
> [. . .]
>
> Uncertainty has heightened over the fate of many of these commercial inroads in Iran since the election of Donald Trump. On the campaign trail, Mr. Trump said he opposed the Iran nuclear deal. Critics in the U.S. Congress have said they would try to unwind the Boeing deal, in particular.
>
> [. . .]
>
> Even though it is a European company, Airbus is vulnerable to any big shift in U.S. policy toward Iran. Airbus requires specific U.S. approval for the sales because its jets include many American parts and technology that are subject to American export controls. It received that approval, from the U.S. Office of Foreign Assets Control, earlier this year.

Analysis can be defined as a process aimed at discovering what something means (Rosenwasser and Stephen 2012, 6), and intelligence analysis can be explained as a process consisting on "developing meaning from available information" (Clark, 1996: 1). In his classic description of the intelligence activity, Sherman Kent identifies the discovery of meaning as a step of the intelligence process—following the emergence of the intelligence problem, the analysis of the problem, the collection of data, and the critical evaluation of the data—which involves the "study of the evaluated data with the intent of finding some sort of inherent meaning" (Kent 1966, 157).

As indicated by Rosenwasser and Stephen, a central activity of analysis is making explicit what is implicit or suggested, and we can make that thinking move by asking "So what?" and infer suggested meanings—implications derived from the observations made (2012, 33 and 62). Interpretation provides the leap for moving from description and summary to analysis. For these authors, a summary is analytical in the sense that it lays out the significant parts of a subject providing a focused description and perspective by explaining the meaning and relationship between the parts of a subject (ibid., 76), but analysis brings a bigger "interpretive leap" through a creative process governed by logic and valid reasoning from evidences (ibid., 78). Interpretation operates according to the following process:

Offers a theory of what X means, not fact
Supplies a context for understanding X that is suggested by the details
Strives for the plausible, not the certain: explains individual details and patterns of evidence
Supplies reasons for why the evidence means what you claim it means.
(Rosenwasser and Stephen 2012, 133)

Declassified intelligence publications like *President's Daily Brief* (PDB), *Senior Executive Intelligence Brief*, or *Defense Intelligence Report* provide a general perspective on how intelligence products do look, their internal structure, the kind of titles used, and other relevant information on intelligence writing practices. For example, a seven-page declassified *Defense Intelligence Report* on Rwanda titled "Rwanda: The Rwandan Patriotic Front's Offensive"[3] and dated May 9, 1994, is organized according to the following structure: title; key judgments (4); body of the report including background information, overview of the crisis, current situation; and implications. The report also contains maps and figures including military capabilities.

Similarly, a declassified British Joint Intelligence Committee's assessment titled "International Terrorism: Impact of Iraq," of April 13, 2005,[4] is structured in the following manner: title; key judgments (6); body of the report; and long-term impact.

On the other hand, open source intelligence products like *Jane's Intelligence Review* include key points at the beginning of each piece and structure articles in the following way: title; subtitle; key points; body of the article, including background information, analysis and assessment of the situation; and outlook. The articles may include pictures, maps, cases, and diagrams when relevant.

News production and finished intelligence production are very different businesses, but similarities are evident as well. On January 1974, the CIA started the publication of the first current intelligence newspaper, the *National Intelligence Daily* (Colby 1974). According to William E. Colby, then director of the CIA,

The *Daily* was printed on four, four-columns pages, laid out with headlines and photographs or other graphics just like normal newspaper. Its purpose was to provide a wider range of daily intelligence to senior policy makers in a more readable form and on a more timely basis than we had achieved previously. After five months, it is clear that the *Daily* has succeed. The newspaper has been readable and timely, as we had hoped. It has also been an attractive product; it has offered more comprehensive and analytical coverage than any of our previous daily publications and it has provided a vehicle by which some of the findings of our in-depth analytical work can be brought more directly to the attention of senior level users of intelligence.

(Colby 1974, 1)

Writing on this 7,000-word flagship publication, Nathan Nielsen highlighted that, unlike the commercial press, the *Daily* went beyond "scoring incidental scoops on foreign news developments," and that whenever possible the "newspaper" should do more than merely telling policymakers what happened yesterday, but must tell them "what is likely to happen tomorrow and why" (Nielsen 1976).[5] The *Daily* was described as "a compilation in tabloid format of key items of current intelligence produced six days a week by the CIA's Office of Current Intelligence" (Product Review Division of Intelligence Community Staff 1975, 6). Another example of a major current intelligence publication (although published on a weekly basis every Friday) is the *Weekly Review*, which "reports and analyzes significant developments of the week through noon on Thursday" (ibid.).[6]

Box 2.1

Example of a current intelligence piece published in the *National Intelligence Daily*

Current intelligence piece from a partially declassified top-secret issue of the CIA's *National Intelligence Daily* published on April 25, 1974.

The piece was published on the front page of the *Daily* and continued on page 4. The warning notice of the last page indicated that "The *Daily* is an experimental publication, offering initial analysis of recent developments." The use of the semicolon in the headlines is uncommon in news writing, although there are famous examples of the contrary. See for example the *New York Times* front page on the sinking of the *Titanic*.

Military Uprising in Portugal; Situation Remains Confused[7]

A military uprising is in progress in Portugal this morning, the state-supported news agency has acknowledged. Troops have blocked access to the Defense Ministry and, according to press reports, a group calling itself the Armed Forces Movement has taken over a radio station. The troops apparently plan to set up a "National Junta of Salvation" and restore civil liberties.

It is not clear, as of 0430 EDT, whom the forces represent or what is the extent of the uprising. There are reports that the military rebellion has spread to the north of the country.

Last month a military company stationed 50 miles from Lisbon marched to protest the firing of General Antonio de Spinola, the deputy chief of staff of the armed forces, and his boss, General Costa Gomes. The march was stopped by troops loyal to the government who forced the dissidents to return to their barracks. They then surrendered and were arrested.

Spinola was fired because far rightists were outraged over his proposal—in a recent book—to loosen Portugal's ties to its African territories. The government arrested some 200 military supporters of General Spinola, but refrained from further arrests, reportedly to avoid any greater stirring up of the military.

Military dissidents are apparently again manifesting discontent with government policy, and loyal troops have been alerted to intercept them. The strength of the dissidents is not yet clear.

A distinctive feature of intelligence assessments is the use of expressions such as "we assess," "we believe," "we judge," and the like to mark that the assertions following those phrases are analytic judgments, interpretations, and inferences based on the collected information. The following excerpts exemplify the writing style associated to these products:

> Only an improbable combination of disasters—for example, widespread social disorder and near economic collapse or resurgent terrorism and government meddling in internal military affairs—could, in our view, generate a successful coup.
>
> (CIA 1983, iv)

> We assess with high confidence that Russian President Vladimir Putin ordered an influence campaign in 2016 aimed at the US presidential election, the consistent goals of which were to undermine public faith in the US democratic process, denigrate Secretary Clinton, and harm her electability and potential presidency.
>
> (ICA 2017–01D, 1)

> We judge that the conflict in Iraq has exacerbated the threat from international terrorism and will continue to have an impact in the long term.
>
> (JIC Assessment, 13 April 2005)

Facilitator's Guide

Pre-simulation Preparation

* Identify a list of key topics and relevant newsworthy events that the students can cover in their intelligence reports. Monitor open sources and track developments in the topics identified to ensure you have at least a basic knowledge and you are updated on those topics before running the simulation exercise with your students.
* Develop a list of open sources of information that you can recommend to your students to use when writing the open source reports. Include major national and international newspapers, either the digital versions of printed newspapers or online newspapers,[8] newsmagazines, news agencies' websites, 24-hour TV news broadcasters, social media accounts of journalist covering specific topics, think tanks focused on national security and foreign policy topics, official websites of international institutions and non governmental organizations, and so forth.
* Consider that the amount of time and quality of the work devoted to this preparation phase will have a direct impact on the simulation experience.
* Determine the number of participants in the classroom. Keeping the number of participants below 30 is strongly recommended.
* Tell the participants to be prepared for the simulation by opening an account on Twitter—in the case they don't have one—and to follow relevant accounts for the aims of the simulation.
* Ensure that the computer equipment that the participants are going to use has all the necessary software installed, such as a web browser and plugins, and that they have signed up for the web-based services that they are going to use. Get familiar with the classroom facility in which the simulation will be run.

Materials

See appendix 2A.

Running the Simulation

Simulation Step 1

Tell the participants that they are going to role-play as intelligence analysts and produce during the next sessions a series of intelligence reports to be delivered electronically through the chosen platform (learning management system [LMS] or a similar system). Highlight the importance of delivering the finished intelligence in a timely manner for being useful and that each piece will have assigned a limited time to be completed and submitted as well as a maximum number of words.

Instructors may want to create a competitive environment by telling participants that the best intelligence pieces will be awarded and published in *The Open Source Simulation Intelligence Brief*, a branded periodical intelligence product published for the occasion in an ePaper edition.

Simulation Step 2

Explain each intelligence requirement, the proposed internal structure for each piece that the participants are going to produce (see table 2.2), and the style guidelines. Use examples to illustrate what the students are expected to produce and suggest sources of information. All this information should also be included in the description of the assignments created on the LMS platform for the simulation exercise. Tell the participants to dedicate some time to familiarizing themselves with the topic requirement before starting to write.

Simulation Step 3

Tell the participants to start working on their reports and give them the deadline for the task. Instruct the students to ask you questions as necessary and to get your comments and feedback about their pieces before sending the finished products through the LMS system. Highlight the need for adjusting the piece to the guidelines on structure, style, wording, and length proposed (see table 2.2 and appendix 2A).

Simulation Step 4

Review the intelligence pieces delivered by each participant and provide the corresponding feedback.

Simulation Step 5

Evaluate the portfolio of products elaborated by the participants and select the best deliverables. Acknowledge the best pieces and select the products that will be published in the edition of *The Open Source Simulation Intelligence Brief* (OS-SIB). Tell the authors to edit their pieces considering the comments provided by the facilitator and to submit the final version by the appropriate deadline.

TABLE 2.2 **Portfolio of Open Source Products (Arcos 2017)**

Product	Description and structure	Length	Time	Example
1. Interpretive article	To write an interpretive article with and interpretive headline on the topical issue X. The piece should provide background information (causes and preceding events), context (present), and implications or likely developments. It should be written in the third person and include an interpretive title. Do not include value judgments. Information and interpretation are not the same as opinions.	300–310 words, including title	120 minutes. Highlight the need for delivering the pieces on time and stress that delayed deliveries will be dismissed.	See appendix
2. Multimedia enhanced interpretive article	See description for product 1 and also include interactive multimedia elements that can potentially add value by boosting the understanding of the events and their meaning. Instructors can use tools such as Flip HTML5, Joomag, or other similar web-based software.	300–310 words, including title. Include at least one embedded video ard one image.	120 minutes. Highlight the need for delivering the pieces on time and stress that delayed deliveries will be dismissed.	See appendix
3. Current intelligence summary piece with comment	To write two short current intelligence summary pieces on the current topics Y and Z. Proposed structure: a short title beginning with the identification of the country/region of interest followed by a colon and a maximum of five words capturing the "what"; body, providing information and written as a news story; comment, providing additional relevant information and assessment.	160–180 words per piece, including the title	120 minutes.	See appendix
4. Open source intelligence article (including key points)	To write an interpretive article on a current topic. The students should inform instructors beforehand on the chosen topic. Approval from the instructor is needed. Article structure: (1) a short title (maximum of three words) followed by a subtitle/deck head; (2); three key points; (3) body of the article, including short summary lead paragraph, background information, analysis and assessment of current events (not opinion), and outlook. Use estimative language to convey likely developments as appropriate. Instruct participants to follow guidelines for sourcing quotation and attribution (see appendix).	1,500–3,000 words	Two sessions of two hours plus additional time of the participant for doing research on the chosen topic, including primary sources and open literature.	*Jane's Intelligence Review* articles are recommended as examples.

(Cont.)

TABLE 2.2 (Continued)

Product	Description and structure	Length	Time	Example
5. Interactive story map	To produce an interactive story map providing the timeline of a topic of interest enhanced with images, videos, and 3D maps by using the web-based storymap tool Mapme (free trial version). The exercise aims to develop storytelling skills using multimedia elements.	Build a PDF document from screen captures of the map	120 minutes	See appendix
6. Intelligence assessment	To produce a team intelligence assessment. The assessments can be developed from the open source articles (see Product 4), according to the instructor's criteria. Internal structure: headline/title; scope note (including research question and objectives); numbered principal conclusions or key judgments (three to seven); discussion section organized in subheads including background/context, analysis and assessment in depth; outlook. Instruct the participants to use standardized estimative language (see table 2.3)	1,500–3,000 words	Two sessions of two hours plus additional team working time for doing research on the chosen topic, primary sources, and open literature.	See appendix

Simulation Step 6

You can download the file with the basic design and layout of the OSSIB from the companion website for the book: https://textbooks.rowman.com/art-of-intelligence-2. Place the articles and design elements accordingly using a word processor. Once the full document is ready, convert it to a PDF file.

Use an interactive digital publishing platform like Yumpu.com, FlipHTML5, or a similar service for embedding videos, images, or other multimedia elements to bring an interactive experience to the readers of your open source intelligence publication.

Debriefing Session

A structured debriefing session is required to make participants reflect on their learning experience and discuss the theoretical and practical issues of the simulation.

The facilitators may run a short debriefing at the end of each session, after the participants have submitted each open source piece. This short debriefing should be focused more on eliciting impressions of the experience than on conceptual aspects. A longer debriefing session is recommended once the instructors have evaluated the open source deliverables produced by the participants. This facilitates the group discussion and further reflection on the complexities and aspects involved in intelligence production.

Ask the participants to reflect on the following issues or others that you might consider relevant to move the discussion forward:

- Did the time pressure have any effects on your reasoning and writing process during the simulation exercise?
- Did you find difficulties in separating information, analysis and interpretation, and opinion during the process of producing each piece?
- What particular words did you use for conveying implications and uncertainty?
- Was it particularly difficult for you to write the title for each piece?
- Can you highlight any significant difference between textual interpretative articles and the multimedia-enhanced interpretive articles? Do you think digital communication requires to develop specific skills for producing meaningful messages?
- Can you identify any weaknesses when writing each intelligence piece? What has been particularly challenging for you?
- Which sources of information did you rely on most when writing the open source pieces?
- Did you find any difficulties in adapting your analysis to each format and word limit?

Conclusion

The simulation exercise provides an active learning environment that can be used for education purposes on the issues related to the elaboration of intelligence products and communication aspects associated with the task of writing open source intelligence analyses. The simulation exercise can be used for training purposes in undergraduate and graduate programs with the objective of practicing and developing their intelligence writing and communication skills. It can be easily adapted to distance learning courses.

The production of each open source piece challenges the participants' skills, including planning, time optimization, source identification, open source collection, evaluation and analysis, interpretive thinking, and communication skills.

It can also be adapted to the needs of the facilitators on specific courses dealing with national security topics or in the field of competitive intelligence.

Appendix 2A

1.   Interpretive article

Examples of interpretive headlines and articles:

- "Unrest in Syria Threatens Regional Stability," *Washington Post*, May 2, 2011.
- "Extradition Request for Russian Suspects Has Zero Chance of Success," *Guardian*, August 6, 2018.
- "Global Crises Put Obama's Strategy of Caution to the Test," *New York Times*, March 16, 2014.
- Trump's Negotiating Playbook Faced Test in North Korea, *New York Times*, March 24, 2018.

2.   Multimedia enhanced interpretive article

   Sign in to Yumpu FREE, FlipHTML5, or other similar digital publishing platform to include video and other interactive resources in your piece.

3.   Current intelligence summary piece with comment

Box 2.2

Example of Current Intelligence Summary Piece with Comment

The following piece, produced by the State Department's Bureau of Intelligence and Research (INR), appeared on the April 26, 1994 edition of the Secretary's Morning Summary.

Source: https://nsarchive2.gwu.edu/NSAEBB/NSAEBB117/Rw23.pdf

For another example see: http://www.rwandadocumentsproject.net/gsdl/collect/usdocs/index/assoc/HASH0181/21ed25a4.dir/4604.pdf

Rwanda: Genocide and Partition

Heavy fighting yesterday continued in Kigali after the government failed to show up for weekend peace talks in Tanzania and the Rwandan Patriotic Front (RPF) did not appear in Zaire for separate talks to which it apparently was not invited, according to press reports. Both sides announced unilateral, conditional cease-fire declarations that were to take effect yesterday.

The ICRC delegate for Africa is certain at least 100,000 Rwandans have been killed since April 6, believes the actual number is closer to 300,000, and notes ICRC personnel in country think the toll could be 500,000, according to Mission Geneva. The ICRC is concerned that the situation could worsen, citing some Hutu-extremists who speak of a "final solution" to eliminate all Tutsis. The ICRC and other NGOs have withdrawn all their workers from the country, except for a small number in Kigali.

Comment: The butchery shows no sign of ending. The inability of either side to conquer the other—and the intensity of the ethnic slaughter—make it increasingly probable Rwanda will divide into zones controlled by the RPF in the north and east and by Hutu forces linked to the interim government in the northwest, the south and most of Kigali. Though a cease-fire may be possible in the days ahead, Hutu hard-liners ascendant behind government lines totally distrust the RPF and will reject any interim political settlement based on sharing power with the rebels.

4. Open source intelligence article (including key points)
   - Headline
   - Deck head
   - Key points (highlighted in a box)
   - Summary lead/news hook. It should answer, although not all, of the basic 5W and H questions: Who, What, When, Where, Why, and How
   - Background/context
   - Analysis organized in relevant subheadings
   - Outlook/conclusion.

Facilitators may use features published in *Jane's Intelligence Review* as examples of the open source pieces required.

5. Interactive story map
   - Access https://mapme.com and click on "start free." Sign up for an account or alternatively sign in with a Facebook or LinkedIn account (note that publishing and sharing features are available only with premium accounts).
   - Once you have signed in, you can start creating your interactive map. Start with the title and with the map description. You can use a summary lead for this purpose.
   - Now you can start developing your story by introducing location name, address (use Google Maps for this purpose), and description and adding media like YouTube video and images. Example: Obama's historic visit to Cuba (https://story.mapme.com/obama-s-historic-visit-to-cuba/overview).
   - Make screen captures and send them to your instructor using the LMS system for the course.

PHOTO 2.1 Screen capture of an interactive story map

Source: Rubén Arcos

6. Intelligence assessment
   - Title
   - Scope note capturing the key research question that the assessment aims to respond to and objectives
   - Key judgments (numbered; three to seven)
   - Discussion (including under relevant subheadings: background/context; analysis and assessment)
   - Outlook.

Each paragraph may be numbered, following the practice of some IC products, and should be written using the standardized linguistic markers of uncertainty characteristic of estimative language (see table 2.3).

Examples of sanitized or declassified assessments:

- "The Spanish Socialists: Six Months in Power," June 1983.

   https://www.cia.gov/library/readingroom/docs/CIA-RDP84S00555
      R000200090002-1.pdf
- JIC Assessment, September 9, 2002, "Iraqi Use of Chemical and Biological Weapons—Possible Scenarios"

   http://webarchive.nationalarchives.gov.uk/20171123124712/http://
      www.iraqinquiry.org.uk/search/?query=&sortByDate=False&search
      Refine=0&fm=0&fy=0&tm=0&ty=0&da=&dr=&dc=1&ft=1

TABLE 2.3 — **Verbal Expressions of Likelihood and Associated Numerical Probabilities for Expressing Uncertainty in Analytic Judgments**

	US ICD 203			UK Defence Intelligence Uncertainty Yardstick	
	Almost no chance	Remote	1%–5%	Remote or highly unlikely	< 10%
	Very Unlikely	Highly improbable	5%–20%		
	Unlikely	Improbable	20%–45%	Improbable or unlikely	15%–20%
	Roughly even chance	Roughly even odds	45%–55%	Realistic probability	25%–50%
	Likely	Probable	55%–80%	Probable or likely	55%–70%
	Very likely	Highly Probable	80%–95%	Highly probable or highly likely	75%–85%
	Almost certain	Nearly certain	95%–99%	Almost certain	> 90%

Source: ICD 203; Jane's 2017; JPD 2–00: 3–23

- "Assessing Russian Activities and Intentions in Recent US Elections"

  Intelligence Community Assessment, January 6, 2017
  https://www.dni.gov/files/documents/ICA_2017_01.pdf

- "Worst Case Scenarios for the Narrower Middle East"

  Single Intelligence Analysis Capacity (SIAC) of the EU, July 12, 2007
  http://data.consilium.europa.eu/doc/document/ST-7636-2017-INIT/
  en/pdf

The SIAC report is organized according to the following structure: introduction; the threats; the players; the environment; conflict extensions; contingencies leading to worst case-scenarios; and conclusions.

Guidelines to consider when writing your open source pieces:

Expressions of Likelihood

Use any of the following sets of terms when expressing uncertainty in analytic judgments. They are promulgated standards used by the IC and commercial open source providers.

Sourcing Quotations and Attribution

As a general rule, all the assertions in your pieces must be supported by evidence.

Source and date the quotations used when writing your pieces. Direct quotations should be place under open (") and closed quote marks (").

Be as specific as possible about your sources of information; consider anonymity only as a last resort due to the national security nature of the topic when you are using a reliable source that request to remain anonymous. In this case, use a formula for describing the source and its reliability without compromising the anonymity. Do not use nonattributable sources without the approval of your instructor.

How much of my human source's identity can I disclose, and how much of the information provided by that source can I publish? Refer to the following Associated Press definitions on the degree of anonymity of the sources:

On the record: The information can be used without caveats, quoting the name of the source.

Off the record: The information cannot be used for publication at all.

Background: After agreeing with the source on a general attribution without comprising his/her identity, the information can be published. Generally, attribution under this formula comes with a description of the source's position.

Deep background: The information can be used but without any attribution.

Source: AP [online] Anonymous Sources. Available at:
https://www.ap.org/about/news-values-and-principles/
telling-the-story/anonymous-sources

[Insert image here. © stock.adobe.com]

Intelligence Sentry

[Place multimedia enhanced interpretive articles within this section by region]

Current intelligence

[Place current intelligence summary pieces with comment within this section]

Analysis and assessment

[Place open source intelligence articles and intelligence assessment within this section]

Forewarning

(Forthcoming events and likely short-term developments)

[Place the logo of your institution here]

The Open Source Simulation Intelligence Brief
[Insert a description of the publication here]

Contact
[Insert the name and position of the instructor/editor here, and contact details]

[Insert Email address

Insert Website]

Editorial Policy
OSSIB is delivered [insert timeframe here] and produced by [insert corresponding information]. Assessments do not necessarily reflect [insert name of institution] views.

[Insert image here. © stock.adobe.com]
[Insert caption accompanying image]

[Insert video here. © stock.adobe.com]
[Insert caption accompanying video

PHOTO 2.2 Structure, design, and layout for the OSSIB

Source: Rubén Arcos. Software: FlipHTML5

INTELLIGENCE SENTRY | Middle East

[Place the logo of your institution here]

Lorem ipsum dolor sit amet, consectetuer adipiscing elit. Maecenas porttitor congue massa [Insert title of the piece here]

Lorem ipsum dolor sit amet, consectetuer adipiscing elit. Maecenas porttitor congue massa. Fusce posuere, magna sed pulvinar ultricies, purus lectus malesuada libero, sit amet commodo magna eros quis urna.
Nunc viverra imperdiet enim. Fusce est.
Vivamus a tellus.
Pellentesque habitant morbi tristique senectus et netus et malesuada fames ac turpis egestas.
Proin pharetra nonummy pede. Mauris et orci.
Aenean nec lorem. In porttitor. Donec laoreet nonummy augue.
Suspendisse dui purus, scelerisque at, vulputate vitae, pretium mattis, nunc. Mauris eget neque at sem venenatis eleifend. Ut nonummy.
Fusce aliquet pede non pede. Suspendisse dapibus lorem pellentesque magna. Integer nulla.
Donec blandit feugiat ligula. Donec hendrerit, felis et imperdiet euismod, purus ipsum pretium metus, in lacinia nulla nisl eget sapien. Donec ut est in lectus consequat consequat.
Etiam eget dui. Aliquam erat volutpat. Sed at lorem in nunc porta tristique.
Proin nec augue. Quisque aliquam tempor magna. Pellentesque habitant morbi tristique senectus et netus et malesuada fames ac turpis egestas.
Nunc ac magna. Maecenas odio dolor, vulputate vel, auctor ac, accumsan id, felis. Pellentesque cursus sagittis felis.
Pellentesque porttitor, velit lacinia egestas auctor, diam eros tempus arcu, nec vulputate augue magna vel risus. Cras non magna vel ante adipiscing rhoncus. Vivamus a mi.
Morbi neque. Aliquam erat volutpat. Integer ultrices lobortis eros.
Pellentesque habitant morbi tristique senectus et netus et malesuada fames ac turpis egestas.
Proin semper, ante vitae sollicitudin posuere, metus quam iaculis nibh, vitae scelerisque nunc

massa eget pede. Sed velit urna, interdum vel, ultricies vel, faucibus at, quam.
Donec elit est, consectetuer eget, consequat quis, tempus quis, wisi. In in nunc. Class aptent taciti sociosqu ad litora torquent per conubia nostra, per inceptos hymenaeos.
Donec ullamcorper fringilla eros. Fusce in sapien eu purus dapibus commodo. Cum sociis natoque penatibus et magnis dis parturient montes, nascetur ridiculus mus.
Cras faucibus condimentum odio. Sed ac ligula. Aliquam at eros.

[Insert video here. © stock.adobe.com]
[Insert caption accompanying video

Etiam at ligula et tellus ullamcorper ultrices. In fermentum, lorem non cursus porttitor, diam urna accumsan lacus, sed interdum wisi nibh nec nisl. Ut tincidunt volutpat urna.
Mauris eleifend nulla eget mauris. Sed cursus quam id felis. Curabitur posuere quam vel nibh.
Cras dapibus dapibus nisl. Vestibulum quis dolor a felis congue vehicula. Maecenas pede purus, tristique ac, tempus eget, egestas quis, mauris.
Curabitur non eros. Nullam hendrerit bibendum justo. Fusce iaculis, est quis lacinia pretium, pede metus molestie lacus, at gravida wisi ante at libero.
Quisque ornare placerat risus. Ut molestie magna at mi. Integer aliquet mauris et nibh.

PHOTO 2.3 Basic structure of multimedia interpretive articles and current intelligence pieces for the OSSIB.

Source: Rubén Arcos. Software: FlipHTML5. The design and layout file can be downloaded at the companion website: https://textbooks.rowman.com/art-of-intelligence-2.

CURRENT INTELLIGENCE	[Place the logo of your institution here]

Spain: Lorem ipsum [Insert title of the piece here]

Lorem ipsum dolor sit amet, consectetuer adipiscing elit. Maecenas porttitor congue massa. Fusce posuere, magna sed pulvinar ultricies, purus lectus malesuada libero, sit amet commodo magna eros quis urna.
Nunc viverra imperdiet enim. Fusce est. Vivamus a tellus.
Pellentesque habitant morbi tristique senectus et netus et malesuada fames ac turpis egestas. Proin pharetra nonummy pede. Mauris et orci.
Aenean nec lorem. In porttitor. Donec laoreet nonummy augue.
Suspendisse dui purus, scelerisque at, vulputate vitae, pretium mattis, nunc. Mauris eget neque at sem venenatis eleifend. Ut nonummy.
Fusce aliquet pede non pede. Suspendisse dapibus lorem pellentesque magna. Integer nulla.
Donec blandit feugiat ligula. Donec hendrerit, felis et imperdiet euismod, purus ipsum pretium metus, in lacinia nulla nisl eget sapien. Donec ut est in lectus consequat consequat.
Etiam eget dui.

    Comment: Nunc ac magna. Maecenas odio dolor, vulputate vel, auctor ac, accumsan id, felis. Pellentesque cursus sagittis felis. Pellentesque porttitor, velit lacinia egestas auctor, diam eros tempus arcu, nec vulputate augue magna vel risus. Cras non magna vel ante adipiscing rhoncus. Vivamus a mi. Morbi neque. Aliquam erat volutpat. Integer ultrices lobortis eros.

Russia: Lorem ipsum [Insert title of the piece here]

Lorem ipsum dolor sit amet, consectetuer adipiscing elit. Maecenas porttitor congue massa. Fusce posuere, magna sed pulvinar ultricies, purus lectus malesuada libero, sit amet commodo magna eros quis urna.
Nunc viverra imperdiet enim. Fusce est. Vivamus a tellus.
Pellentesque habitant morbi tristique senectus et netus et malesuada fames ac turpis egestas. Proin pharetra nonummy pede. Mauris et orci.
Aenean nec lorem. In porttitor. Donec laoreet nonummy augue.
Suspendisse dui purus, scelerisque at, vulputate vitae, pretium mattis, nunc. Mauris eget neque at sem venenatis eleifend. Ut nonummy.
Fusce aliquet pede non pede. Suspendisse dapibus lorem pellentesque magna. Integer nulla.
Donec blandit feugiat ligula. Donec hendrerit, felis et imperdiet euismod, purus ipsum pretium metus, in lacinia nulla nisl eget sapien. Donec ut est in lectus consequat consequat.
Etiam eget dui.

    Comment: Nunc ac magna. Maecenas odio dolor, vulputate vel, auctor ac, accumsan id, felis. Pellentesque cursus sagittis felis. Pellentesque porttitor, velit lacinia egestas auctor, diam eros tempus arcu, nec vulputate augue magna vel risus. Cras non magna vel ante adipiscing rhoncus. Vivamus a mi. Morbi neque. Aliquam erat volutpat. Integer ultrices lobortis eros.

PHOTO 2.4 Basic structure of multimedia interpretive articles and current intelligence pieces for the OSSIB.

Source: Rubén Arcos. Software: FlipHTML5. The design and layout file can be downloaded at the companion website: https://textbooks.rowman.com/art-of-intelligence-2.

ANALYSIS & ASSESSMENT	[Place the logo of your institution here]

Lorem Ipsum

Scope note: Lorem ipsum dolor sit amet, consectetuer adipiscing elit. Maecenas porttitor congue massa. Fusce posuere, magna sed pulvinar ultricies, purus lectus malesuada libero, sit amet commodo magna eros quis urna.
Nunc viverra imperdiet enim. Fusce est. Vivamus a tellus.
Pellentesque habitant morbi tristique senectus et netus et malesuada fames ac turpis egestas. Proin pharetra nonummy pede. Mauris et orci.
Aenean nec lorem. In porttitor. Donec laoreet nonummy augue.
Suspendisse dui purus, scelerisque at, vulputate vitae, pretium mattis, nunc. Mauris eget neque at sem venenatis eleifend. Ut nonummy.
Fusce aliquet pede non pede. Suspendisse dapibus lorem pellentesque magna. Integer nulla.
Donec blandit feugiat ligula. Donec hendrerit, felis et imperdiet euismod, purus ipsum pretium metus, in lacinia nulla nisl eget sapien. Donec ut est in lectus consequat consequat.
Etiam eget dui. Aliquam erat volutpat. Sed at lorem in nunc porta tristique.
Proin nec augue. Quisque aliquam tempor magna. Pellentesque habitant morbi tristique senectus et netus et malesuada fames ac turpis egestas.

Key Judgments

1. Lorem ipsum dolor sit amet, consectetuer adipiscing elit. Aenean commodo ligula eget dolor. Aenean massa. Cum sociis natoque penatibus et magnis dis parturient montes, nascetur ridiculus mus. Donec quam felis, ultricies nec, pellentesque eu, pretium quis, sem. Nulla consequat massa quis enim. Donec pede justo, fringilla vel, aliquet nec, vulputate eget, arcu. In enim justo, rhoncus ut, imperdiet a, venenatis vitae, justo. Nullam dictum felis eu pede mollis pretium. Integer tincidunt. Cras dapibus. Vivamus elementum semper nisi. Aenean vulputate eleifend tellus.
2. Lorem ipsum dolor sit amet, consectetuer adipiscing elit. Aenean commodo ligula eget dolor. Aenean massa. Cum sociis natoque penatibus et magnis dis parturient montes, nascetur ridiculus mus. Donec quam felis, ultricies nec, pellentesque eu, pretium quis, sem. Nulla consequat massa quis enim. Donec pede justo, fringilla vel, aliquet nec, vulputate eget, arcu. In enim justo, rhoncus ut, imperdiet a, venenatis vitae, justo. Nullam dictum felis eu pede mollis pretium. Integer tincidunt. Cras dapibus. Vivamus elementum semper nisi. Aenean vulputate eleifend tellus.
3. Lorem ipsum dolor sit amet, consectetuer adipiscing elit. Aenean commodo ligula eget dolor. Aenean massa. Cum sociis natoque penatibus et magnis dis parturient montes, nascetur ridiculus mus. Donec quam felis, ultricies nec, pellentesque eu, pretium quis, sem. Nulla consequat massa quis enim. Donec pede justo, fringilla vel, aliquet nec, vulputate eget, arcu. In enim justo, rhoncus ut, imperdiet a, venenatis vitae, justo. Nullam dictum felis eu pede mollis pretium. Integer tincidunt. Cras dapibus. Vivamus elementum semper nisi. Aenean vulputate eleifend tellus.
4. Lorem ipsum dolor sit amet, consectetuer adipiscing elit. Aenean commodo ligula eget dolor. Aenean massa. Cum sociis natoque penatibus et magnis dis parturient montes, nascetur ridiculus mus. Donec quam felis, ultricies nec, pellentesque eu, pretium quis, sem. Nulla consequat massa quis enim. Donec pede justo, fringilla vel, aliquet nec, vulputate eget, arcu. In enim justo, rhoncus ut, imperdiet a, venenatis vitae, justo. Nullam dictum felis eu pede mollis pretium.

PHOTO 2.5 Basic structure of intelligence assessments and open source features for the OSSIB.

Source: Rubén Arcos. Software: FlipHTML5. The design and layout file can be downloaded at the companion website: https://textbooks.rowman.com/art-of-intelligence-2.

[Place the logo of
your institution here]

ANALYSIS & ASSESSMENT

Lorem Ipsum

Lorem ipsum dolor sit amet, consectetuer adipiscing elit. Maecenas porttitor congue massa. Fusce posuere, magna sed pulvinar ultricies, purus lectus malesuada libero, sit amet commodo magna eros quis urna [Insert deck head here]

Key Points

- Lorem ipsum dolor sit amet, consectetuer adipiscing elit. Maecenas porttitor congue massa. Fusce posuere, magna sed pulvinar ultricies, purus lectus malesuada libero, sit amet commodo magna eros quis urna.
- Nunc viverra imperdiet enim. Fusce est. Vivamus a tellus.
- Pellentesque habitant morbi tristique senectus et netus et malesuada fames ac turpis egestas. Proin pharetra nonummy pede. Mauris et orci.

Etiam eget dui. Aliquam erat volutpat. Sed at lorem in nunc porta tristique.
Proin nec augue. Quisque aliquam tempor magna. Pellentesque habitant morbi tristique senectus et netus et malesuada fames ac turpis egestas.
Nunc ac magna. Maecenas odio dolor, vulputate vel, auctor ac, accumsan id, felis. Pellentesque cursus sagittis felis.
Pellentesque porttitor, velit lacinia egestas auctor, diam eros tempus arcu, nec vulputate augue magna vel risus. Cras non magna vel ante adipiscing rhoncus. Vivamus a mi.
Morbi neque. Aliquam erat volutpat. Integer ultrices lobortis eros.

Cras faucibus condimentum odio. Sed ac ligula. Aliquam at eros.

[Insert summary lead paragraph here]
Lorem ipsum dolor sit amet, consectetuer adipiscing elit. Maecenas porttitor congue massa. Fusce posuere, magna sed pulvinar ultricies, purus lectus malesuada libero, sit amet commodo magna eros quis urna.
Nunc viverra imperdiet enim. Fusce est. Vivamus a tellus.
Pellentesque habitant morbi tristique senectus et netus et malesuada fames ac turpis egestas.
Proin pharetra nonummy pede. Mauris et orci.
Aenean nec lorem. In porttitor. Donec laoreet nonummy augue.
Suspendisse dui purus, scelerisque at, vulputate vitae, pretium mattis, nunc. Mauris eget neque at sem venenatis eleifend. Ut nonummy.
Fusce aliquet pede non pede. Suspendisse dapibus lorem pellentesque magna. Integer nulla.
Donec blandit feugiat ligula. Donec hendrerit, felis et imperdiet euismod, purus ipsum pretium metus, in lacinia nulla nisl eget sapien. Donec ut est in lectus consequat consequat.

[Insert image here. © stock.adobe.com]
[Insert caption accompanying image]

Subhead
Pellentesque habitant morbi tristique senectus et netus et malesuada fames ac turpis egestas.
Proin semper, ante vitae sollicitudin posuere, metus quam iaculis nibh, vitae scelerisque nunc massa eget pede. Sed velit urna, interdum vel, ultricies vel, faucibus at, quam.

PHOTO 2.6 Basic structure of intelligence assessments and open source features for the OSSIB.

Source: Rubén Arcos. Software: FlipHTML5. The design and layout file can be downloaded at the companion website: https://textbooks.rowman.com/art-of-intelligence-2.

Notes

This chapter is based on the paper "Open Source Intelligence Portfolio: Challenging and Developing Intelligence Production and Communication Skills through Simulations," prepared by the author for presentation at the panel "Intelligence Simulations: Theory and Practice," International Studies Association, Baltimore, Maryland, February 25, 2017.

1   I started teaching the course on journalism of analysis and opinion in the academic year 2014–2015 at Rey Juan Carlos University in Madrid, Spain. Journalism students are tasked with producing an interpretive or opinion piece in the classroom on a weekly basis. The time allowed for writing individually each piece is 105 minutes and includes interpretive articles, editorials, analysis and opinion columns, and other genres of opinion.

2   In 2011, I introduced the Multimedia Intelligence Product simulation exercise within the Interuniversity Master's degree in Intelligence Analysis, in which students are tasked with producing a web-based intelligence assessment working in analytic teams. For further information about this simulation exercise, see chapter 15 of *The Art of Intelligence*. See also Arcos, Rubén, and Randolph H. Pherson, eds. *Intelligence Communication in the Digital Era: Transforming Security, Defence, and Business.* Basingstoke: Palgrave Macmillan, 2015.

3   To access the report, see http://nsarchive.gwu.edu/NSAEBB/NSAEBB53/rw050994.pdf.

4   See the declassified JIC Assessment at http://www.iraqinquiry.org.uk/media/76539/2005-04-13-JIC-Assessment-International-terrorism-impact-of-Iraq.pdf.

5   https://www.cia.gov/library/readingroom/docs/CIA-RDP78T03194A000400010022-7.pdf.

6   "Memorandum for the United States Intelligence Board: A Guide to the National Intelligence Community's Production Organizations and Their Products." https://www.cia.gov/library/readingroom/docs/CIA-RDP82M00591R000400010010-7.pdf (last accessed: August 6, 2018).

7   The use of the semicolon in the headlines is uncommon in news writing, and some authors argue that the best headlines do not use punctuation marks. However, there are famous examples of the contrary. See, for example, the *New York Times* front page on the sinking of the *Titanic*, published on April 15, 1912. A more recent example was the headline of *El País*: "Junqueras a prisión; petición de captura de Puigdemont" (see *El País*, November 3, 2017). According to the *New York Times Manual of Style and Usage*, 5th edition, "The semicolon can mark a division in a sentence made up of statements that are closely related but require a separation more emphatic than a comma" (p. 286).

8   See http://www.onlinenewspapers.com, http://www.newspapersintheworld.com, http://www.bbc.com/news.

References

Arcos, Rubén and Randolph H. Pherson. eds. 2015. *Intelligence communication in the digital era: transforming security, defence, and business.* Basingstoke: Palgrave MacMillan.

Benson, Randy and Daniel C. Hallin. 2007. "How states, markets and globalization shape the news: the French and US national press." *European Journal of Communication* 22(1): 27–48.

CIA Directorate of Intelligence. 1983. *The Spanish Socialist: Six months in power. An intelligence assessment.* EUR 83–10176. Approved for release 2008/09/26. https://www.cia.gov/library/readingroom/docs/CIA-RDP84S00555R000200090002-1.pdf

Clark, Robert M. 1996. *Intelligence analysis: estimation and prediction.* Baltimore, MA: American Literary Press.

Colby, William E. 1974. Publication of the National Intelligence Daily. June 18, 1974. https://www.cia.gov/library/readingroom/docs/CIA-RDP84-00780R00610012 0016-7.pdf

Esser, Frank and Andrea Umbricht. 2014. "The evolution of objective and interpretative journalism in the western press: comparing six news systems since the 1960s." *Journalism & Mass Communication Quarterly* 91(2): 229–249.

Grijelmo, Álex. 2014. *El estilo del periodista*. Madrid: Taurus.

Hjarvard, Stig. 2010. "The views of the news: the role of political newspapers in a changing media landscape." *Northern Lights* 8: 25–48. doi: 10.1386/ nl.8.25_1

Houston, Brant. 2015. "Interpretive journalism." In *The concise encyclopedia of communication*, edited by Wolfgang Donsbach, 301. West Sussex: John Wiley & Sons.

Jane's. 2017. *Writing articles for Jane's Intelligence Review. Guidelines for freelance contributors*. Revised 10 May 2017.

JIC Assessment. 2005. *International terrorism: impact of Iraq*. April 13, 2005. Declassified January 2011. http://iraqinquiry.org.uk

Lahneman, William J. and Rubén Arcos. Eds. 2014. *The art of intelligence: Simulations, exercises, and games*. Lanham, MD: Rowman & Littlefield.

Kent, Sherman. 1966. *Strategic intelligence for American world policy*. Princeton, NJ: Princeton University Press.

MacDougall, Curtis D. 1968. *Interpretative reporting* (5th ed.). New York: The Macmillan Company.

Nielsen, Nathan. 1976. "The national intelligence daily." *Studies in Intelligence* 20(1): 39–51. https://www.cia.gov/library/readingroom/docs/CIA-RDP78T03194A000400010022-7.pdf

Office of the Director of National Intelligence. 2006. *Intelligence community directive ICD 301: National open source enterprise*. July 11, 2006. https://fas.org/irp/dni/icd/icd-301.pdf. Accessed December 23, 2016.

Office of the Director of National Intelligence. 2015. *Intelligence community directive ICD 203: Analytic standards*. January 2, 2015. https://www.dni.gov/files/documents/ICD/ICD%20203%20Analytic%20Standards.pdf. Last Accessed August 13, 2018.

Office of the Director of National Intelligence. 2017. *Intelligence community assessment ICA 2017–01D. Assessing Russian activities and intentions in recent US elections*. January 6, 2017. https://www.dni.gov/files/documents/ICA_2017_01.pdf

Patterson, Thomas E. 1998. "Political roles of the journalist." In *The politics of the news and the news of politics*, edited by Doris Graber, Denis McQuail, and Pippa Norris, 17–32. Washington DC: CQ Press.

Patterson, Thomas E. 2000. "The United States: news in a free-market society." In *Democracy and the media: a comparative perspective*, edited by Richard Gunther and Anthony Mughan, 241–265. New York: Cambridge University Press.

Product Review Division of the ICS. 1975. *A guide to National Intelligence Community's production organizations and their products*. July 28, 1975.

Rosenwasser, David and Stephen, Jill. 2012. *Writing analytically with readings*. Boston: Wadsworth, Cengage Learning.

Salgado, Susana and Jesper Strömbäck. 2012. "Interpretive journalism: a review of concepts, operationalizations and key findings." *Journalism* 13(2): 144–161.

Siegal, Allan M. and William G. Connolly. 2015. *The New York Times Manual of Style and Usage* (5th ed.) New York: Three Rivers Press.

UK Ministry of Defence. 2011. Joint Doctrine Publication 2–00 Understanding and intelligence support to joint operations (3rd ed.). August 2011. Developments, Concepts and Doctrine Centre. https://assets.publishing.service.gov.uk/government/uploads/system/uploads/attachment_data/file/311572/20110830_jdp2_00_ed3_with_change1.pdf. Last Accessed August 13, 2018.

Wall, Robert. 2016. "Multibillion-dollar jet deals with Iran will test Trump policy." *The Wall Street Journal*, December 22. http://www.wsj.com/articles/airbus-finalizes-18-billion-jet-deal-with-iran-1482414783 Accessed December 22, 2012.

Wyatt, Robert O. and David P. Badger. 1993. "A new typology for journalism and mass communication writing." *Journalism Educator* (Spring 1993): 3–11. https://doi.org/10.1177/107769589304800101

3

The Collaborative Discovery Process

Leveraging Community Resources to Combat Human Trafficking

Randolph H. Pherson and Karen Saunders

The collaborative discovery process derives from the practice of harnessing data from individuals with diverse backgrounds, expertise, and demographic profiles. This practice, commonly known as *crowdsourcing*, is defined by *Merriam-Webster* as "the practice of obtaining needed services, ideas, or content by soliciting contributions from a large group of people and especially from the online community rather than from traditional employees or suppliers."[1] Crowdsourcing[2] is a powerful method of generating a wide range of perspectives and perceived knowledge to solve a problem or better understand an issue, particularly when the problem or issue is distributed enough to affect—or be encountered by—the broad population. Human trafficking is one such issue, as many members of a community will encounter victims of this crime or instances of human trafficking in their everyday lives without knowledge or realization.

Crowdsourcing, however, has some drawbacks that the collaborative discovery process can overcome. For example, the soliciting of information from an undefined group in an online environment can be problematic in law enforcement and other intelligence arenas. First, there is no guarantee of confidentiality. Second, there is no way to evaluate either the sources' credentials or the authenticity, credibility, and substantive value of the information provided.

Collaborative discovery addresses these problems. It is a process that combines several structured analytic techniques to produce a targeted plan of action for harnessing all the resources of known members of the community whose information will be relevant and highly useful in addressing the issue at hand.

In the human trafficking example, the collaborative discovery process can help stakeholders in communities, including law enforcement, victim service providers, and the public, gain a better understanding of the human trafficking phenomenon. It helps illuminate who may be most vulnerable to human trafficking and how, where, when (at what times or on what days), and by whom people are trafficked within a community. Such specificity helps law enforcement develop better investigative and response techniques, helps victim services providers target their resources to those most vulnerable to human trafficking and better respond to victims, and empowers the public to report potential human trafficking situations.

The value of the collaborative discovery process is not limited to human trafficking. The process is also useful in addressing gang activity, terrorism, drug trafficking, arms trafficking, and other network-based crimes.

Combating Human Trafficking: Opportunities and Weaknesses

In many ways the global response to human trafficking has been admirable. Legislators, law enforcement personnel, prosecutors, policymakers, assistance providers, civil society members, and even ordinary citizens have galvanized to identify and respond to international and domestic human trafficking cases and to rescue and protect victims of this crime.

The international community and individual countries have made considerable efforts to prevent and combat human trafficking, identify and rescue victims, and prosecute traffickers. For example, the US government has launched a large-scale initiative to combat human trafficking across and within its borders. The guiding force behind this initiative is the Trafficking Victims Protection Act (TVPA), federal legislation first enacted in 2000 that defines and criminalizes human trafficking, provides for victims' assistance services, and requires the integration of new research and analysis into the development of methods to prevent, identify, enforce, and prosecute human trafficking crimes and assist its victims. Similarly, the international community, led by the United Nations under its Protocol to Prevent, Suppress, and Punish Trafficking in Persons from 2000, has endeavored to define human trafficking and set conditions for its elimination.

These efforts, however, have been stymied by incomplete information on the nature, scale, and scope of this phenomenon globally, on a national level, and in individual localities within countries. Lack of understanding as to *where, how, when, by whom*, and *to whom* human trafficking occurs leads to missed opportunities for victim identification, intervention, and assistance as well as prevention of trafficking and prosecution of traffickers.

Due to fundamental failures to conduct proactive research and analysis on this issue, counter-trafficking initiatives have failed to keep pace with human traffickers' increasingly cunning methods and means of enticing, recruiting, and/or forcing victims into situations of modern-day slavery—and keeping them there.

The Community: An Underutilized Analytic and Investigative Resource

In many instances, analysis and investigative work have failed to involve the community to broaden our conceptualization and understanding of human trafficking. Law enforcement analysts and investigators working on human trafficking do not generally interface with community members about the problem, despite research that suggests that community members have been invaluable in identifying victims of human trafficking crimes. The National Human Trafficking Resource Center reports that 26.6 percent of calls to its hotline in 2015 were made by community members with no professional obligations to identify and report suspected human trafficking cases.[3] A study of 140 human trafficking cases that were successfully prosecuted in the United States found that 39 percent of the case investigations were sparked by a tip from a community member, hotline call, or victim services organization.[4]

Most research and analysis of human trafficking crimes and victims' assistance practices within the United States and its territories has thus far consisted of case data reviews and interviews with survivors, law enforcement, prosecutors, witnesses, convicted traffickers, and victims' assistance providers.[5] This type of analytic approach is *reactive*[6] and gives rise to the cycle of knowledge, analysis, and capacity-building depicted in figure 3.1.

Although certainly useful in augmenting our current understanding of the forms and manifestations of human trafficking in the United States, this type of analysis is insufficient for developing a full and forthright understanding of the

FIGURE 3.1 Cycle of Knowledge, Analysis, and Capacity-Building

nature, scale, and scope of the complex phenomenon of human trafficking and articulating appropriate responses to it.

In their study of methodological challenges in empirical studies of human trafficking, Tyldum and Brunovskis highlight the pitfalls inherent in an overreliance on the use of reactive analysis to illuminate a country's human trafficking problems.[7] First, although researchers use the number of identified and rescued human trafficking victims to extrapolate the nature, scale, and scope of human trafficking in a given jurisdiction, this data is actually more indicative of the efficacy of law enforcement and victims' assistance groups operating within that jurisdiction. Second, and most important to the central arguments in this chapter, they highlight the problem of representativity and bias. Using law enforcement and victims' assistance data to analyze and depict human trafficking as a whole will necessarily bias the results, because law enforcement will likely continue to identify and respond to cases similar to those uncovered or described in the past, and victims' assistance groups will identify, rescue, and serve victims of similar types of human trafficking. They write, "It is difficult to determine to what extent the identified cases are representative of the universe of trafficking cases, and which biases they introduce to our data."[8] In other words, those cases that law enforcement is most adept at uncovering—or those to which victims' assistance groups are most skilled at responding—will be overrepresented in the dataset. Research and analysis based on this case data will fail to illuminate other forms of trafficking that are prevalent in the jurisdiction but that are as yet unknown.

In contemplating the cycle depicted in figure 3.1, the limitations of relying on this type of reactive research and analysis to improve our understanding of human trafficking and build appropriate responses to it become evident. We may be missing a large number of human trafficking cases by failing to challenge our assumptions and expand our thinking and response beyond self-confirming analysis. Tyldum and Brunovskis sum it up thus:

> in spite of the strong increase in identified cases of trafficking, it remains difficult to determine if the identified cases represent a tip of the iceberg, or if all or close to all incidents of trafficking for sexual exploitation are usually identified.[9]

The same premise holds true for labor trafficking, trafficking into situations of domestic servitude, and labor and sex trafficking of US citizens or foreign national minors.

Invoking the power of the community could prove instrumental in identifying unknown and emerging types of human trafficking crimes. The National Human Trafficking Resource Center underscores that human trafficking victims live within communities and, as such, routinely encounter community members: "Victims are in plain view and may interact with community members, but the widespread lack of awareness and understanding of trafficking leads to low levels of victim identification by the people who most often encounter them."[10]

Case evidence suggests that community members often have knowledge about human trafficking victims and cases, but researchers and analysts tend to overlook this group. Victims' assistance organizations and law enforcement agencies, however, are learning to harness the power of the community to increase their efficacy in identifying situations of human trafficking and/or victims of these crimes. For example, law enforcement officers in Montgomery County, Maryland, support a contingent of confidential informants that include service workers such as hotel personnel and taxi drivers who provide information to law enforcement when they see situations that appear to be trafficking-related.[11] Similarly, victims' assistance organizations and other nongovernmental organizations (NGOs) build awareness of human trafficking among community members through training at churches, synagogues, mosques, community centers, unions, and the like; many cases of trafficking into domestic servitude have been identified and reported by ordinary citizens who see something amiss in the home of a neighbor or fellow community member.

The collaborative discovery process aims to address these weaknesses and help communities adopt a more proactive approach to addressing their human trafficking problems. The collaborative discovery simulation and exercise are discussed below.

Simulation

Basic Data

Instructional Objectives
To educate students on the complexities of the human trafficking problem and invoke the power of structured analytic techniques to help communities manage the problem.

Debriefing Format
The instructor provides basic background information on the issue, the inadequacies of a reactive approach to the problem, and how a proactive approach using structured analytic techniques is more effective and methodologically valid.

Target Audience
Undergraduate or graduate students in basic or advanced courses in intelligence analysis, critical thinking skills, or the broader disciplines of political science.

Playing Time
Two three-hour sessions

Debriefing Time
30 minutes

Number of Players Required
The simulation works best in a classroom setting with at least 12 and as many as 32 participants. A minimum of three groups of four is recommended. Additional groups of four can be added as necessary.

Participation Material Included

Handouts:

- Appendix 3A. Introduction to Human Trafficking
- Appendix 3B. Key Assumptions Check Instructions
- Appendix 3C. Key Assumptions Check Worksheet
- Appendix 3D. Cluster Brainstorming Instructions
- Appendix 3E. Red Hat Analysis/Indicators Instructions
- Appendix 3F. Indicators Worksheet
- Appendix 3G. Force Field Analysis Instructions

Computer/Internet

Not required

Other Materials/Equipment Required

A large classroom that allows organizing the students into small groups sitting around a table. Each group will also need an easel with large sheets of paper to write on (or adjacent whiteboards) with three colored markers.

Pre-simulation Briefing

The instructor begins with a brief overview of the human trafficking problem. Resources for preparing an overview are included in appendix 3A. The instructor should discuss the strengths and weaknesses in current practice to respond to human trafficking as detailed above, as well as the distinctions between collaborative discovery and traditional crowdsourcing in eliciting "the wisdom of the crowd."

The simulation is structured as follows:

Session One:

30 minutes	Introduction, course objectives, topic familiarization
60 minutes:	Key assumptions check exercise
60 minutes:	Cluster brainstorming exercise
30 minutes:	Generating list of key professions

Session Two:

90 minutes	Red hat/indicators exercise
60 minutes	Force field analysis exercise
30 minutes	Debrief: What have we learned?

Conducting the Simulation

As discussed earlier, human trafficking is a community-based, network-based crime. Victims live in communities and routinely intersect with members of the community, and traffickers rely on an extensive network of individuals within their community—aware or not—to perpetrate their crimes.

The impetus for the collaborative discovery approach is the need for a process to help identify and better understand the phenomenon of human trafficking and then arm key members of a community with the strategies that are likely to prove most effective in their community to combat the problem. In the first session, students engage in two exercises to further their understanding of the phenomenon: a key assumptions check and cluster brainstorming. In the second session, they focus their attention on what to do about it using red hat analysis, indicators, and force field analysis.

Key Assumptions Check

A key assumptions check will help students understand the complexity of human trafficking by identifying and evaluating the validity of their assumptions about the phenomenon. This is accomplished by conducting a key assumptions check exercise in groups of a dozen or so students (see appendix 3B: Key Assumptions Check Instructions and appendix 3C: Key Assumptions Check Worksheet).

A key assumptions check involves first identifying assumptions about an issue or phenomenon. Participants then critically evaluate their assumptions, assigning a value of "solid and well supported," supported with "caveats," and "unsupported" by data and evidence. After each group has completed the exercise, the instructor facilitates a discussion comparing and contrasting each group's results. The facilitator then asks the students to reflect on how their improved understanding of the key assumptions surrounding human trafficking impacts their understanding of the phenomenon.

Cluster Brainstorming

After the students have developed a better understanding of the human trafficking phenomenon and challenged their assumptions about it, they will be ready to apply their understanding to human trafficking at the community level.

Cluster brainstorming is a widely used structured analytic technique (SAT) for idea generation. In this exercise it is used as a launching point for students to explore how members of a community will likely intersect with human trafficking victims and traffickers. Unlike many SATs, cluster brainstorming does not require that participants have particular expertise in the topic of analysis. In this case, its value in expanding the known universe of human trafficking forms and methods is predicated on its ability to involve individuals *without significant knowledge or expertise* on human trafficking and to thereby harness the knowledge intrinsic within the population.

The instructor facilitates one or more parallel cluster brainstorming sessions involving the same dozen or more students in each session (see appendix 3B: Cluster Brainstorming Instructions). The instructor posts the following question on a whiteboard or an easel for all the students to see: *Which members of a community might encounter some aspect of human trafficking in their daily lives or would be in a position to observe or come in contact with those involved in it?*

The objective of this cluster brainstorming exercise is to expand and enrich understanding of what, where, to whom, by whom, and how human trafficking works in a given community. Students leverage the power of a structured form of silent brainstorming to identify all the possible members of the community who might encounter human trafficking victims in the community. At the end of the exercise, the group should have an exhaustive list of professionals and other community members such as medical personnel, mail carriers, garbage collectors, florists, hotel workers, clergy, beauty salon employees, convenience store clerks, fast-food service workers, nightclub workers, restaurant personnel, and the like.

Questions that students should explore following the cluster brainstorming exercise include: Where might the illegitimate business of human trafficking intersect with legitimate business? How might people be vulnerable to trafficking Schemes? How might traffickers exploit these vulnerabilities?

The first class session concludes with the instructor asking the students to reflect on the results of both exercises and make a list of all the professions most likely to come in contact with human trafficking. The instructor then asks the students to prioritize which community members are likely to have the most contact with human trafficking as well as the best insights into what may be going on within their locale. They will use this list to delve deeper into the simulation during the second session.

Red Hat Analysis/Indicators

Red hat analysis is a useful technique for identifying and anticipating the behavior of those involved in human trafficking. It is a reframing technique that helps students break out of their established mindsets and gain a new perspective on the problem by putting themselves "in the shoes" of those engaged in trafficking and going further to identify ways that community members might spot trafficking behavior.

Students begin the second session by conducting a red hat analysis to explore what specific community members can do to combat the practice of human trafficking (see appendix 3E: Red Hat/Indicators Instructions and appendix 3F: Indicators Worksheet). The instructor assigns one or two participants (depending on the size of the class) to role-play each of the "community members" identified and prioritized in the previous session. Their task is to:

- Generate a list of ways they might encounter human trafficking. For example, a repairman might notice that too many people live in a house he visits; a dog walker might notice a large volume of cars coming and going; a delivery person might suspect the type and volume of packages he or she drops off at a house.
- Rank order the list of "ways" each profession might encounter human trafficking from what appears to be the most compelling to the least compelling idea.

The list of behaviors that is developed for each profession is basically a list of indicators. Indicators are a pre-established set of observable phenomena that is periodically reviewed to help spot emerging or suspicious behavior, track events, and warn of unanticipated change. They provide an objective base line to alert one to unanticipated developments, validate existing hypotheses, and confirm

TABLE 3.1	Five Characteristics of a Good Indicator
Key Characteristic	**Description**
Observable/collectible	Can be sensed visually or by other means and accurately reported
Valid	Accurately and reliably captures the phenomenon
Reliable	Is reported consistently by different people
Stable	Remains consistent over time
Unique	Measures only one thing

that a target's activity is consistent with established patterns of those involved in human trafficking.

After constructing lists of indicators for each profession, the students engage in a validation exercise. Their task is to:

- Check the diagnosticity of the indicator against five criteria (see Table 3.1). Does the indicator meet the test of being observable/collectible, valid, reliable, stable, and unique? The first two characteristics are required for every indicator. The third and fourth characteristics are extremely important but cannot always be satisfied. The fifth characteristic is key to achieving a high degree of diagnosticity for the indicator but is the most difficult goal to reach. A way to test uniqueness is to ask if the same indicator might appear if something else was happening. If that is the case, then the indicator has less value.
- Review the list of compelling indicators and decide if some of them should be clustered to provide more efficient monitoring of the activity.

Force Field Analysis

Force field analysis is a useful tool for prioritizing which forces and players are likely to have the most beneficial impact in dealing with an issue or situation. It offers a powerful way to visualize the key elements and players involved by providing a tally sheet for displaying the differing levels of intensity of the key players and forces both individually and as a group. The display helps key decision makers—and the community as a whole—identify which forces deserve the most attention and are likely to have the most impact in addressing the problem.

In their final exercise, students assign a value to each indicator giving an intensity score of 1 (minor) to 5 (major) (see appendix 3G: Force Field Analysis Instructions). They then create specific action plans for the key role players associated with the most highly rated indicators. The action plan should describe the overall process of observation, reporting, and any follow-on actions that would be warranted.

An overarching action plan should also be sketched out for the community as a whole. The plan should facilitate sharing observations across the community while ensuring effective feedback to all members. It should illustrate how the insights gained from the exercises can best be leveraged by members of the community to deal with the human trafficking problem. It should identify the key players committed to combatting the scourge of human trafficking and those who are most likely to resist or obstruct such efforts. The plan should list specific goalposts over the coming year.

Debriefing

The final component of this simulation exercise is to involve the students in a discussion of their learning outcomes from it. The instructor should reconvene the entire class and reiterate the learning objectives and the purposes of each structured analytic technique, and then generate student responses to the following questions:

1. What were the most surprising unsupported assumptions you had about human trafficking? How did your key assumptions check inform the cluster brainstorming exercise?
2. What results of your cluster brainstorming exercise do you feel would be most helpful to communities that seek to address their human trafficking problems? What was your group's most innovative idea?
3. What new ideas for addressing human trafficking did you discover by performing the indicators and force field exercises?
4. How would you use these individual techniques or the collaborative discovery process to address another issue that you care about?

Conclusion

The potential for using community collaboration as a powerful weapon against complex problems such as human trafficking should not be underestimated. Victims' assistance organizations and law enforcement agencies are increasingly engaging the community in identifying situations of human trafficking. By adopting a more proactive collaborative discovery process, communities can more effectively address their human trafficking problems. With little modification, the five structured analytic techniques used in this approach can also provide new ways for dealing with other complex phenomena like radicalization, gang violence, drug trafficking, and other illicit trade.

Appendix 3A

Introduction to Human Trafficking

The international community has criminalized human trafficking under the auspices of the United Nations Protocol to Prevent, Suppress, and Punish Trafficking in Persons. Human trafficking is defined as the recruitment, harboring, transportation, and/or sale of people for purposes of sexual exploitation, forced labor, or domestic servitude.

Human trafficking is considered to be a pervasive crime that affects every country in the world. Estimates of its scope by the International Labour Organization (ILO) suggest that proceeds from human trafficking exceed $150 billion annually and that there are more than 20 million victims worldwide.[12]

Countries may be source countries, whose populations are enslaved in global trafficking; transit countries, which serve as pipelines for victims from source countries to "markets" where they are exploited; destination countries, which provide a market for sexual and/or labor exploitation; or a combination of these.

More developed economies, such as those in Western Europe, the United States, and Canada, are generally considered destinations for international victims of trafficking, and less developed countries are source or transit countries. However, in 2009, the US-based NGO Shared Hope International published the first report on the growing phenomenon of Domestic Minor Sex Trafficking, which is the sex and labor exploitation of US-born children under the age of 18.[13] Estimates of the number of domestic minor victims of trafficking in the United States range from 150,000 to 300,000 per year.[14] Runaway children are considered to be most vulnerable to human trafficking schemes.

Selected External Resources on Human Trafficking

United Nations Office on Drugs and Crime (UNODC): https://www.unodc.org/unodc/en/human-trafficking/index.html?ref=menuside

International Labour Organization (ILO): http://www.ilo.org/global/topics/forced-labour/lang—ja/index.htm

The European Commission Anti-Trafficking Resources: http://ec.europa.eu/anti-trafficking/

US Department of State Office to Monitor and Combat Trafficking in Persons (TIP): https://www.state.gov/j/tip/

The US National Human Trafficking Hotline: https://humantraffickinghotline.org/

Shared Hope International: http://sharedhope.org/

Polaris Project: https://polarisproject.org/

Appendix 3B

Key Assumptions Check Instructions

A **key assumptions check** is an explicit exercise to list and challenge the key working assumptions that underlie the basic analysis.

The process of conducting a key assumptions check is relatively straightforward in concept but often challenging to operationalize. The key to conducting a key assumptions check is to be open-minded. It also pays major dividends when you can involve others less familiar with the topic who can openly challenge the key analytic assumptions of the group. Keep in mind that many "key assumptions" turn out to be "key uncertainties." Based on facilitator experience, approximately one in four key assumptions usually collapses on careful examination.

The Method

- Gather a small group of individuals who are working the issue along with a small number of "outsiders" who can come to the table with an independent perspective.
- At the outset, the group must agree on a definition of a key assumption. An assumption is a supposition of something as true in order for another condition or development to be true; it can also be a fact or statement that analysts tend to take for granted. The latter are often generated by cultural bias or analytic mindsets and are difficult to uncover.
- On a whiteboard or an easel, list all the key assumptions that underlie the subject.
- After developing a complete list, go back and critically examine each assumption.
- Encourage the participants to ask themselves the following questions. You may want to display this list on another easel or on the whiteboard, or provide it as a handout.
  - How much confidence do I have that this assumption is valid?
  - Why do I have this degree of confidence?
  - Under what circumstances might this assumption be untrue?
  - Could it have been true in the past but no longer be true today?
  - If it turns out to be invalid, how much impact would this have on the analysis?
- Try to place each assumption in one of three categories:
  - Basically solid.
  - Correct with some caveats.
  - Unsupported or questionable.
- The unsupported assumptions often are better characterized as key uncertainties.
- Refine the list of key assumptions, deleting those that do not hold up to scrutiny and adding new assumptions that emerge from the discussion.

Appendix 3C

Key Assumptions Check Worksheet

Key Assumption	Rationale	Rating: Supported (S), Caveated (C), or Unsupported (U)
1.		
2.		
3.		
4.		
5.		
6.		
7.		

Supported: An assumption that is basically solid.
Caveated: An assumption that is correct with some caveats.
Unsupported: An assumption that is unsupported or questionable.

FIGURE 3A.1 Key Assumptions Check Worksheet

Appendix 3D

Cluster Brainstorming Instructions

Cluster brainstorming follows specific rules and procedures to stimulate new ideas and concepts, emphasizing the use of silence and "kinetic brainstorming" with sticky notes.

1. Pass out sticky notes and marker pens to everybody. Tell the participants that no one will be allowed to speak except the instructor during the exercise.

2. Project or write the question on a whiteboard: which members of a community might encounter some aspect of human trafficking in their community or would be in a position to observe or come in contact with those involved in the practice?

3. Ask the participants to write down their responses to the question on a sticky note and give it to the facilitator who reads them out loud. Participants are asked to capture the concept with a few key words that will fit on the sticky note. Use markers so everyone can easily see what is written.

4. The facilitator sticks all the sticky notes on the wall or a whiteboard in random order as they are called out. All ideas are treated the same. Participants are urged to build on one another's ideas. Usually there is an initial spurt of ideas followed by pauses as participants contemplate the question. After five or ten minutes, expect a long pause of a minute or so. This slowing down suggests that the group has "emptied the barrel of the obvious" and is now on the verge of coming up with some fresh insights and ideas. Facilitators should not talk during this pause even if the silence is uncomfortable.

5. After a couple of two-minute pauses, facilitators conclude this divergent stage of the brainstorming process. They then ask a small group of students to go up to the wall and arrange the sticky notes into affinity groups that would describe different professions or roles people play within the community. Group members cannot talk while they are doing this. If one sticky note seems "to belong" in more than one group, make a copy and place one sticky note in each affinity group.

6. If the topic is sufficiently complex, ask a second small group to go to the board and review what the first group did. They cannot speak but are encouraged to rearrange the notes into a more coherent pattern.

7. When all the sticky notes have been arranged, the group at the board should pick a word or phrase that best describes that grouping.

8. Also look for outliers, or sticky notes that do not belong in a particular group. Such an outlier could be either (1) useless noise or (2) the gem of an idea that deserves further elaboration as a theme.

Appendix 3E

Red Hat Analysis/Indicators Instructions

Step 1: Generate a list of ways each member of the community might encounter human trafficking. We will call these indicators. For example, a repairman might notice that too many people live in a house he visits; a dog walker might notice a large volume of cars coming and going; a delivery person might suspect the type and volume of packages he or she drops off at a house.

Step 2: For each profession, list five to ten indicators down the left side of the matrix.

Step 3: Examine each indicator to determine if it meets the following five criteria. Discard those that are found wanting.

- **Observable and Collectible**. There must be some reasonable expectation that, if present, the indicator will be observed and reported by a reliable source. If an indicator is to monitor change over time, it must be collectible over time.
- **Valid**. An indicator must be clearly relevant to the end state the analyst is trying to predict or assess, and it must be inconsistent with all or at least some of the alternative explanations or outcomes. It must accurately measure the concept or phenomenon at issue.
- **Reliable**. Data collection must be consistent when comparable methods are used. Those observing and collecting data must observe the same things. Reliability requires precise definition of the indicators.
- **Stable**. An indicator must be useful over time to allow comparisons and to track events. Ideally, the indicator should be observable early in the evolution of a development so that analysts and decision makers have time to react accordingly.
- **Unique**. The indicator should measure only one thing and, in combination with others, only point to the phenomenon being studied.

Step 4: Review the list of compelling indicators and decide if some of them should be clustered to provide more efficient monitoring of the activity.

Appendix 3F

Indicators Worksheet

Profession:

Criteria:
A. *Observable/Collectible/Practical*
B. *Valid*
C. *Reliable*
D. *Stable*
E. *Unique*

Candidate Indicator	A	B	C	D	E
1.					
2.					
3.					
4.					
5.					
6.					
7.					
8.					
9.					
10.					

FIGURE 3A.2 Indicators Worksheet

Appendix 3G

Force Field Analysis Instructions

Ask the students to create specific action plans for the key role players.

1. Assign a score to each indicator from 1 (minor value) to 5 (major value).
2. Reorder the indicators, placing those with the highest value on the top of the list and those with the lowest value on the bottom.
3. Develop a plan of action for each profession associated with an indicator, focusing attention on those indicators with the highest value. The action plan should describe the overall process of observation, reporting, and any follow-on actions that would be warranted.

An overarching action plan should also be sketched out for the community as a whole. The plan should facilitate sharing observations across the community while ensuring effective feedback to all members. It should illustrate how the insights gained from the exercises can best be leveraged by members of the community to deal with the human trafficking problem. The plan should list specific goalposts over the coming year. Students conduct a force field analysis to establish an analytic foundation for creating the action plan:

1. List all the players who are committed to combatting the scourge of human trafficking in the community.
2. Rank these players on a scale of 1 (minimal support) to 5 (enthusiastic support).
3. List all the players who are likely to resist or obstruct the effort (5 = active obstruction).
4. Reorder the lists, putting the high numbers on top and low numbers on the bottom.
5. Identify the key players willing to promote change and implement a counter human trafficking strategy and accompanying strategies to enlist their support.
6. Identify the players likely to offer the most opposition and develop strategies to minimize their impact.
7. Draft an overarching plan that encompasses all these strategies.

Notes

1 "Crowdsourcing," *Merriam-Webster Dictionary*, https://www.merriam-webster.com/dictionary/crowdsourcing. Accessed June 15, 2017.
2 For a brief etymology of crowdsourcing, see Safire, William. "Fat Tail," *New York Times Magazine*, February 5, 2009. http://www.nytimes.com/2009/02/08/magazine/08wwln-safire-t.html?_r=3&ref=magazine&.
3 *United States Report 1/1/15–12/31/15*, National Human Trafficking Resource Center. https://humantraffickinghotline.org/sites/default/files/NHTRC%202015%20United%20States%20Report%20-%20USA%20-%2001.01.15%20-%2012.31.15_OTIP_Edited_06-09-16.pdf. Accessed July 20, 2017.
4 Farrell, Amy and Jack McDevitt. "Hidden in Plain Sight: Challenges to Identifying, Investigating, and Prosecuting Human Trafficking," *JRSA Forum*, vol. 32, no. 3, September 2014. http://www.jrsa.org/pubs/forum/sep2014_32-3/trafficking.htm.

[5] See, for example: Dank, Meredith, Bilal Khan, P. Mitchell Downey, Cybele Kotonias, Deborah Mayer, Colleen Owens, Laura Pacifici, and Lilly Yu. *Estimating the Size and Structure of the Underground Commercial Sex Economy in Eight Major US Cities.* Washington, DC: The Urban Institute, March 2014; Smith, Linda A., Samantha Healy Vardaman, and Melissa A. Snow. *The National Report on Domestic Minor Sex Trafficking: America's Prostituted Children.* Arlington, VA: SharedHope International, May 2009; *Report from the U.S. Mid-Term Review on the Commercial Sexual Exploitation of Children in America.* Shared Hope International, ECPAT-USA, and the Protection Project of the Johns Hopkins University School of Advanced International Studies, Washington, DC. September 2006; Clawson, Heather J., Mary Layne, and Kevonne Small. *Estimating Human Trafficking into the United States: A Methodology.* Fairfax, VA: Caliber, an ICF International Company, 2006; Bales, Kevin and Steven Lize. *Trafficking in Persons in the United States: A Report to the National Institute of Justice.* Report prepared under National Institute of Justice Grant #2001-IJ-CX-0027; and Estes, Richard J. and Neil Alan Weiner. *The Commercial Sexual Exploitation of Children in the U.S., Canada, and Mexico.* Philadelphia, PA: University of Pennsylvania Center for the Study of Youth Policy, September 10, 2001.

[6] Pherson, Katherine Hibbs and Randolph H. Pherson. *Critical Thinking for Strategic Intelligence.* Washington, DC: CQ Press, 2013.

[7] Tyldum, Guri and Anette Brunovskis. "Describing the Unobserved: Methodological Challenges in Empirical Studies on Human Trafficking." *International Migration*, vol. 43, no. 1/2 (2005): 17–34.

[8] Ibid., 24.

[9] Ibid., 24.

[10] National Human Trafficking Hotline, "The Victims," https://humantraffickinghotline.org/what-human-trafficking/human-trafficking/victims. Accessed August 27, 2018.

[11] Montgomery County, Maryland. Vice Detective, Name Withheld. Personal Interview by Author. April 25, 2008.

[12] International Labour Organization, "ILO 2012 Global Estimate of Forced Labour," http://www.ilo.org/wcmsp5/groups/public/—ed_norm/—declaration/documents/publication/wcms_181921.pdf. Accessed July 20, 2017.

[13] Smith, Linda A., Samantha Healy Vardamon, and Melissa A. Snow, *The National Report on Domestic Minor Sex Trafficking,* Shared Hope International. 2009.

[14] US Congress, "Domestic Minor Sex Trafficking: Hearing before the Subcommittee on Crime, Terrorism, and Homeland Security," September 15, 2010. Serial Number 111–46.

4

Practicing Foresight Analysis in Intelligence Courses

William J. Lahneman

Much analytical work in the social sciences, business, and government relies on trend analysis. Trend analysts employ methods ranging from complicated multiple regression analyses, with heavy emphasis on datafication, statistics, and computer computations, to more qualitative analyses that look more generally at multiple trends and seek to draw conclusions. Trend analyses produce *forecasts*.

> Forecasting is a great deal about gathering data, assessing risks and opportunities inherent in trends, and shaping scenarios that fit within the given parameters of probability. Within this context, the future is generally assumed to look somewhat as it does today, except more so.
>
> (Briggs and Briggs 2013, 1)

Trend analysis remains fairly accurate as long as prevailing trends remain in force. However, history is full of events that bring about discontinuous change, thus altering the "direction" of trends virtually overnight. Some good examples of events that have produced discontinuous change are:

- The collapse of the Soviet Union
- Apple inventing the iPhone
- The Rwandan genocide
- Al Qaeda carrying out the 9/11 attacks
- The US real estate bubble bursting in 2007.

Some other events that might cause discontinuous change are:

- Russia invading Crimea
- Russia invading Ukraine
- Edward Snowden revealing Project Prism
- The Fukushima nuclear disaster
- Donald Trump being elected US president

Analysts often have referred to events such as these as "black swan" events, where the term "black swan" is a "metaphor that describes an event that comes as a surprise, has a major effect, and is often inappropriately rationalized after the fact with the benefit of hindsight" (Black Swan Theory, 2016). Nassim Nicholas Taleb, the developer of black swan theory (Taleb 2010), describes these events more formally:

- The event is a surprise (to the observer)
- The event has a major effect
- After the first recorded instance of the event, it is rationalized by hindsight, as if it could have been expected; that is, the relevant data were available but unaccounted for in risk mitigation programs. The same is true for the personal perception by individuals (Black Swan Theory, 2016).

In fact, however, scientific methods such as trend analysis are not capable of forecasting such events. Rationalizations that they could have been forecast if only analysts had been smarter, worked harder, or shared information better only serve to obscure this fact.

In social science jargon, these kinds of events are "low-probability, high-consequence" events. They are of such low probability or rarity that analysts cannot forecast or predict them. Nevertheless, analysts must try to account for them in their work because they have tended to cause vastly larger roles in history than the kinds of events produced by normal trends (perhaps because policymakers account for trends when designing their policies and seek to optimize their group's welfare or at least minimize the discomfort as the expected trends unfold).

Foresight analysis offers one way for analysts and policymakers to try to account for unexpected but important events. Foresight analysis does not try to predict black swan events. Rather, it develops scenarios that include such low-probability, high-consequence events. "Foresight analysis, like forecasting, also relies on using the most up-to-date information available, but looks not only at trends and probabilities, but more importantly evaluates how future drivers of change may influence a *range of possible alternative futures*" (Briggs 2013, 2). The goal of such scenario-building is to identify plausible ways that black swan events could affect politics, economics, the biosphere, and so forth. In complex societies, interaction of black swan events with each other and with normal trends is particularly important.

> Most disasters emerge not from single events, but rather from unexpected combinations of events and drivers. The nuclear accident at Fukushima and the immense fallout from Superstorm Sandy are examples of where critical vulnerabilities and/or complex combinations of ingredients created overwhelming problems that surprised many planners.
>
> (Briggs and Briggs 2013, 2)

Being able to describe *potential* mechanisms for cascading impacts from disasters and other events is crucial in avoiding potential surprises.

Foresight Scenario Exercise

Basic Data

Instructional Objectives The purpose of this classroom exercise is to acquaint students with the basic nature of foresight analysis. In the process it seeks to raise student awareness of the complex nature of trying to design policies in such a way that they can hedge against the occurrence of black swan events and thus reduce the overall effects of such low-probability, high-consequence events. In particular, the exercise emphasizes identifying policies that might be relatively easy and inexpensive to implement but would have a significant effect on mitigating the effects of black swan events. The exercise also exposes students to the concept of knowledge creation by providing an interactive forum for participants to exchange knowledge and feel invested in the issues. The exercise can also identify key risks that are capable of being explored further.

Simulation Objectives
Working in small groups, participants prepare a foresight analysis using four potential global developments—including some black swan events—which each group randomly selects from a series of alternative partial scenarios (see appendix 4A). Each group uses these four "partial futures" to construct a coherent global future scenario using mind mapping techniques. Participants use the global future scenarios that they have developed to identify the kinds of discontinuous changes that can occur when expected trends and relationships interact with low-probability, high-consequence events.

Debriefing Format
The instructor facilitates a group discussion among all participants at the end of the simulation, directing the discussion to ensure that the class discusses the learning objectives described above.

Target Audience
Undergraduate and graduate students in introductory or advanced courses about intelligence analysis, national security, US foreign policy, international relations, and business strategy.

Playing Time
90–120 minutes

Debriefing Time
30–45 minutes

Number of Players Required
Two to 30 participants. The exercise can be conducted with a single group of two students, and can accommodate up to five or six groups of up to five participants each. Groups containing four to five participants seem to be the best size for stimulating discussion and creating knowledge.

Required Materials
Appendix 4A (Sample Partial Scenarios for Foresight Analysis Exercise) and appendix 4B (Sample Mind Map). (Note: Instructors are welcome to draft their own partial scenarios and mind maps to augment or replace those in appendices 4A and 4B.) The classroom should be large enough to allow each group to have its own area to conduct discussions without disturbing the other groups. Each group should have markers and large sheets of paper for recording their thoughts and constructing their mind maps (classrooms with adequate blackboard/erasable board space can use them instead). Computer/Internet access is not required.

Facilitator's Guide

Pre-exercise Briefing (5–10 Minutes)

The pre-exercise briefing should cover the basic principles of foresight analysis as described in the introduction.

Step 1 (5 Minutes)

Divide the class into a number of groups made up of three to five students each. Explain that each group will be a team of analysts. The instructor then distributes a copy of appendix 4A (Sample Partial Scenarios for Foresight Analysis Exercise) to each group *after* circling four of the partial scenarios for each group to analyze. (Note: The instructor can assign a different set of scenarios to each group or can assign the same four to all groups. The former approach produces a diverse set of scenarios at the end of the session, while the latter approach produces different scenarios based on the same four factors.)

Step 2 (10 Minutes)

The instructor will demonstrate the format of the exercise by explaining that students will be required to construct mind maps or link diagrams that describe their scenarios. In a mind map, boxes represent nodes (in this case, the partial scenarios and any other additional factors that students want to use), while lines indicate linkages between/among the nodes. Arrows at the end of lines indicate the direction of causation. The instructor should stress that students should use their imaginations in constructing scenarios and not feel constrained by rules of constructing the mind map.

    The instructor should then briefly display appendix 4B on an overhead projector or PowerPoint slide. Using appendix 4B (Sample Mind Maps), the instructor should identify the position of the original four nodes, indicate the various ways to employ arrows, and show students that they should feel free to add additional factors to the scenario.

Step 3 (30–45 Minutes)

Each group discusses how to construct their mind maps using the four scenarios that the instructor has assigned. Students usually begin sketching their results on paper, but later the instructor should instruct each group to either transfer their results to a whiteboard or blackboard, or place their mind map on a PowerPoint slide, so that their drawings are large enough for the entire class to see clearly during the exercise debrief. The instructor should facilitate mind map construction but try to avoid interfering with the creative process. Toward the end of this step, when students have almost completed their mind maps, the instructor should ask each group to consider what kinds of policies might help to prevent their low-probability, high-consequence scenarios from occurring. It often happens that relatively small adjustments to current policies can produce big results. Sometimes the scenarios provide insights about where intelligence agencies and other parts of national security establishments should direct their resources in order to gain early warning that these scenarios might be playing out.

Step 4 (30 Minutes) Each group explains their mind maps to the class and lists policies that might prove useful for either diminishing the chances that a particular outcome

might occur or mitigating negative effects if a particular scenario should occur. The instructor should emphasize particularly interesting outcomes/developments in each mind map. The instructor should also draw attention to whether policies that groups offer to hedge against undesirable outcomes are something that policymakers might realistically consider. Some scenarios and policies are very creative (e.g., one recent group ended their scenario with zombies taking over the planet!).

Debriefing

Exercise Debrief (30 Minutes) The instructor should elicit student thoughts on whether foresight analysis as demonstrated in the exercise is useful. Sometimes different groups will produce scenarios that suggest that policymakers adopt opposing policies (e.g., Russia should form an alliance with ISIS vs. Russia should ally with the United States to defeat ISIS). In such cases, the instructor should discuss whether such opposing outcomes can be reconciled and the trade-offs between selecting one over the other.

Conclusion

The exercise exposes students to one form of foresight analysis in an easy-to-run and concise format that can fit into almost any course in intelligence analysis, competitive intelligence, foreign policy, international relations, global studies, or business strategy at the graduate and undergraduate levels. Student exposure to foresight analysis is admittedly superficial, but the exercise is fun and students are likely to retain the basic information about foresight analysis that they have learned from this experience. By providing them with the basic ingredients for performing foresight analysis, students are able to compare and contrast this form of analysis with the trend analyses which they knowingly or unknowingly have used as the basis for much of their studies. https://textbooks.rowman.com/art-of-intelligence-2

Appendix 4A

Sample Partial Scenarios for Foresight Analysis Exercise

North Korea Nukes United States

North Korea procures or creates a functional 10-kiloton intercontinental ballistic missile and launches it at Los Angeles, striking the city center successfully. Upon impact, there are an estimated 40,000 casualties and 70,000 injuries. Everyone in a 1.5 km radius suffers third-degree burns. Assuming a 15 mph wind blows in any direction, radioactivity at the level of 10 rads per hour spreads a maximum distance of 60 km in a cloud 5 km wide. At least 5 km² of the affected area is irradiated at a rate of 1,000 rads per hour, rendering it effectively useless and uninhabitable for decades.

Overfishing of the North Atlantic Ocean

Norwegian fisheries exercise poor management practices and exhaust their supplies of fish, gradually resulting in an 80 percent reduction in Norwegian fishery output. As Norway is the world's second largest exporter of seafood, this is highly problematic as it creates a global shortage of seafood. Nations dependent upon imported seafood suffer a sharp increase in the price of seafood and a less severe increase in the general price of food, resulting in severely decreased food security.

Revolution in Russia

Vladimir Putin and the United Russia Party are overthrown by leaders in the Russian military, who seize complete control of the state and instantly nationalize all state resources. The regime makes territorial demands of the former Soviet states, which largely depend on Russian natural gas. The new Russian military regime is desperate for support, so it shares Russian nuclear technology and stealth aircraft designs with Iran and North Korea. It also triples conventional weapon exports, both legitimate and underground, with no discrimination.

Ebola Virus Outbreak

An airborne strain of the Ebola virus is discovered in the Democratic Republic of the Congo. It spreads across Africa at an alarming rate, soon engulfing the central and lower parts of the continent. Refugees—many already infected with the virus—flee in multiple directions. Containment efforts are failing in central and southern Africa, and the virus approaches northern Africa before long.

Establishment of Islamic State

Over a decade or so, the Islamic State (IS) gradually de-radicalizes its domestic policies while maintaining a tight grip on the territory it has captured. Using its substantial oil revenues, IS begins to build infrastructure and gain some semblance of legitimacy within Iraq/Syria/Lebanon and the surrounding region. They maintain their ideology and their aggression to Western and westernized states, but build strategic relationships with other states opposed to Western societies to help to secure their status as a legitimate state.

Melting Arctic Ice Pack

Current projections concerning the melting of ice in the arctic prove inaccurate, and the rate of arctic ice melt accelerates. In the next five years, the Arctic Ocean becomes ice-free year-round. This development produces several effects. By opening the Arctic Ocean to unlimited navigation by shipping of all kinds, an ice-free Arctic allows for relatively easy access to the vast natural resources that lie below the Arctic Ocean, including oil, natural gas, strategic minerals, and new fishing grounds. An ice-free Arctic leads to a large increase in merchant shipping using the new Arctic trade routes, and the potential for shipping accidents and environmental disasters rises substantially. Also, the Arctic Ocean essentially becomes an inland sea; countries such as the United States and Russia now find that they are in geographical proximity. Many countries, including those that do not border the Arctic, such as China and India, consider establishing military presences in the region.

Overfishing of the World's Oceans

The growing global population places ever-increasing strains on the world's fish stocks. When this demand is combined with continuing pollution of the world's oceans due to increasing population densities on the world's coasts, plus changes in the oceans' pH (acidity) due to melting arctic and Antarctic ice packs and increased CO_2 absorption due to increased CO_2 air concentrations, the world's great fisheries begin to wither and die. The North Atlantic Basin and the Mediterranean Sea become the first dead zones, followed by the collapse of fish populations in the South China Sea, Sea of Japan, Arabian Sea, Bay of Bengal, and the seas surrounding the Indonesian archipelago.

Rising Sea Levels Due to Climate Change

Melting Arctic and Antarctic ice packs cause a rise in world sea levels. Coastal areas around the world are permanently flooded, making them unfit for further human habitation. Some low-lying areas fare much worse. For example, large areas of Bangladesh, the Netherlands, and a number of island nations see their land areas drastically reduced as flood waters continue to encroach upon some of their most fertile, habitable land.

Iran Nukes Israel

Iran creates several functional 15-kiloton intercontinental ballistic missiles and launches them at Israeli population centers. The number of missiles launched by Iran overwhelms Israel's Iron Dome anti-ballistic missile system, and ten Iranian nuclear weapons strike their targets. Upon impact there are an estimated 2 million casualties and 4 million injuries. Everyone in a 1.5 km radius of each explosion suffers third-degree burns. Assuming a 15 mph wind blows in any direction, radioactivity at the level of 10 rads per hour spreads a maximum distance of 60 km from each detonation point in a cloud 5 km wide. At least 2,000 km² of Israeli territory is irradiated at a rate of 1,000 rads per hour, rendering it effectively useless and uninhabitable for decades. The government of Israel is destroyed.

The Islamic State (IS) Nukes Madrid

The Islamic State (IS) procures or creates a functional 10-kiloton intercontinental ballistic missile and launches it at Madrid, striking the city center successfully. Upon impact, there are an estimated 40,000 casualties and 70,000 injuries. Everyone in a 1.5 km radius suffers third-degree burns. Assuming a 15 mph wind blows in any direction, radioactivity at the level of 10 rads per hour spreads a maximum distance of 60 km in a cloud 5 km wide. At least 5 km² of the affected area is irradiated at a rate of 1,000 rads per hour, rendering it effectively useless and uninhabitable for decades.

Appendix 4B

Sample Mind Map

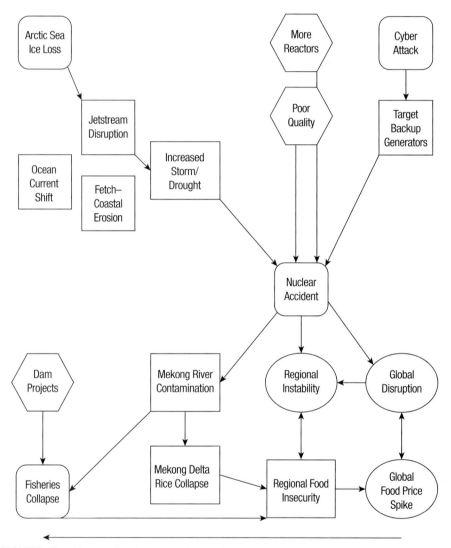

FIGURE 4A.1 Hunnan Province and Mekong River

Source: Briggs and Briggs, *Foresight Scenario Workshop on Energy and Environmental Security*, 2013.

Note

The author wishes to thank Dr. Chad and Tracy Briggs of GlobalInt LLC (http://www.glo balint.org) for inviting him to their *Foresight Scenario Workshop on Energy and Environmental Security* at Johns Hopkins University, Washington, DC, on September 21, 2013. The foresight analysis simulation explained in this chapter is an adaptation for classroom use of their two-day foresight exercise intended for subject matter experts. The main goal of this condensed adaptation is to provide undergraduate and graduate students with insights into the concept of foresight analysis and its goals rather than to produce actionable results.

References

Chad Briggs & Tracy Briggs, GlobalInt LLC, *Foresight Scenario Workshop on Energy and Environmental Security*, Johns Hopkins University, Washington, DC, September 21, 2013.

"Black Swan Theory," Wikipedia entry available at http://en.wikipedia.org/wiki/Black_swan_theory.

Taleb, Nassam Nicholas. *The Black Swan: the Impact of the Highly Improbable* (2nd ed.) (London: Penguin, 2010).

5

Intelligence Sovereignty Game

Roger Mason

Since 1992, nations of Europe have been moving toward increasing levels of unification and collaboration. The 1992 Treaty of Maastricht followed by the 2009 Treaty of Lisbon provided foundational agreements for unification. These agreements established three pillars of legal collaboration: economic, security, and law enforcement/judicial cooperation. The goal was to gradually de-emphasize individual sovereignty while gradually increasing collaboration.

Since 2009, the European Union suffered gradually increasing levels of political, economic, and security-related stress. Several of the biggest challenges to unification include the financial stability of individual members, problems related to unrestricted immigration, and terrorism. These challenges have impacted the total coalition while having profound effects on the culture and society in individual countries.

Conflict in the Middle East has flooded Europe with millions of refugees. The immigrants move to cities where ethnically familiar enclaves exist. During this period the economy of Europe has been unstable. Individual European Union states have nearly gone bankrupt. Terrorism has rocked Europe while increasing streams of migrants struggle to integrate and survive.

Intelligence Sovereignty versus Collaboration

Individual EU member states must consider many issues as the European Union becomes more unstable and associates like the United Kingdom back away from participation. Some of the biggest questions involve the future of the European Union and the individual member's future as a sovereign nation.

Intelligence cooperation and collaboration are some of the most challenging issues facing these nations. Intelligence collection and analysis represent some of the most important secrets of a sovereign country. Sharing intelligence reveals what you know, exposes your ability to gather intelligence, and places you in a position where your vulnerabilities are transparent. The possibility of catastrophic terrorist attacks require collaboration and cooperation between sovereign states to prevent them.

The Intelligence Sovereignty Game

The Intelligence Sovereignty Game is a card-based simulation of intelligence operations by members of the European Union. The players attempt to conduct intelligence operations, preserve national sovereignty, and hopefully prevent a catastrophic terrorist attack. The game employs a constantly changing situation where players must constantly chart a course through an evolving "Prisoner's Dilemma."

Instructional Objectives

Provide understanding regarding the dilemma facing European intelligence agencies who must balance national sovereignty issues and the need to collaborate with other European nations to prevent terrorist attacks.

Simulation Objectives

Provide the individual players a chance to participate in active decision making during periods of uncertainty. The players must balance risk versus an evolving threat.

Debriefing/Discussion Format

Debriefing the game should involve three areas: what students learned from the related reading, what they learned during the game, and how the game outcomes can impact future policy decisions.

Reading/Foundation-Related Questions
   What is the Prisoner's Dilemma?
   What are the policy challenges of information sharing by EU countries?

Gameplay Questions
   Did you have a strategy before the game began regarding how much cooperation you were willing to offer?
   Did your intention to seek a win without cooperating change during the game?
   How much risk related to the level of the crisis index were you willing to accept?
   How did this game resemble the "Prisoner's Dilemma," and were there factors that made it different?

Policy Questions
   How should security agencies within the EU deal with the issue of balancing intelligence sovereignty against preventing terrorism?
   What solutions could address the current intelligence-sharing obstacles?

Target Audience

Higher education students studying intelligence analysis, national security issues, or geopolitical theory.

Playing Time

Approximately 90 minutes.

Number of Players

There should be a minimum of four players. To accommodate larger groups, the number of players can be doubled.

Debriefing Time

Approximately 30 minutes.

Game Description

The Intelligence Sovereignty Game is about maintaining the greatest level of individual sovereignty but balancing this against the need to collaborate and prevent a catastrophic terrorism event. The players represent the intelligence services of four European Union nations. The goal is to gather intelligence while maintaining the greatest level of individual sovereignty but preventing a major terrorist attack. The player who gathers the most intelligence breakthrough chips by the end of the game wins. The only exception is if the crisis index falls at any point in the game to –10. This signifies a major terrorism incident has occurred, at which time the game ends and everyone loses no matter how many chips they have.

The players conduct intelligence operations and can choose to negotiate, cooperate, or place obstacles in the path of other players. The more a player cooperates, the less chance they have of scoring individual points. Players going for an individual win may refuse to cooperate. This is a risk because they may be pulled over the edge into a terror incident.

Players can sometimes slow or reverse the trend toward disaster by sharing resources or working together. Players can also help or hinder their fellow player's intelligence operations. The game employs two decks of cards: operations and crisis. The operations deck of cards allows you to conduct intelligence operations. The second deck involves random events that cause the crisis scale to rise or fall.

Conclusion

There are current 28 EU member nations. The threats from security challenges, such as international terrorism and transnational crime, have never been greater. During the Cold War Western democracies faced the challenge of nuclear war. One solution came from the employment of game theory to reach possible cooperation. The current threat of terrorism is much more complicated and involves many more individual and state-sponsored actors. Combatting terrorism requires intelligence cooperation and information sharing. Both approaches infringe on national intelligence sovereignty.

The Intelligence Sovereignty Game provides students and decision makers the opportunity to develop solutions in a simple but realistic simulation. Just like the real world, players must balance their preferences against the risk of a major terrorist incident. The simple Prisoner's Dilemma provided answers during the Cold War. A new approach to the game may offer solutions in the global war on terror.

Suggested Reading

For students playing this game, the suggested reading includes the following articles. The first article is by Robert Axelrod, who has conducted extensive research in game theory and the psychology of cooperation and decision making. The other articles discuss the issues related to maintaining national sovereignty and intelligence cooperation in Europe. These articles provide a broad foundation for the design of the game and the policy issues it simulates.

Aldrich, Richard. "US-European Intelligence Co-operation on Counter-terrorism: Low Politics and Compulsion." *British Journal of Politics and International Relations.* Vol. II, 2009.

Axelrod, Robert. "Effective Choice in the Prisoner's Dilemma." *Journal of Conflict Resolution.* Vol. 24, no. 1, March 1980.

Fagersten, Bjorn. "For EU Eyes Only? Intelligence and European Security." White paper. Union Institute for Security Studies, March 2016. Accessed August 13, 2018. https://www.iss.europa.eu/sites/default/files/EUISSFiles/Brief_8_EU_Intelligence_Cooperation.pdf

Seyfried, Pia. "A European Intelligence Service: Potentials and Limits of Intelligence Cooperation at EU Level." White paper: Academy for Security Policy. No. 20, 2017. Accessed August 13, 2018. https://www.baks.bund.de/sites/baks010/files/working_paper_2017_20.pdf

The URL for the companion website is: https://textbooks.rowman.com/art-of-intelligence-2.

Appendix 5A

Intelligence Sovereignty Game

Introduction

The Intelligence Sovereignty Game is a strategy game which incorporates the challenges of intelligence sharing and individual sovereignty in the European Union.

Players attempt to increase their individual wealth of intelligence while being forced to cooperate during increased periods of terrorist threats.

Game Parts

Crisis deck: Cards that provide the criticality level throughout the game.

Intelligence operations deck: These are cards that players can play during the game to gather intelligence. The cards represent four types of intelligence operations: Humint (human intelligence), Cybint (cyber intelligence), Sigint (signals intelligence), and Geoint (geospatial intelligence).

Crisis index: An index that indicates the current terrorism threat level through the EU.

Breakthrough chips: The breakthrough chip reflects raw intelligence being collected by individual players. These chips can be collected by players who conduct successful intelligence operations.

Game map: This includes the crisis index, a box for crisis cards, a box for operations cards, and four playing slots (face cards) for intelligence operations cards.

How the Game Is Played

Players representing four EU intelligence services play a card game against a constantly changing crisis index. The goal of the players is to amass the most breakthrough chips by the end of the game. The game ends in two ways: when all of the operations cards have been drawn, or if the crisis index drops to –10. The game has a self-interest factor as the individuals attempt to gather the most breakthrough chips.

The game also contains a mutual cooperative factor, because no matter how many breakthrough chips you have, the failure to prevent the collapse of the crisis index means everyone loses. Players can take game actions to improve their self-interest but may be forced to cooperate if a crisis is approaching.

Game Turn

The game turns follow a sequence.

1. Draw a crisis card.
2. Negotiations: If the crisis index is falling, the players may wish to negotiate to take action to reverse the fall.
3. Each player may take a turn. They can draw a card from the operations deck, play a card on the game board, or take an action with a clandestine operations card. Any cards requiring the loss of breakthrough chips must be applied immediately. The only exception is if the player can pass off the card to another player.
4. Once a player is done, play moves to the next player on the right. After all four players have played, the sequence is repeated.

Card Hands

The players may hold a maximum of six operations cards. The players can play cards in the form of hands. The cards are played on the game board in the face card slots.

There are four types of cards: Humint, Cybint, Sigint, and Geoint.

Humint: Human intelligence or spies
Cybint: Cyber intelligence
Sigint: Signals intelligence (electronic eavesdropping)
Geoint: Geospatial intelligence (spy satellites)

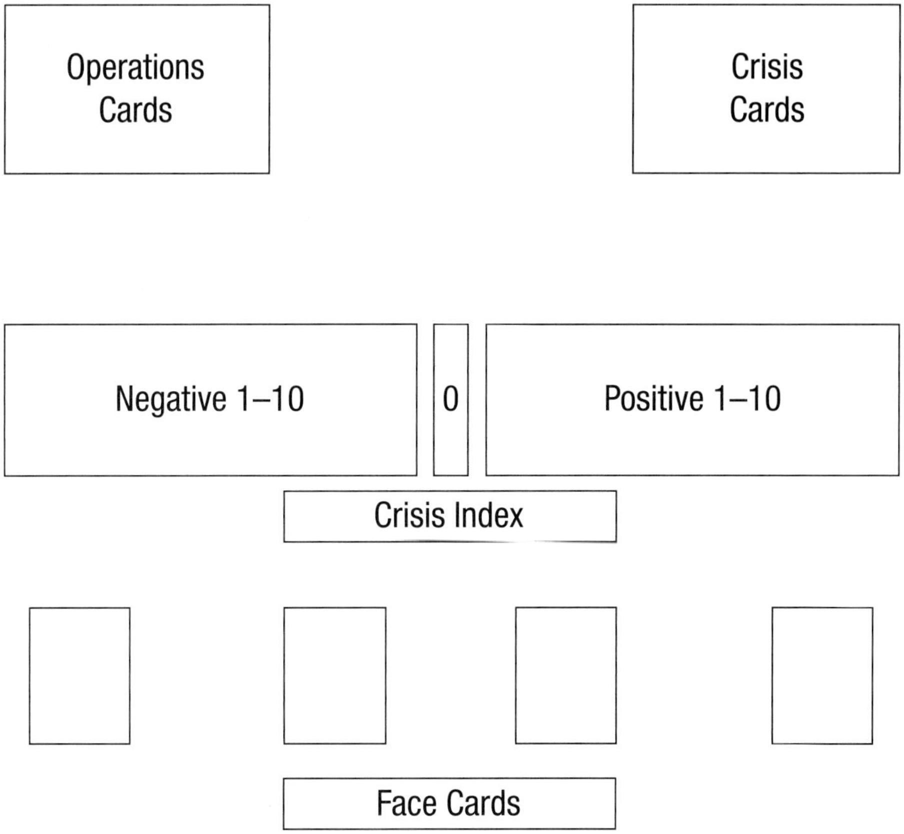

FIGURE 5A.1 Game Map

Examples of Card Hands

Two pair: Any two pairs of the same cards (e.g., Humint, Humint, Cybint, Cybint). Two pair are worth one breakthrough chip.

Four of a kind: Four of the same card (e.g., Sigint, Sigint, Sigint, Sigint). A four of a kind is worth one breakthrough chip.

Straight: (e.g. Sigint, Humint. Geoint, Cybint). A straight is worth two breakthrough chips.

Card Stacking: If there are four cards played, players can stack a card above an existing card to make a hand. If this is done, a playable hand is removed and the remaining card is left in place (e.g., currently there are four cards on the table [three Humint and one Sigint]). Only four cards can be played on the table. The current face cards cannot be played to make any points.

The next player could "stack" a Humint card by placing it over the Sigint card, which now becomes four of a kind. The player can remove the cards and receive their breakthrough chip.

The Humint card that was stacked over remains as a face card and play continues.

Crisis Index

The crisis index is a moveable scale that indicates the probability for a major terrorist attack. The index starts at zero. Based on the crisis cards and the game play, the index can go up to +10 or down to –10. Any time the index reaches –10, everyone loses. If the index reaches +10, all players receive a breakthrough chip and the index is reset on the next turn to zero.

> *Crisis deck*: There are three types of crisis cards played at the start of each player round: +, –, and 0. These cards can freeze the index or make it go up or down. The crisis cards are drawn from the crisis deck. After they are played they are discarded. If the cards in the crisis deck are exhausted but the game is continuing, reshuffle the cards and put them back in play. Card values go from 0 to 4.

+ :   A + card (Ex: +1, +2) means that the number on the card is applied to move the crisis index up that number of spaces.

– :   A – card (Ex: –2, –4) means the number on the card is applied to move the crisis index down that number of spaces.

0 :   A 0 card means there is no change to the crisis index.

Note: There are operations cards that can be used to move the crisis index upward should it become dangerously low.

Negotiations

After the crisis card is drawn, any player can ask for negotiations. The individual play is temporarily suspended while the players negotiate. This is typically done if the crisis index has dropped to a point that the players are concerned that another crisis card could bring the crisis level to the bottom where all players lose.

The level of the index can be reversed by:

Playing an intelligence coup card: crisis level goes up by 2
Playing a direct action card: crisis level goes up by 1
Spending three breakthrough chips: crisis level goes up by 1
Spending five breakthrough chips: crisis level goes up by 2
Playing a de-escalation card: crisis index can go up to 3 if three chips are paid with the card.

Players can trade cards or favors with each other to prevent the index from reaching a crisis. The players can pool their breakthrough chips to cover the cost of raising the index.

Note: Players may use only one of these actions per turn.

Clandestine operations: There are eight types of cards representing types of clandestine operations or actions. They can impact your intelligence operations positively or negatively. They can be used offensively or defensively against other players.

Hacker

There is a computer security breach in your organization. If you draw this card you must give up half of your breakthrough chips or pass it to another player using an intelligence operations card. If you pay the penalty, it goes into the game chip pool.

(If you possess a false flag card, you can pass this card to another player. The person receiving the card must pay you half of their chips.)

Mole

This indicates there is a traitor within your organization. Upon drawing this card, you must immediately give up all of your breakthrough chips or pass it off to another player. If you possess a false flag card, you can pass this card to another player.

If the second player has an intelligence coup or false flag card, they can pass it to another player. Wherever the card ends up, the player must suffer the impact.

False Flag

This operation allows you to pass a card to any of the other players.

It can be used pass off a hacker or mole card to prevent losing your breakthrough chips. If the player receiving the card does not have an intelligence coup or false flag card, they must suffer the consequences. If the second player has an intelligence coup or false flag card, they can also pass it to another player. Wherever the card ends up, the player must suffer the impact.

Direct Action

The direct action card allows you to receive one breakthrough chip from each of the other players.

Double Cross

A player may hand this card to any other player, forcing them to lose their next turn.

De-escalation

This card allows you to slow down the crisis. When you play the de-escalation card, you may play up to four breakthrough chips. The number of chips you play is how many cards from the operations card discard pile are shuffled back into the operations deck. Players may contribute the chips on their own, or players can pool chips to restack the operations deck.

Defector

A defector card allows you to take a random card from any other player. (Note your hand may never exceed a total of six cards.)

Intelligence Coup

This is the most powerful card in the game. The player may use this card to increase the crisis index by 2, or substitute for a direct action, double-cross, defector, or false flag operation card.

How to Win

The game ends when the intelligence operations cards have been exhausted. The player with the most breakthrough chips wins. If the crisis index reaches −10 at any time during the game, the game immediately ends and everyone loses no matter how many breakthrough chips they possess.

Strategy

This game is really a balancing act between trying to gather your own intelligence and working cooperatively with one another. Players must try and guess what cards their opponents are holding and use successful intelligence operations to gather as many chips as possible while watching to ensure the crisis index does not suddenly reach critical mass. You goal is to win the game on your own, but the crisis level may force you to cooperate to prevent the game from reaching a crisis. To win, you have to have flexible combination of positive moves, backstabbing your fellow players, and cooperating to prevent the crisis index reaching critical mass.

Making a Copy of the Game

Making a copy of the game is simple and inexpensive.

Supplies

Two decks of 3×5 inch black index cards or printable business cards
One 24×36 inch sheet of plain drawing paper
One 8.5×11 inch sheet of green construction paper
One 8.5×11 inch sheet of red construction paper
60 poker chips

Making the Cards

The two types of cards can be produced by printing them on two sided business cards or merely writing the words on 3×5 inch cards. The operations cards should have the type of operations on one wide and the word "operations" on the other side. The crisis cards should have the word "crisis" on one side and the appropriate number on the reverse.

Step 1: Operations Cards

Make 12 each of the Humint, Cybint, Geoint, and Sigint operations cards (a total of 48 cards).

Make two of each of the clandestine operations cards (two hackers, two moles, two defectors, etc.; a total of 16 cards).

These 64 cards combine to make up the operations card deck.

Step 2: Crisis Cards

The crisis deck should consist of

+2 (two cards)
+1 (five cards)
+0 (six cards)
–1 (six cards)
–2 (three cards)
–3 (one card)
–4 (one card)

These are the 24 cards in the crisis card deck.

Step 3: Crisis Index

Take the red piece of construction paper and cut out a 4×10 inch strip.
    Take a pen and mark off 1-inch sections starting with –10 and going to –1.

| -10 | -9 | -8 | -7 | -6 | -5 | -4 | -3 | -2 | -1 |

FIGURE 5A.2 Negative Crisis Index

Repeat this with the green piece of paper, going from +1 to +10.

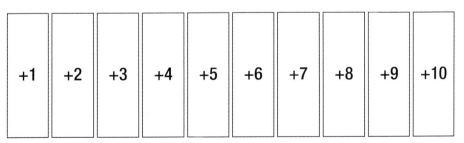

| +1 | +2 | +3 | +4 | +5 | +6 | +7 | +8 | +9 | +10 |

FIGURE 5A.3 Positive Crisis Index

Step 4: Make the Map

Take the large sheet of paper.
    Glue the parts on the sheet.

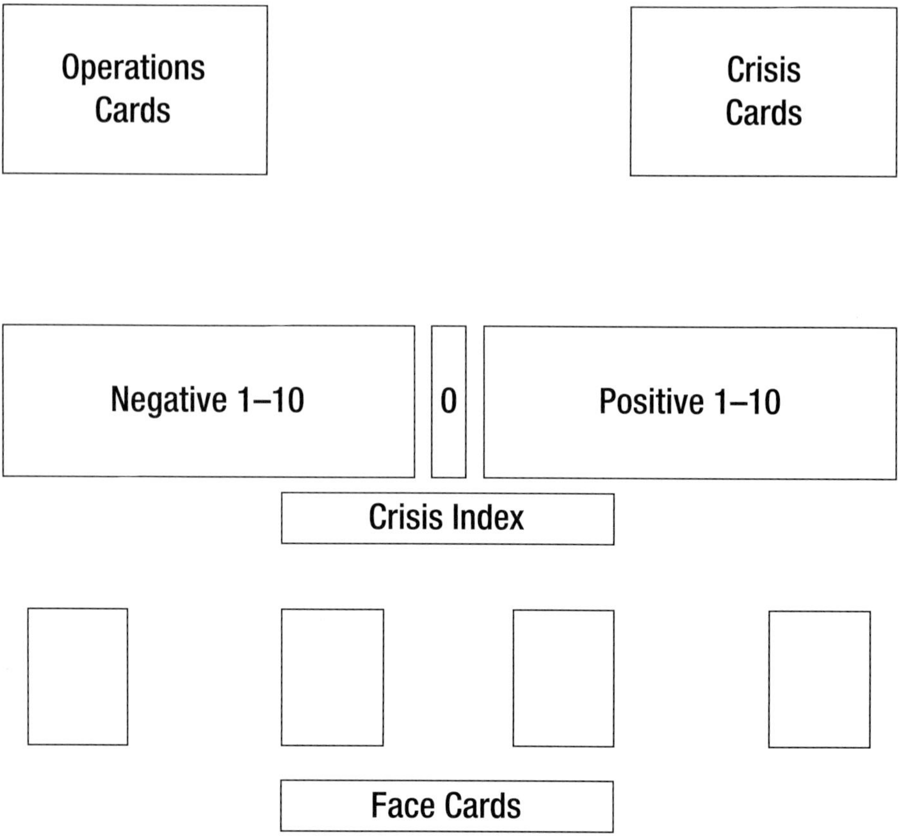

FIGURE 5A.4 Game Map

The crisis index should look like this.

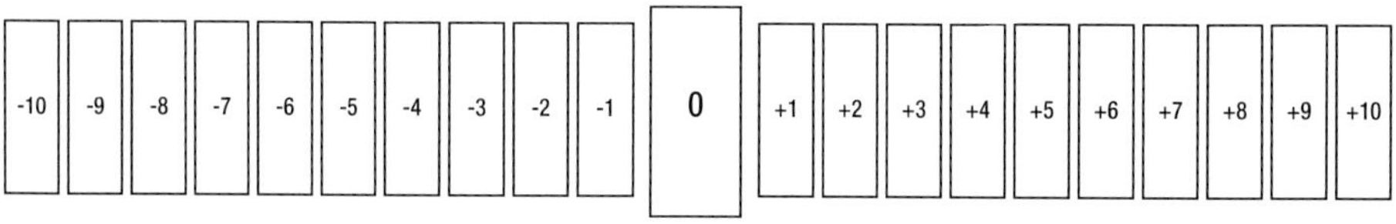

FIGURE 5A.5 Final Crisis Index

Note

I wish to thank Joseph Miranda for his assistance and advice in the development of this game. Eric Harvey assisted with the play testing and graphic organization of the game. Their help and expertise were invaluable.

6

Intelligence, Security, and Democracy

Florina Cristiana Matei and
Carolyn Halladay

Basic Data

Instructional Objectives

The objectives of this simulation exercise are to expose participants to the various roles and missions fulfilled by intelligence agencies in a democracy versus in non-democratic regimes; to provide an understanding of the reforms and institutions required in developing a capable intelligence community in a democracy and the challenges associated with these processes; and to expose participants to various mechanisms of transparency, accountability, democratic control and oversight of intelligence, and the challenges associated with these processes.

Simulation Objectives

This simulation exercise aims to improve participants' understanding of the complex and often interrelated challenges of developing and operating an effective intelligence community in a democratic environment. The exercise exposes participants to a series of scenarios that involve, on the one hand, reforming or transforming intelligence institutions to adjust to the dynamic current security context, and on the other hand, institutionalizing and preserving robust democratic control and oversight mechanisms, ethical safeguards, and transparency. Specifically, the simulation exercise involves either one of two scenarios: one focused on the challenges to and ingredients of success when democratizing intelligence in a consolidating democracy (for example, in a state emerging from authoritarian rule or protracted domestic conflict); and one focused on the challenges to preserving a democratized intelligence community when a consolidated democracy—or democratic consolidation—is in peril (perhaps by the advent of extremist politics at home or amid the pressures of regional or international conflict).[1]

The selection of scenario depends on the composition of each group of participants. If the majority of participants are from consolidating democracies, they stand to gain the most from the scenario about democratizing intelligence institutions. If, on the other hand, most participants are from developed or consolidated democracies, they are more appropriately presented with the second scenario about preserving democratic oversight and institutions.

Debriefing Format

The instructor or instructors explain different challenges and frameworks associated to each scenario. The instructor or instructors highlight the objectives behind each of the simulation exercise objectives and relate them to the groups' positions and responses to the scenario requirements.

Target Audience

The ideal participants in this simulation exercise series include a mix of practitioners (e.g., military, civilian, and/or law enforcement) and intelligence outsiders dealing with intelligence, defense, and security issues on a regular basis (e.g., current or future policymakers, executive and legislative branch staffers, and media professionals, as well as representatives of the civil society that deal with security). Nevertheless, the simulation exercise series is suitable for any audience with an interest in intelligence in general and democratic reform of intelligence in particular.

Playing Time

The playing time for this simulation exercise series ranges between 180 and 240 minutes.

Debriefing Time

The debriefing time for this simulation exercise series is 60 minutes.

Number of Players Required

The ideal number of players for this simulation exercise series is between 9 and 50 participants. A minimum of three participants per group and a minimum of three groups are required. A maximum of 10 participants per group is recommended. A maximum of five groups is recommended.

Participation Materials Included

See appendix 6A and appendix 6B.

Computer/Internet

A computer and Internet access are recommended for this simulation exercise series but are not required. Easel-stand pads or a whiteboard with erasable markers of different colors are required for each group.

Other Materials/Equipment Required

The following additional materials/equipment is required: one large classroom for the entire group of participants and a few small rooms to accommodate each small group (the large classroom can be used as a breakout room for a small group during the exercise), in order to allow each group to brainstorm and work independently of the others. If computer/Internet access exists, the large class-room is required to have a computer and a wall projector.

Facilitator's Guide
Pre-simulation Briefing
This simulation exercise usually occurs during long courses (up to 11 weeks) or short courses (up to three weeks) focused on such topics as civil-military relations and democratic consolidation; strategic decision making in a democracy; intelligence and democracy; democratic homeland security and defense; and so forth. Before the simulation exercise series, the instructor or facilitator provides a presentation or a series of presentations, addressing the role and place of intelligence in a democratic environment. Topics covered may include democracy and democratic consolidation frameworks, strategic security context, theories of intelligence, defining intelligence, roles and missions of security institutions, homeland defense and security policies, democratization of intelligence, civilian control and oversight of the security institutions, ethical issues and intelligence, developing an intelligence culture, and the like.

One day prior to the simulation exercise, the instructor or instruction team provides the participants with the read-ahead for the selected scenario, which they are required to read prior the exercise, and for which they are required to work in groups to respond to all requirements. The prior presentation material provide participants with the basic tools for responding to each of the requirements of the simulation exercise. Each participant receives his or her own copy of the respective scenario.

Simulation Steps

Simulation Step 1: Getting Organized (5 Minutes)
The participants are divided into at least three and a maximum of five small groups, depending on the overall number of participants, their home country or countries, and the agencies for which they work. Each group should be as inclusive as possible, blending participants from different countries and different agencies as well as government versus nongovernment participants. Each group must respond to the scenario requirements by consensus. Each group is told to select a group speaker to take notes and to present the results and findings to the class. Each group is assigned a different room in order to ensure good communication among all participants in each group, without disturbing/influencing or being disturbed/influenced by the other groups. Next the instructor reviews the main ideas and issues in the simulation exercise scenario that the participants have already read.

Simulation Step 2: Group Brainstorming, Debating, and Reaching a Consensus (85 Minutes)
The instructor or instruction team invites the participants to evaluate and assess the respective scenario, discuss and debate possible responses to the

requirements, and reach consensus. By the end of this step, each group should select a rapporteur, who will capture and report the group's findings, positions, and briefing points; and a speaker who will brief the entire group of participants. The instructor or instructors should not interfere or try to influence any of the groups, but should be available to each group to clarify any doubts or questions each group may have regarding the respective scenario.

Simulation Step 3: Group Presentations (between 90 Minutes and 150 Minutes)

This step requires between 90 (for the minimum of three groups) and 150 minutes (for the maximum of five groups), per each of the two scenarios, as follows: 15 minutes for each group's presentation, followed by a 10-minutes "questions and answers" session for each group, and 5 minutes of additional "critiques" for each group.

Debriefing (60 Minutes)

Debriefing Session 1: Facilitator Assessment (20 Minutes)

This step requires 20 minutes. The facilitator provides an analysis of the group presentations, and, if needed, recommendations. The facilitator also requests the groups to work together to provide one unified "Intelligence, Security, and Democracy" roadmap.

Debriefing Session 2: Participant's Unified "Intelligence, Security, and Democracy" Roadmap (40 Minutes)

This step requires 30 minutes for the whole group of participants to create one unified "Intelligence, Security, and Democracy" roadmap, and 10 minutes to present it to the instructor or instruction team.

Conclusion

This simulation exercise aims to improve participants' understanding of the multifarious and often interconnected challenges of institutionalizing an effective intelligence community in a democratic milieu. The exercise involves a series of scenarios aimed, on the one hand, to revamping intelligence institutions to better tackle the current security challenges, and on the other hand, to developing vigorous democratic control and oversight mechanisms over the intelligence.

Appendix 6A

Scenario 1 (Democratizing Intelligence)

Dreamlandia is situated on the beautiful Halladaylian Sea Coast, bordering Latin Crislandia, the Europenian Republic, Africaland, and the Asian Kingdom. Its capital is the beautiful city of Lyndaville.

From 1987 to 2017, Dreamlandia was an authoritarian regime, under the rule of the Totalitarian Dreamlandian Vile Party (TDVP) led by the ruthless General Nefarious Odious and abetted by the malicious Highly Secret Security (HSS) intelligence apparatus, a combined military and police intelligence agency. The HSS was the chief prop of the TDVP/Nefarious's regime. Throughout the dictatorship, HSS personnel kidnapped, incarcerated, or killed (disappeared) more than 20,000 real or imaginary opponents to the regime, all Dreamlandian citizens, both in country and abroad.

In February 2017, Dreamlandia transitioned to democracy. The transition was peaceful, initiated by a military coup, which led to the removal of General Nefarious, followed by negotiations among the TDVP, the military, and opposition. The TDVP was dismantled and ruled illegal, while the HSS was divided into four agencies: Dreamlandia's National Intelligence Agency (DNIA), a hybrid civilian agency (domestic and foreign intelligence) under the presidency; the Police and Criminal Intelligence Service (PCIS) under the Ministry of Security and Home Affairs; the Military Intelligence Service (MIS) under the Ministry of Defense; and the Ministry of Finance's Intelligence Service (MFIS).

After the regime change, political pluralism emerged, and free and fair elections took place in May 2017, when Dreamlandia's citizens elected a president and parliament. A new constitution was enacted in December 2017, which provides Dreamlandia is a semi-presidential republic,[2] with separation of power between the three branches of the government: executive (president and prime minister), legislative (parliament), and judicial (courts).

Dreamlandia is now striving to develop robust democratic institutions: political parties, civil society, a free market economy, and democratic civil-military relations (including civilian-led security institutions, committees in the parliament to oversee the security sector, openness, and transparency). Of these difficult tasks, the most daunting will be overhauling Dreamlandia's intelligence sector, to change its focus from an instrument of dictatorship to a community in service of democracy and citizenry, accountable, under democratic civilian control, and transparent while also effective. There are several challenges that Dreamlandia's policymakers must overcome with regard to intelligence democratization:

- Dreamlandia faces a series of security issues and concerns: a direct external threat from the Latin Crislandia, which has several territorial claims, some involving access to the Halladaylian Sea; ethnic discontent/issues at the border with the Europenian Republic, heavily populated with Dreamlandia's Europenian minority; organized crime, in particular drug and arm trafficking; and international religious terrorism.
- Despite attempts to reduce the power of the TDVP, its former members, aided by several HSS agents, continue to influence the decision-making process in post-authoritarian Dreamlandia. Attempts to develop de facto and de jure oversight mechanisms of intelligence, for example, are deterred by threats of exposure of past affiliation or cooperation with HSS.
- The public image of the intelligence agencies is negative. Intelligence, as an occupation and a discipline, carries a stigma associated with General Nefarious's egregious human rights abuses. Despite the broad popular and political

understanding and awareness of the security challenges, which call for effective intelligence, the population resents any real or perceived enhancement of the intelligence agencies' power, position, or mission.

• The four newly established intelligence agencies are not cooperating among themselves. In fact, lack of information-sharing and cooperation when the Financial Intelligence Service had access to relevant information concerning financing of a terrorist attack by the International Religious Extremist Group (IREG) on Dreamlandia's territory, precluded the agencies from averting a terrorist attack a week after the enactment of the constitution. The attack resulted in 278 dead and more than 400 wounded Dreamlandians and foreign nationals. Nor did the Police Intelligence Service share information on organized crime cyber gangs, eyeing Dreamlandia's critical infrastructure, with the National Intelligence Agency, which led to a cyberattack on the banking system and hospitals, jeopardizing the country's economy and citizens' security. Similarly, long-festering economic downturn in neighboring Crislandia prompted a migration wave. It did not last long, but the several intelligence agencies did not cooperate or coordinate any activities or information before or after, and while the agencies bickered among themselves about which one was to lead a combined effort, a measles outbreak seized the refugee settlements and rapidly spread to the Dreamlandian population.

• There is limited interest, as well as lack of expertise in defense and security on the part of the civilian elected and/or appointed officials, who still struggle (even now, one year after the transition to democracy) to develop capable, cooperative intelligence agencies under democratic auspices.

Tasks

You have been appointed to a working committee made up of members of parliament, the civil service, the armed forces, and the police to devise means of democratic control of the intelligence service compatible with the requirements of national security and the stability of the republic. You are asked to:

I. Define Dreamlandia's intelligence needs.
    1. What intelligence services does Dreamlandia require?
    2. Define their roles and missions. Should the services be civilian or military?
    3. To whom should they report? Should they preserve the original report channels or change?
    4. Should there be a framework in place to enforce coordination, cooperation, and sharing among agencies?

II. Is there a need for a legal framework for intelligence in Dreamlandia? If yes, what should it include/involve—control? Effectiveness? Both? In broad strokes, how?

III. Devise mechanisms of democratic civilian control and oversight of intelligence for Dreamlandia.

IV. Is there a need for more robust democratic civilian control/oversight mechanisms for intelligence in Dreamlandia? If yes, devise a method to make the intelligence service accountable to a democratic process. Who should determine intelligence priorities? Which mechanisms of executive, parliamentary, and judicial oversight, if any, should be instituted? What will their roles be? If not, explain, why not? Which other checks and balances does Dreamlandia need to ensure the transparency and accountability of its new/reformed intelligence system?

Does Dreamlandia need effective intelligence agencies? If yes, which measures should Dreamlandia undertake to ensure effectiveness of intelligence? If not, explain why not.

Appendix 6B

Scenario 2 (Democracy and Intelligence in Crisis)

Dreamlandia is situated on the beautiful Halladaylian Sea Coast, bordering Latin Crislandia, the Europenian Republic, Africaland, and the Asian Kingdom. Its capital is the beautiful city of Lyndaville.

Since 1987, when it transitioned to democracy from the authoritarian rule of the Totalitarian Dreamlandian Vile Party (TDVP), led by the ruthless General Nefarious Odious, Dreamlandia has been a liberal democracy for 100 years: a semi-presidential republic[3] with separation of power between the three branches of the government—executive (president and prime minister), legislative (parliament), and judicial (courts)—and peaceful political transfer of power between four major political parties (the Up Party, the Down Party, the Right Party, and, respectively, the Left Party). Dreamlandia has 13 intelligence agencies, as follows: the National Intelligence Agency (NIA), a domestic, all-source, civilian agency, with law-enforcement authorities, under the presidency and the Ministry of Justice; the Foreign Intelligence Agency (FIA), a foreign all-source civilian agency, under the presidency; the Finance Intelligence Service (FIS), under the Ministry of Treasury; the Health Safety Intelligence Unit (HSIU), under the Ministry of Health; the Army, Navy, Air Force, and Coast Guard Intelligence Agencies, under the Ministry of Defense; the Military Attachés Directorate (MAD) of the Ministry of Defense; the Imagery, Communication, and Cyber Intelligence Unit (ICCIU) of the Ministry of Defense; the Environmental Security Intelligence Unit of the Ministry of Environment; the Homeland Protection Intelligence Service (HPIS); and an Intelligence Fusion Center under the Ministry of Homeland Protection, an organization that provides analysis integration specific to all-hazards threats to Dreamlandia.

Dreamlandia's elected and appointed civilian elites established and developed robust control and oversight mechanisms over the myriad of intelligence agencies, ranging from a legal framework for intelligence to civilian-led institutions, interagency coordination and cooperation organizations at the executive level, parliamentary committees, internal audit departments, and judicial review courts. Likewise, the free media and the civil society institutions in Dreamlandia and abroad, especially democratic Latin Crislandia, and the Regional Court for Human Rights (RCHR), have acted as true watchdogs of the intelligence community, conducting debates on security and democracy issues, watching the intelligence community, and exposing wrongdoing within the government. Policymakers have also sought transparency in the intelligence community. As such, all intelligence agencies have information, strategic communications, and outreach programs. All in all, Dreamlandia successfully deepened and broadened its democracy at home, while promoting democratic values among its allies and partners, regionally, and on the global stage.

Lately, however, Dreamlandia's democracy has been increasingly tested by a series of security issues and challenges, mostly involving transnational organized crime, in particular drug and arms trafficking, illegal migration and immigration, and international and homegrown terrorism. Against this background, Dreamlandia has struggled with elements of extremism amid the political, social, and security transformations. "Ultra-nationalist," "populist," and "radical" politicians have more and more claimed to speak for those left out of democratic success, using such democratic institutions as press freedom or political campaigns to advance their fundamentally anti-democratic programs. In December 2127, Dreamlandia elected a populist leader, President Mania Fanaticus, primarily on a platform of excluding the long-time ethnic Europenian minority from political life and extracting Dreamlandia from "corrupt" regional and international organization. All these developments have resulted in challenges to the effectiveness and transparency of the intelligence community and security sector, as well as the overall democratic progress.

Then:

- President Fanaticus attempts to consolidate her power:
    - She undertakes to stop immigration and limits tourism, inciting widespread, if largely symbolic, boycotts of Dreamlandian products on the world market and, more seriously, precipitating labor shortages and other economic problems domestically.
    - Bypassing parliament by issuing executive decrees "to express the will of the right-thinking Dreamlandian people," she bans all public protests, restricts people from associating in groups without a permit, and outlaws two small but vocal opposition parties.
    - The president and her inner circle of political appointees have frequently attempted to curb or quell media coverage that reflected negatively on their extremist policies, first by allowing only "tame" journalists access to Fanaticus and other officials, and later by abandoning conventional media channels altogether. Moreover, any time the president and her media staff have been unhappy with the media coverage of the Fanaticus administration, they have attempted to provide the Dreamlandian population with distorted or fabricated facts, even occasionally contradicting their own earlier representations in the name of asserting their counternarrative. Another executive order provides for the immediate termination of educators at any level who "disrespect" (that is, voice any dissent from) the president or her policies.
    - The president has occasionally tried to limit or even roll back the checks and balances that parliament exerts on the executive sector, especially

in connection with investigations of wrongdoing within the presidential cabinet. (While the parliament has striven to conduct fair and balanced oversight of the executive, its activity has been hindered by rising partisanship and re-election concerns.) President Fanaticus has attempted to exclude the prime minister from many decisions, invoking "national security" and the inherent power of the executive.

- The president continues to express her intention to withdraw Dreamlandia from various regional and global alliances, particularly those that obligate Dreamlandia to uphold certain norms of democratic process and justice, like the Regional Court for Human Rights (RCHR), and those that facilitate open borders and free trade, like the Regional Economic and Security Union (RESCU).
- The judiciary remains independent and attempts to exercise its own checks and balances on the executive. But President Fanaticus persists, frequently ignoring unfavorable rulings even by the constitutional court. Her media staff attempts to whip up public distrust of, if not open animosity toward, the judicial process, harping on "elitist" and "out-of-touch" judges. Fanaticus also has attempted to replace various judges with jurists who are loyal to her.
- In the name of "clearing out the dead wood," the Fanaticus administration has zero-funded many senior civil service positions, depriving most agencies and ministries of their highest-level nonpolitical appointees.

The Fanaticus administration also has had some specific designs on the intelligence community in Dreamlandia:

- Citing "national security" and the "urgent threat of foreign influence in the Dreamlandian polity," the president has considerably increased the powers of all intelligence agencies:
  - She empowers the intelligence community to spy on the population, which has resulted in attempts by several intelligence personnel to use the collected personal/private information for personal or political gain/vendettas—largely with little or no national security justification. As these cases go unpunished, they grow in number and audacity.
  - She also empowers the intelligence agencies, domestic and foreign, to detain without a warrant any Dreamlandian citizen suspected of "posing a national security threat." The definition or requirements of this designation are not clear in law or practice, though noncitizens as well as the assimilated Europenian minority appear to be presumptive "threats."
- The president has also attempted to politicize the intelligence community on several occasions:
  - Fanaticus is reported to have met with the head of each agency separately, pressing them each to swear their loyalty to her personally rather than to the Dreamlandian constitution.
  - She has urged the intelligence agencies' leadership to spy on media professionals, political opponents, or even on each other. While the

intelligence agencies have sought to remain apolitical, several elements within the intelligence community have surreptitiously become the president's political policemen. Traditional media and social media coverage revealed that people were being blackmailed with intelligence documents, real or fabricated. All of this domestic surveillance has ramified in diminished trust in government institutions and among government institutions.

- There is increasing evidence that certain elements of the intelligence community are using their new and expanded powers, often in conjunction with local law enforcement, to harass or harm the Europenian minority, as well as other populations that "just don't fit into the Dreamlandian people's self-image."

- The president has also pressured the intelligence community and the security sector to refuse to provide information to the legislative oversight committees, fearing that the information could be damaging or incriminating to her and her inner circle.

- Fanaticus has shuffled the membership of the Dreamlandian National Defense and Security Council (DNDSC), giving permanent membership to two of her ideological advisers but diminishing all of the intelligence agencies to "by request" participation. In practice, those agencies that currently enjoy the president's favor are included in the DNDSC deliberations, while any "doubting" agency is excluded.

- Documents leaked by intelligence community agents in May 2128 have revealed that the president had accepted significant financial favors and other gifts from another head of state prior to the elections, a man with an unsavory and decidedly undemocratic reputation, whose country has been a decade-long enemy of Dreamlandia: the Infernal Central Republic. Further information from HSIU revealed that the then candidate Fanaticus not only accepted these gifts for herself but also allowed the president of the Infernal Central Republic, Dark Hades, to pay considerable sums/amounts of money to Fanaticus's party (and later to the coalition parties), as well as voters, to vote for Fanaticus. What Fanaticus promised the Infernal President in return was total support for Hades's plan to destroy the RESCU. Several senior members of the intelligence community had worked through appropriate channels with this information before and after the election. Most have been fired or demoted.

Tasks

This state of affairs has created confusion among the intelligence services regarding their respective roles and missions, hindering proper interagency coordination and cooperation. For example, the Health Intelligence Service (HIS) detained an illegal immigrant suspected of carrying a biological weapon, but it did not share any information with the rest of the agencies. In January 2128, an attack in Border Province using weapons of mass destruction (WMD) led to more than 500 dead and 1,700 injured and severe, long-term environmental and health problems in the region. Amid these poor interagency communications, it remains unclear whether the HIS detainee was part of a larger plot or an accidental distraction.

The balance between liberty and tolerance on the one hand, and self-protection on the other, in a democracy is hardest to strike where such elements enter the domestic security forces, the intelligence organizations, or the military—that is, those institutions sworn in the first instance to uphold the democracy. You have been appointed to a working committee made up of members of parliament, the civil service, the armed forces, and the police to address the requirements of national security and the stability of the republic, particularly within the context of democratic control and oversight of the intelligence service:

I. How can Dreamlandia recover from this grave national security incident without jeopardizing its democracy?

   1. Should the failure to prevent the WMD attack be attributed to the intelligence community fully? Why?
   2. Should there be an investigating committee to assess the situation that led to the attack?

II. How can Dreamlandia's democracy and democratic intelligence/security sector survive the populist regime of President Fanaticus?

   1. What constitutional and legal arrangements should Dreamlandia use to curb the president's alarmingly mounting political extremism?

      a. Should an investigating committee be established to look into the intelligence community's allegations of foreign influence on elections that resulted in president Fanaticus's election?
      b. Should the intelligence agents who leaked this information be reprimanded? What about those who blackmailed opponents to President Fanaticus?

   2. What is the role of the intelligence community in keeping the democratic institutions intact and avoiding democratic erosion or breakdown? What options do the intelligence agencies, singly and collectively, have to exercise this role?

      How can the intelligence community simultaneously maintain its political neutrality and operational effectiveness under these circumstances?

      i. Is there a need for a new legal framework for intelligence, including prospects for better interagency coordination, political neutrality, and the like? If yes, how should this law be enacted, given the strong hand of the president? If not, how does the intelligence community achieve these things now?
      ii. How can the oversight mechanisms perform their checks and balances functions effectively, and apolitically?

   3. How can the interagency process—within the intelligence community as well as between the intelligence community and other executive branch

agencies—be built or rebuilt to protect and promote democratic and effective intelligence in Dreamlandia? Do the same structures or processes serve both ends—democracy and effectiveness?

4. What should/can the intelligence community do to interrupt the trend toward a "vicious cycle" of politicization, public distrust, and institutional decay?

5. What should the intelligence community *not* do in these circumstances? Why?

6. What, if anything, can the intelligence community do in the context of its international relationships to improve the situation in Dreamlandia?

Notes

1 The simulation exercises are inspired by the Center for Civil-Military Relations (CCMR) Intelligence exercise used in the Executive Program in Defense Decision Making, and Intelligence and Democracy courses.

2 It has a president, a prime minister, and a cabinet, the latter two being responsible to the legislature. There are a few examples of semi-presidential political systems around the world, including France, Romania, and several francophone African countries, notably Mali. The prime minister (PM) and the legislative branch in such a system have some authority and powers, together with the president; for example, in some countries, the parliament can remove the PM and the cabinet, while the president cannot. For detailed information on semi-presidential systems, see Robert Elgie, "Semi-presidentialism: Concepts, Consequences and Contesting Explanations," Centre for International Studies School of Law and Government Dublin City University Working Paper 2 of 2004, available at http://doras.dcu.ie/2124/1/2004-2.pdf, accessed December 24, 2017, in particular the bibliography.

3 It has a president, a prime minister, and a cabinet, the latter two being responsible to the legislature. There are a few examples of semi-presidential political systems around the world, including France, Romania, and several francophone African countries, notably Mali. The prime minister (PM) and the legislative branch in such a system have some authority and powers, together with the president; for example, in some countries, the parliament can remove the PM and the cabinet, while the president cannot). For detailed information on semi-presidential systems, see Robert Elgie, "Semi-presidentialism: Concepts, Consequences and Contesting Explanations," Centre for International Studies School of Law and Government Dublin City University Working Paper 2 of 2004, available at http://doras.dcu.ie/2124/1/2004-2.pdf, accessed 24 December 2017, in particular the bibliography. Dreamlandia has four political parties, and Fanaticus's party is ruling with a coalition with another (therefore, the president is not an independent), while two others are in opposition. The constitution stipulates that the president of Dreamlandia can temporarily transfer power to the prime minister. However, if the president of Dreamlandia is impeached, the constitution stipulates the head of the Chamber of Deputies becomes president. President Fanaticus's brother is the head of Fanaticus's political party and the head of the Chamber of Deputies, one of the parliament's chambers/houses (the other is the Chamber of Senators).

7

Security Gaming Scenario

A Pun upon . . . Cards in a Multicultural Setting

Cristina Ivan and Irena Chiru

This exercise has been calibrated to serve the training needs of both undergraduate and postgraduate target audiences and, taking into consideration the overall very positive feedback it received from trainees (players), we have taken this opportunity to redesign and fine-tune it in order to provide a replicable exercise usable in any format of security analysis. In our perspective, the exercise has all the ingredients and the potential to be used as a virtual lab for the enhancement of security threat assessment drafting skills and decision making in highly heterogeneous groups of individuals with different professional perspectives and (national) agendas.

Its potential for replication has been tested with great success in different formats and professional backgrounds, therefore we assess that with the current methodology it can be tailored and applied not only in the Black Sea context but regardless of the region/country of interest and socioeconomic conditions that the trainer might like to apply.

In recent years the Black Sea region has witnessed dramatic shifts in the balance of power. While the sovereignty and democratic development of countries in the region have been placed under pressure by confrontational geopolitics, hybrid warfare, global terrorism, or at times internal corruption and political imbalances, actionable responses have become a critical factor in addressing regional security in the past two decades.

Traditional dichotomies between sovereignty versus hegemonic control, centralized versus diffuse power, or the tangible versus the intangible capital harnessed by local (non)state actors are re-emerging as the region once again in its conflicting history moves toward an ambiguous border position. The revamping of hard power and its methods by dominant actors in the region threatens to turn the once celebrated need for a regional shared identity into a strategically irrelevant claim. And once again, the Black Sea region may turn into a bridge (dis)connecting Europe and the Middle East.

Therefore the new ecology of power, which is significantly different from that experienced a decade ago, speaks of an increasing need to reframe and map out national interests, interconnect regional alliances, and improve complex interdependences. Whether the region is likely to move toward diplomatic iso-lation in an embattled and fratricidal geography of anger, or whether regional stakeholders will find resources to reframe and reposition national power toward a co-management of regional interests is something to be seen in the coming years. Smart power in general and public diplomacy in particular can in this context be regarded as potential solution for the creation of better and inte-grated strategies and visions in international relations and policymaking across the region and the world.

At the same time, as power is often conditioned by and exercised through knowledge, we must not forget that agents of power tend to express them-selves through an entire new array of complex tools that make specific (mis)use of knowledge: active citizenship, weaponization of identity, (r)evolutions of community thinking, collective empowerment and depowerment, the increasing agency of nonstate actors, and the equally increasing subtle repressive mecha-nisms of propaganda and manipulation. They all need to be considered from both a political and an ethical standpoint.

It is in this context that the exercise is debating current convergent forms of power in the Black Sea region and their impact in creating the right tools for conflict resolution and sustainable development throughout the region.

The main goal will remain that of building a model of alliances, partnerships, and cooperation between state, nonstate, and transnational actors in order to establish legitimacy and success of integrated public and foreign policies.

The Role of the Facilitator

The facilitator has an important role in setting the initial boundaries and in guiding and assisting practice-oriented learning. During the exercises and the interactions between instructor-trainee and trainee-trainee, the facilitator's role is fundamental in guiding investigations and insuring the correct sharing of experiences, best practices, and innovative solutions. The facilitator's tasks include:

- Keeping time on each session
- Ensuring cohesion and the freedom of expression for each member of the team
- Encouraging participants to express opinions and engage in dialogue on all topics debated throughout exercise sessions
- Moderate discussions and clarifying potential misunderstandings
- Providing theoretical and communicational support to avoid tense situations
- Discouraging group thinking and polarization among team members.

Basic Data

Instructional Objectives

The exercise is designed as a framework in which public consultation, partici-patory management, and leadership skills are exercised by program attendants in order to reach a vision for the future of the Black Sea region. As such, they will be encouraged to use knowledge acquired during the program and their own skills as policymakers and strategists to create new approaches to regional security challenges and prioritize initiatives for regional competitiveness by 2030. Therefore, envisioned instructional objectives include the following:

- To foster the participants' ability to structure a solid expertise and forward-thinking scenarios as to the development of interdependencies between the various factors impacting the sustainable development and security of a region;
- To consolidate the ability to think in terms of a common good and a shared objectives paradigm in which they are focused more on common objectives and are encouraged to reframe differences as opportunities, not as limits and obstacles;
- To assimilate an extensive and comprehensive overall understanding that complements professional sectorial expertise, implicitly determined by job profile and domain of activity;
- To learn not to react to risk via learned inertial practices and mental cognitions but to remain open-minded and continuously integrate horizon scanning and alternative methods to obtain innovative knowledge.

Simulation Objectives

- To provide a controlled environment in which the socioeconomic, cultural, political, and security preconditions are already set in a close replication of the reality specific to a certain regional/national environment;
- To enhance the participants' ability to cooperate and collectively create common ground for development;
- To counteract group thinking and collective validation effect;
- To get out of the "spiral of silence" (Elisabeth Noelle-Neumann, 1984), defined as the tendency of people to remain silent when they feel that their views are in opposition to the majority view on a subject;
- To step outside the "comfort zone" built via personal and professional routine that is feeding a patterned world of our existence, and stepping into an "optimal performance zone";
- To create large regionally oriented patterns of action focused on capitalizing differences and subordinate them to a broader, common good objective;
- To analyze national agendas and integrate national interests into a larger canvas, measuring impact, reaction, and interdependence created between stakeholders;
- To enhance quick decision making and flexibility of thinking by having to always adapt own thinking to the set of data provided by facilitators;
- Enhance communication, presentation, and persuasion skills, facilitating understanding of different perspectives and angles by a group with an already set mind frame;
- Facilitate understanding and learning of practical skills in conflict resolution and designing of policy solutions in which the national interest is implicit for the regional good.

Debriefing Format

The facilitators initiate a wrap-up session in which participants are encouraged to give feedback on the clarity of the objectives and the (easy) flow of exercising sequential tasks. At the same time, for the continuous improvement and necessary tailoring of the exercise format according to its different target audiences, participants are also encouraged to express their views on whether and how they would change the format, the variables, or the flow of tasks in the decision-making process if they were given the chance to change the exercise methodology. Subsequently, they are asked to evaluate how relevant the group thinking and decision-making processes were in their efforts to expand knowledge, vision, and structured thinking on regional security and sustainability as well as whether they leave the exercise format with clear policymaking solutions.

Target Audience

As previously mentioned, the target audience ranges from undergraduate students in intelligence, security, and/or political studies international training formats to policymakers, practitioners, and experts involved in multilateral cooperation formats. According to the structure and background of the group, the development of the actual exercise is highly dependent on the skills of the facilitator, whose expertise is highly significant in setting a course of action and establishing proactive interaction between participants.

Playing Time

10 hours, carried out either as an intensive, two-day program or unfolded over five days.

Debriefing Time

30–45 minutes

Numbers of Players Required

Minimum 18; maximum 45. Participants are divided in three groups of 6 to 15 individuals that are required to accomplish one task at a time, then switch groups according to an algorithm given below.

TABLE 7.1 Playing Time

Day	Time	Session
Debriefing time		
1	45 min	Debriefing: students are introduced to exercise modus operandi and objectives
Playing time		
1	120 min	Session 1: State of the art
2	120 min	Session 2: Game changers
3	120 min	Session 3: Policy recommendations
4	120 min	Session 4: Drafting deliverable
5	60 min	Session 5: Presenting results

Participation Materials Included

Three sets of cards per group to be delivered sequentially before each session from 1 to 3; a set of three wild cards/each exercise session/each table (total nine wild cards). Wild cards are to be delivered during sessions 2 and 3. Participation materials can be downloaded at the companion website: https://textbooks.row man.com/art-of-intelligence-2.

Computer/Internet

Not required.

Other Materials/Equipment Required

Three rooms/round tables at a distance from each other; three flipcharts (one for each room/table); colored markers; three sets of cards (see companion website: https://textbooks.rowman.com/art-of-intelligence-2.); list of participants/session/table to be posted in a visible spot.

Facilitator's Guide

Materials

Players are given (1) an exercise handbook containing the information set below with which they can efficiently manage interaction during the exercise sessions and (2) one set of cards for each session from 1 to 3 (see companion website: https://textbooks.rowman.com/art-of-intelligence-2).

Pre-simulation Briefing

Before the actual exercise, the exercise coordinator sets up a meeting with three dedicated facilitators who are introduced into the exercise objectives, modus operandi, opportunities, and challenges they might face during the sessions (e.g., cultural differences, communication barriers between practitioners from different fields, possible sources of conflict and ways to overcome them) dependent on country profile, level of expertise, and exercise theme.

Before the actual start of the exercise, participants are reunited in a plenary meeting and the facilitator explains the overall format and objectives as well as the dynamic and the specific phases that the exercise will unfold.

Participants are introduced into the setting of the real region (e.g., the Black Sea region) which they may already know and understand from the multiple perspectives of their professions and national backgrounds. In this real-life context, what they are encouraged to do is exercise their vision beyond the time span of current policy planning to find ingenious "new ways" and create a vision which can inspire strategic decisions toward how new forms of power could and should be used in the years to come to enforce regional stability and sustainability. Given this overall vision, participants are then informed that tasks in the exercise will be oriented so as to guide them through a participatory process of interrogation and understanding of the sources of security versus insecurity, growth versus decline, and competitiveness versus ineffectiveness that can shape the future of the region. Special focus shall be given to those factors which can constitute "game changers."

Description of Exercise Steps

The exercise is designed in three distinct stages, each stage consisting of steps to be followed according to the scenario detailed below.

To provide consistency and structure to participants' collaborative analysis and decision-making process, during each stage facilitators will hand to the three groups an identical set of cards containing major indicators of most impactful events and trends that correspond to the use of hard/soft power instruments (set of cards 1 in stage 1), game changers likely or potentially occurring to change the current state of the art (set of cards 2 in stage 2), and goals to describe a look into desired future (set of cards 3 in stage 3). Cards will be debated, selected, and completed with participants' own vision recorded on distinct cards, named *jokers*.

Stage 1: Diagnose the Current State of the Art in the Region

Participants will make an X-ray of the current state of the art and most impactful milestones in the past five years. Choices will be based on own knowledge and suggested indicators provided by the exercise facilitators (cards and jokers).

TABLE 7.2	Exercise Steps
Stage 1	• Diagnose the current state of the art in terms of regional security • Make an X-ray of the hard and soft power instruments that regional and international actors use within the Black Sea region
Stage 2	• Identify possible and/or likely game changers in terms of hard, soft, and smart power[1]
Stage 3	• Identify potential strategic responses that can turn game changers into leverage for an increased regional stability and sustainability
Stage 4	• Build a vision that can inspire national and collective regional strategic decisions for the overall good by 2030 (to be presented in front of the group)

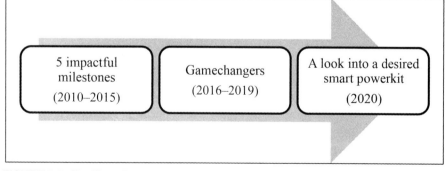

FIGURE 7.1   The Three Themes to be Covered to During the Exercise

Association agreements between the EU
and regional states

> The EU signs association
> agreements with Ukraine,
> Moldova and Georgia.
> These commit aspiring
> future EU members to
> economic, judicial, and
> financial reforms, as well as
> to a convergence of their
> policies and legislation to
> those of the European
> Union.

FIGURE 7.2 Set of Cards 1: Sample Card

Propaganda, conducted by extremist terrorist groups, exploits the concept of cultural identity
and the issue of integration in North Caucasus, thus determining an increase in the cases of
radicalization within the region.

Increased tendency towards radicalism and militancy in North Caucasus

FIGURE 7.3 Set of Cards 2: Sample Card

Stage 2: Identify Game Changers Likely to Shape the Hard and Soft Power Methods Used at Regional Level in the Near Future

Potential game changers will be discussed in terms of innovation, magnitude, and impact with the aim to prioritize their relevance and need for reaction on the part of policymakers.

> With the aim of fostering cooperation, establish 2016–2026 as the decade of good governance, involving all the partners in the region in common projects
>
> Establish the decade of "good governance in the Black Sea region"

FIGURE 7.4 Set of Cards 3: Sample Card

Stage 3: Build "a Smart Power Kit" That Can Inspire Strategic Decisions for the Regional Good by 2020

Based on a careful analysis of smart power techniques, participants will identify potential strategic responses that can turn game changers into well-addressed challenges and therefore increase regional stability and sustainability.

Modus Operandi

The modus operandi is to be gradually explained and monitored by exercise moderators. As mentioned, each stage in the exercise shall follow an action scenario divided in seven distinct steps:

Step 1 Participants are divided in three teams (A, B, and C) that will progressively solve assigned tasks.

Step 2 Each participant chooses a set of three most relevant cards and adds up a joker (own vision). Then, the participant defends the choice in front of the team. The team debates and decides by vote on a set of the nine most important cards.

Step 3 From its own members, each team chooses one spokesperson. After the teams rotate according to the algorithm explained below, the spokesperson will present, argue, and defend the key points of the team in front of the newcomers. The spokesperson holds a position at the table during the following exercise steps.

Step 4 In order to encourage interaction and provide participants with the opportunity to practice their communication, persuasion, and leadership skills as well as contribute to a common vision, all team members, *with the exception of the spokesperson*, change tables according to the following algorithm:

Each team splits in half:

- A = A1 + A2
- B = B1 + B2
- C = C1 + C2

Then each half goes to form another team:

- A1 + B2, B1 + C2, C1 + A2

Result: Three new teams, listed on the chart set near each team table.

Step 5 Newly formed teams listen to the brief delivered by the spokesperson, filter ideas, debate, and choose by vote five out of the nine initial cards presented by each table's spokesperson. Team may also discuss and choose to add an additional joker.

Step 6 Team members switch tables again according to the following algorithm:

- B1 + A2, A1 + C2, B2 + C1

Result: Three new teams, listed on the chart set near each team table.
The elected spokesperson holds position to defend the team's choice in front of the newly formed team. Team filters ideas again and chooses by vote three cards. Team may also discuss and choose to add up a joker.

Step 7 Teams A, B, and C reunite to debate the three resulting sets of cards. Finally, group ranks by vote the most relevant cards.

Stage 4: Power Kit Presentation

Once the first three stages of the exercise completed, in the fourth stage, the group (all three teams together, in plenary session) will have to elaborate and deliver in front of the audience a vision for a new power kit, that can safely counter negative, conflict-oriented policies of attraction, subversion, and projection in the Black Sea region by 2020.

Methods Used to Enhance Communication, Exercise Results, and Avoid Communication Gaps and Cultural Misperceptions

During the exercise, facilitators encourage participants to use in the collective decision-making process collection of a wide range of information from open sources, to discuss and critically address facts and opinions, to brainstorm solutions, debate, and defend opinions. All in all, the exercise format should encourage participative decision making throughout the sessions.

Deliverables

Intermediate

- Oral briefs to be delivered in front of the team.

Final:

- Reunited groups draft a presentation (general outline) of a smart power kit *that can inspire strategic decisions for the regional good by 2020.*
- Best vision will be voted by the jury and awarded "a very special, top secret prize" 9.

Debriefing the Simulation

Objectives

After the presentation of the three visions and power kit versions that emerged as a result of collective thinking and group problem-solving stages of the exercise, participants are invited to a session of 30–45 minutes to wrap up and anchor findings resulting from the experience of playing in their overall knowledge and understanding of competing variables affecting the security and development of the region.

- How much were they affected by group thinking and group validation?
- When did that happen, and what effects did it have for the decision-making process?
- Who were the formal and informal leaders of the group?
- Which were the most significant problems of the region identified (e.g., via cards discussion, wild cards, expression of personal opinions, recurrent identification by a large number of group members)?
- What were the most recurrent styles of negotiation displayed by participants (e.g., competitive, conciliatory, conflict avoidance, collaborative)?
- Do the conclusions reached by the group reflect the initial beliefs of the individuals, or do they rather emerge as a creative, integrated vision of the group?

Conclusions

The exercise offers participants a wide range of problem-solving options in the field of public, security, and foreign affairs policy, thus having the potential for a useful tool in the design of learning applications in areas such as international relations, security studies, intelligence studies, diplomacy and international negotiation, conflict resolution, and peace building. Depending on the background and general learning objectives of the group, the facilitator can steer interest and resources in this simulation format toward different dimensions, the exercise being both interdisciplinary and multifaceted (e.g., one can focus on the psychology of decision-making processes, conflict resolution, security dilemma identification and resolution, policy architecture and social outreach).

Moreover, the exercise format and modus operandi can be extracted, tailored, and/or updated to correspond to the knowledge and learning interests of each group. Putting together multiple groups to perform the same task simultaneously and then switch groups, establish new dynamics, and work on the findings of another group, which can be and most often are very different from those established in the initial group, provides two correlated advantages. On the one hand, it challenges participants to continue to think flexibly on the findings, constantly interrogating their own convictions. On the other hand, it fosters an environment of creative and collective problem-solving, which allows both individual expression and collective decision making. Last but not least, it values multiple national/professional/educational perspectives that are frequently a source of conflict and turns them into premises of shared knowledge, understanding, and decision making.

Appendix 7A: Sample cards for exercise stage 1, appendix 7B: Sample cards for exercise stage 2, and appendix 7C: Sample cards for exercise stage 3 can be found on the companion website listed below.
https://textbooks.rowman.com/art-of-intelligence-2

Note

[1] "Smart power" is a concept defined by Joseph Nye as the ability to combine hard and soft power depending on whether one or the other would be more effective in a given situation.

References

Bonwell, Charles and Eison, James (1991). *Active Learning: Creating Excitement in the Classroom.* Information Analyses—ERIC Clearinghouse Products, p. 3, available at https://www.asec.purdue.edu/lct/hbcu/documents/active_learning_creating_excitement_in_the_classroom.pdf, last accessed August 13, 2018.

Dewey, John (1897). *My Pedagogic Creed*, available at dewey.pragmatism.org/creed.htm, last accessed August 13, 2018.

Noelle-Neumann, E. (1984). *The Spiral of Silence: Public Opinion—Our Social Skin.* Chicago: University of Chicago.

Patrick, Felicia (2011). *Handbook of Research on Improving Learning and Motivation.* IGI Global.

8

Disseminating the Intelligence

A Briefing Exercise Using Critical Discourse Analysis

Julian Richards

It is now well established that effective intelligence analysts have to be advanced critical thinkers across a spectrum of activities and approaches. Within this concept, a number of considerations overlap for the intelligence analyst. As Lowenthal famously observed, analysts have to be simultaneously good at thinking critically and at having an advanced knowledge about the thinking process itself and its attendant cognitive weaknesses and pitfalls (Lowenthal 2006). In a sense, analysts have to be operational psychologists. Meanwhile, as the author has written elsewhere, a strong capability in intelligence analysis actually comprises a number of interconnecting skills, whereby a basic ability in critical thinking is ideally supplemented with prowess in creativity, powers of judgment, and communication (Richards 2010). We can consider that the link between critical analysis and communication represents the later stages of the traditional intelligence cycle (notwithstanding the numerous debates about the continued effectiveness of this model), whereby the results of analysis are disseminated effectively to the policymakers who levied the intelligence requirement in the first place. Without this array of skills and process flows working at a high level of performance, it is highly likely that things will sometimes go wrong.

In this chapter, an exercise concerning analysis and dissemination is presented based on the principles of critical discourse analysis (CDA). This strand of analytical theory and method emerged in the social sciences in the 1970s and has frequently been used in the political realm, as a mechanism for deeply analyzing political statements and rhetoric. It is argued in this chapter that CDA, which is all about analyzing language, presents an excellent opportunity for intelligence analysts to further hone their skills both in analysis and in the communication of the results of their analysis. An exercise is presented here in the foreign policy field, for which CDA is particularly well suited.

Intelligence Assessment

The question of how well or otherwise information is received, analyzed, and assessed for its significance to policymakers is a long-standing one. If we accept that all war is essentially an intelligence failure, the two world wars at the beginning of the twentieth century provided a rich seam of information on state-on-state perceptions and misperceptions for subsequent scholars to analyze. Ernest

May's (1986) seminal analysis of the intelligence assessments of European foes in the run-up to the two world wars provided a very detailed exposition of the range of problems in the state intelligence machinery. In particular, the observation was made that intelligence failures were as much about how the intelligence was received, interpreted, and acted upon by the policymakers as about the reports themselves from the analysts (May 1986: 542). Clearly, problems are often about political machinations in the system that contrive to ignore or reinterpret the analysts' findings, but the system has no hope of moving forwards if both the analysis and the communication of it are not highly effective.

In the Cold War that followed, a great deal of analysis was conducted around how the two superpowers saw one another and formed their respective intelligence assessments. This was the period in which Realism gained the upper hand in Western conceptions of international relations, and calculations to do with a state ensuring continued power were paramount. A number of revisionist scholars, writing from the 1960s onward, suggested that the previously normative view that the United States increased its defense spending considerably in the face of perceived Soviet aspirations for world dominance, was ill-informed, and that it was in fact a fear within the Soviet leadership that the communist world would be crushed by the capitalist West that led to an increase in armaments (Hopkins 2007: 915). However, Robert Jervis, one of the more prominent commentators during this period, was critical of the "spiral of misperception" theory that took hold, in which it was proposed that both sides' misperceptions of each other's capabilities and intentions led to the upwardly escalating security dilemma (Jervis 1968: 455). Criticizing the "psycho-logic" of such theories, in which states are inappropriately imbued with the psychological attributes of human beings, Jervis suggests that the evidence for such a theory does not stack up (Jervis 1968: 455).

If states are not human beings as such, however, individual leaders and policymakers (and indeed intelligence analysts) clearly are. In this respect, cognitive factors to do with assessment and decision making certainly have a large bearing on intelligence success and failure. In considering Israel's miscalculations prior to the Yom Kippur War of 1973, Shlaim picks up on the normative psychological view that most people are "cognitive misers," in that they tend to fit incoming information around their favored conceptions of the world and to pay less attention to that which conflicts with their worldview (Shlaim 1976: 357). Such a theory is based on a fairly solid bedrock of repeated psychological experiments, such as Bruner and Postman's infamous "switched cards" experiment, published in the 1940s, in which individuals shown a series of standard playing cards often fail to notice that some of the cards switch the colors of suits, whereby spades become red and hearts become black (Bruner and Postman 1949). In the intelligence world, misperceptions can result from immoveable theories within the establishment, such as, for example, the theory that Cuban human intelligence (humint) was generally unreliable in the early stage of the Cuban Missile Crisis (Moore 2006: 20); or from arrogance in the ruling political class that their policies and theories are right-minded and not to be contradicted, as was arguably the case in the French establishment on the subject of the Maginot Line (Young

1986: 309). In such situations, it is worth considering that contradictory analysis, however well it is framed, may fall on fallow ground.

Similarly problematic may be institutional ways of thinking about "us and them" typifications within political and security establishments. Hirshberg suggested that an American bipolar good-versus-evil "patriotic schema" may have contributed over the years to simplistic and ultimately faulty perceptions of major foes and competitors such as China (Hirshberg 1993: 250–251). Similarly, Song suggests that a fixed Realist mindset established by respected scholars such as Mearsheimer on the question of the nefarious implications of China's rise may cause a Western groupthink narrative which is fundamentally flawed in its framing (Song 2015: 155). In this way, Western Realist scholars may set the ground rules for how to think about such matters, then "prove" that their conclusions are correct, when a completely different epistemology may come up with different answers.

Such thinking may be particularly important in the contemporary context when Western governments and scholars are considering threats within an increasingly multipolar world and more often than not forming negative views of the implications of the emergence of non-Western states such as Russia and China. The argument here is not necessarily that such conclusions will turn out to be completely unfounded but that advanced analysis about foreign policy issues not only needs to be good analysis in all the traditional ways, but also needs to go deeper and think critically about epistemological frames that underpin the whole approach to the question. Jervis was surely right to challenge the assessment of the early Cold War secretary of state, John Foster Dulles, that the CIA generally avoided any problems of bias through good analysis, when the reality is that every political system looks at the world through a particular frame of reference (Jervis 1968: 464).

Much good work has been conducted in the intelligence studies realm about approaches and mechanisms that can raise the awareness of intelligence analysts of the cognitive pitfalls that may bedevil their work, such as groupthink, confirmation bias, or failures to consider alternative hypotheses. Some work (although arguably less) has also looked at issues to do with the subsequent communication of analytical findings to the policymakers. In the United States, the fluctuating fortunes of the National Intelligence Estimates (NIEs) have been the subject of interesting analysis by the likes of Johnson (2008), Shlaim (1976) and Kreps (2008). The NIE approach was itself born from intelligence failure, in the shape of the failure by the American establishment to foresee the invasion of the southern Korean peninsula by the communist North Koreans in 1950.

Kreps examined two very interesting episodes in the post–Cold War period in which NIEs on assessments of weapons of mass destruction (WMD) capabilities had shifted subtly and materially affected policy as a result (Kreps 2008). The first concerned assessments of the general threat from ballistic missile development and proliferation in the 1993–1995 period; the second concerned that of Iran's offensive nuclear capability in the 2005–2007 period. In both cases, an initially robust and doom-laden assessment was tempered two years later by a more equivocal and cautious judgment about the threat. Consequently, both cases also saw political acrimony emerge between policymakers in the military establishment who were calibrating their policy with more pessimistic readings of the situation, and the intelligence community, who some in the former community accused of essentially playing politics by appearing to change their mind. The assessment of Kreps (2008: 609) was that this was not bad but good intelligence, in that information was reassessed in both cases without fear of the implications for the political process. The results of this reassessment were communicated appropriately, even if the policymakers did not like what they heard. This is surely how things should work.

In both cases, the careful language in the estimates was critical, and portrayed the degree of uncertainty in appropriate ways. The example of the infamous Team A/Team B experiment in the US intelligence community in the mid-1970s provided an example of where robust language could trigger very robust response. Team B proclaimed that the Soviets were determined to "crush the capitalist realm by other than military means; the Soviet Union is nevertheless preparing for a Third World war as if it were unavoidable" (Kreps 2008: 612). Such as assessment left little to the imagination and helped to contribute to a spiraling expenditure in US military posture. It is interesting to contrast this with the language of the 2007 NIE on Iran's nuclear program, which concluded "with moderate confidence" that Tehran had stopped its nuclear program a few years before and decided not to restart it (Kreps 2008: 618). Here, much more cautious language led to a different policy outcome.

As was noted by Sherman Kent, the historian and intelligence analyst who posthumously gave his name to the CIA's analysis academy, "estimating is what you do when you do not know" (cited in Kreps 2008: 610). However good the analysis is, it cannot definitively predict the future. This is perhaps particularly so in the highly complex and Machiavellian world of geopolitics. It is also good reason why intelligence analysts need not only highly advanced skills in analysis, but also to know how to accurately, objectively, and carefully communicate the results of that analysis and their certainty or otherwise in their forecasts. This is particularly the case if analysts are working on foreign policy and leadership issues, although the requirements are not confined to that subject area.

Critical Discourse Analysis as a Tool

Analysis of what leaders and governments are saying, therefore, and the assessment of meanings and intentions behind the words have a large connection with the analysis of language and semantics. Of course, in the world of intelligence, things are most definitely not always as they seem, and there will often be loaded meaning, subtext, and even deception to be considered behind the words.

CDA is all about critical and deeper readings of narratives and rhetoric for the meanings they may imply between the lines, and as such it is a potentially very useful analytical tool for analysts in developing their craft. This is achieved by focusing on implicature in texts and statements; identifying relative subject and object positions; and identifying and assessing the use of semantic and lexical devices such as metaphor, euphemism, and polemic. Taking the model further, however, it can be argued that an advanced awareness of CDA also helps analysts to think how they communicate themselves and how they avoid ambiguity in their intelligence reports as far as possible.

Early philosophical work on political myth recognized the importance of language. While Sorel and Barthes disagreed about the potential agency of political myth, they both agreed that language and discourse were central to its propagation. Sorel proclaimed that you did not have to be a great philosopher to see that language "deceives us constantly as to the true nature of the relationship between things" (Sorel 1961: 251). Barthes, similarly, spoke of the destructive power of "depoliticized speech" which "abolishes the complexity of human acts" (Barthes 1972: 143).

John Austin (1962) introduced the idea of speech act theory, which suggests that language has important agential properties, sometimes by directly initiating actions in the physical world (such as a declaration of war for example). From this idea flowed critical discourse analysis (CDA), including Fairclough's analysis of the relationship between language and relative positions of power (Fairclough 1989). In security studies, the Copenhagen School of scholars, led by Buzan, Waever, and de Wilde, included speech act theory as a component in their critical thesis of "securitization," which suggested that certain factors could be converted into existential security concerns in the public consciousness by political leaders, through their narratives and utterances (Buzan et al. 1998).

More recently, much critical analysis has been undertaken of the high-level political discourse following the 9/11 attacks, using speech act theory and CDA. Jackson, in his extensive critique of the discourse surrounding the global war on terror, notes a similarity with the dichotomous principles of the Cold War (Jackson 2005). Then, the oppression and lack of democracy in communist states were counterposed against the West's freedom and respect for human rights, in defining who was right and who was wrong. Similarly, "terrorists" in the contemporary era are characterized as espousing inverse mirror-image values to those of the West, whereby they are barbaric and inhuman.

In times of conflict, a sociology of violence suggests that dehumanization of the out-group is an important device in allowing for violent and murderous acts to be carried out by otherwise ordinary people (Malešević, 2010: 142–143). Using the rhetoric of "war," furthermore, moves the conflict into a different realm from that of ordinary civil life, where different rules apply and a more existential conception of the threat and appropriate response can be applied. In all these cases, the words used to describe the threat and identify the enemy are critically important.

As Gastil (1992: 469) observed, politics and discourse are "inextricably intertwined." Thus political leaders can articulate power through their utterances and can also develop and propagate myth. In his work on language and myth, Edelman (1998) noted a complex and symbiotic relationship between the public's notion of what government was there to do and how spokespeople and leaders in the government could play on those ideas and propagate mythical constructs, which "typically fail to analyse problems adequately and rarely solve them" (Edelman 1998: 131). In this way, lofty ideas such as the fact that government is there to protect the people and ensure their well-being can subtly hide the effect of any actual policy. Similarly, explanations can be proffered for ills befalling the nation, such as the idea that they are because of foreign interference, or immigration, or any number of other factors.

Interestingly, the role of the media and its relative position in the public consciousness as regards political leaders, can play a highly significant role in public understanding. Hallin (1984) conducted a detailed analysis of the American media during the war in Vietnam and analyzed the notion that it became increasingly "oppositional" and anti-government during the war. Analysis showed, however, that while the number of critical stories did grow during the period, this was not as a result of any hidden critical agenda on the part of the media but an accurate reflection of the more negative incidents and stories that were emerging.

What all of this shows are two things. First, official discourse and rhetoric are not what they seem but are the articulation of political agendas and myths. Second, the media's reporting of events is complex and is also not always what it seems, in both negative and positive ways. In the contemporary era of "fake news" and "alternative truths," coupled significantly with a highly antagonistic official relationship to the established media in certain places, the modern analyst of political affairs increasingly needs a highly advanced and developed capability in critical analysis. Looking between the lines at what political leaders and governments mean in their statements continues to be an important and challenging requirement for intelligence agencies. This, coupled with the rapidly rising amount of information available to all analysts and the complex ways in which it is being used and interpreted in the modern age, makes the importance of skilled analysis arguably more important than ever.

Second, analysts need to put these advanced skills in understanding the overt and covert meanings of language to use in their own communication of the analysis they conduct. Understanding the meaning of words, and especially words conveying uncertain judgments or probabilities, is absolutely essential to the effective dissemination of intelligence findings. In this part of the process, meanings need to be avowedly not ambiguous but as clear as possible. Thus, in a sense, CDA has to be used in reverse by advanced intelligence analysts, to ensure that their communications are as little imbued with hidden meaning and complexity as possible.

The Simulation—Basic Data

Instructional Objectives

For intelligence studies programs, this simulation can be used to embed learning about the analysis and dissemination parts of the intelligence cycle. This particular exercise offers an opportunity to supplement and shape a program in this subject area with an episode of exercising and practicing of critical thinking and analysis skills in a way that is very easy and flexible to design and deliver. For the instructor, it thus offers an opportunity to break up and supplement traditional classroom learning with a more interactive exercise.

Simulation Objectives

The general aim of this simulation is to provide students with an experiential episode of learning in which two key objectives are progressed: to further develop critical reading and analysis skills using the framework of critical discourse analysis (CDA) as a tool; and to develop communication and dissemination skills by applying the principles of CDA in drafting a clear and objective policy briefing on a specified issue (in this case, in the foreign policy realm). While these things can be discussed in class, this simulation uses real situations and real communications to provide students with a more immersed and experiential taste of applying critical thinking to the real world, thus enhancing their learning experience.

The Exercise
Debriefing Format

The initial discussion about CDA need not necessarily go into the level of academic detail presented in the introduction to this chapter (depending on the requirements of the program and group at hand), but must simply relay the fact that CDA is a mechanism used in the social sciences to forensically analyze language and communication and to uncover meanings and positions beneath the immediate presentation of the words. For intelligence analysts, it can act as a useful tool for exercising analytical skills and for honing accurate communication of the results of analysis.

The initial debriefing will relay the objectives of the exercise, namely, to provide the students with a critical thinking exercise using CDA as a tool, which will help to enhance their skills in two areas: in applying critical reading and analysis to a text and in thinking about how to draft a policy briefing in the clearest and most objective ways.

It should then be explained that there will be two parts to the simulation. In the first part, the students will practice using CDA to critically analyze text, both in plenary and split into smaller groups. In the second part, students will take a text concerning a current issue and prepare a short policy briefing on its key points, taking the lessons learned from CDA into account in producing the clearest and most objective briefing possible.

Target Audience

This simulation can be effective both as a training tool for current intelligence analysts who have a need to hone and develop their analysis and reporting skills and for a wider constituency of students pursuing intelligence studies or related disciplines who wish to gain a feel for the sorts of challenges faced by analysts and reporters in the intelligence business and the implications of these challenges for the intelligence cycle.

It is also worth noting that given the generic nature of CDA as a framework, this simulation could be adapted to any number of situations and subject areas in which critical thinking, reading, analysis, and communications skills are required. To adapt the simulation, a suitable set of context-specific texts would be chosen.

Playing Time

Ideally, the interactive parts of this simulation requires a good two hours to encompass the initial debriefing, the reading and analysis exercises, and the preparation of the short policy briefing on the required text.

Debriefing Time

A further hour is recommended (depending on the number of groups in the overall class) for the presentation of the short policy briefs back to the plenary group and critical discussion thereafter, in which an evaluation is made of how well the objectives of the exercise have been met and how effective CDA has been for the students as an analytical tool.

Number of Players Required

This simulation requires at least two subgroups of students with an ideal maximum of six students in each. Further groups of around six can be added fairly easily, although consideration must be made in the debriefing stage of how long it will take for all of the groups to report their findings back to plenary. Generally, very short and snappy presentations of a few minutes each are ideal, as the subsequent discussion and reflection are the more important part of the process.

Requirements Such as Computers and Facilities

One of the benefits of this simulation is that it does not necessarily require any audiovisual facilities and is thus easy to mount in a variety of environments. As the simulation is primarily concerned with the analysis of a set of texts, these can all be printed out and handed round to the students as paper copies. However, if there is a requirement to bring in more sophisticated and visually interesting elements to the process, the analysis could just as easily examine oral texts on video or audio, such as the speeches of political leaders, for example; texts can be circulated as document files on computers. For the final briefing stage, instructors can also consider recording the policy briefings and disseminating these afterwards as examples of analysis; consideration can also be made to working the simulation across groups dispersed in space and time, using collaborative wikis, webinars, and so on. In short, the basic requirements are very simple but can be made more sophisticated as required by the particular program in question.

Facilitator's Guide

Pre-Simulation Briefing

The facilitator should consider the intellectual and academic backdrop to this particular simulation as outlined in the introduction to this chapter and develop an initial briefing to the students tailored to the particular cohort in question. Again, the length and degree of that briefing should be flexible and context-specific. Thus, if the cohort in question comprises intelligence analysts who are using this simulation as an analytical training exercise, for example, the deep academic background of CDA will probably not be necessary other than briefly outlining what CDA means and how it is used. Conversely, if this simulation is being delivered in a university course in which there is a mix of academic and practitioner students, the academic background within the broader context of analysis and the intelligence process may be more appropriate in the form of a fuller briefing.

Whichever degree of detail is chosen, the pre-simulation briefing should clearly outline the aims and objectives of this simulation, particularly the two target areas of analysis and dissemination.

Descriptions of the Steps with an Estimation of the Time Required for Each Step

As discussed, there are two stages to the simulation. The first stage is mostly analytical and should take up to approximately two hours. The second stage comprises the briefing of results and subsequent discussion and should take at least one hour.

Stage 1. Preliminary Exercises

The first stage of the simulation comprises a number of short analytical exercises in which the basic principles of CDA are experienced and understood. The first small exercise is aimed at introducing and embedding some of these core principles. Rod Case (2005) presented an interesting example of a text that is often used in schools and universities on programs teaching English as a second language (ESL), whereby CDA helps the students to understand the English language in more depth and sophistication. The text used is a short extract from a contemporaneous account in the early 19th century of the expedition into the Western part of North America by Lewis and Clark, in which the positive attributes of a slave called York were described (see appendix 8A). The text is designed to cause the students to think about race, class, and relative power positions relevant to the time in question by analyzing the subject and object position in the text, the adjectives and metaphors used, and so on.

Any number of examples could be used and historical ones are often good candidates, as they help to show how societal factors have changed over time and thus how "facts" and events can be presented differently in different situations. The particular case chosen should be read through by the whole class and a brief discussion held about what the text is trying to say and how it says it.

This leads on to the second exercise, in which the students consider two contrasting texts and try to analyze them along similar lines to the first example text. For this stage of the process, the facilitator should split the students up into roughly equally sized groups, not exceeding six students in each group if possible. All students are given the same text but are asked to work separately as each group.

In this particular exercise, an example of two contrasting perspectives on events in India in 1857 are presented (see appendices 8B and 8C). The event in question is generally called the Indian Mutiny in Britain today; it was often referred to as the Sepoy Rebellion by the colonial authorities at the time. In India, however, the preferred term is the First War of Independence. Straight away, just from these two different references to the same events, which were constituted by an uprising initiated by native Indian troops (called sepoys) in the British army across several districts in the subcontinent and which marked an important turning point in British colonial policy in India, we can see a difference in historical narrative and communication.

The two texts should not be handed out at the time same. Students are asked, as a whole group, to read the first text from 1857 and offer some initial comments, considering the time and place of its writing. In terms of perspective, this account is obviously written from the perspective of the colonial overlords in India, who held the power at the time. At one level it is arrogant—suggesting that British rule in India is the best thing that has happened to the subcontinent and that other areas in Asia should be jealous—but at the same time a little circumspect, noting that there are a great many things introduced by the British about which the Indians would have cause to feel disgruntled. The prescription for addressing these concerns, however, is to further embed Christianity and British imperial rule in the subcontinent and to reject the "idolatrous" and "tyrannical" rule of precolonial leaders and systems. Indeed, in 1858, India became a formal Dominion of the British Empire and Queen Victoria was crowned Empress of India.

The second text can then be introduced to the students, which is an educational article for schools about the events of 1857, published in 2016 to mark their 159th anniversary, by the news agency *India Today*.

Following analysis of this article, students are then asked to contrast its perspective with that of the British colonialists articulated in the first text and to think about specifically how this contrasting perspective is presented. Discussion could center around the fact that this second statement does not describe a mutinous uprising by subjects but a first attempt at liberation from colonial rule, which only failed for logistical rather than ideological reasons. Here, the events of 1857 are not taken as a single moment but part of a longer narrative of liberationist actions. The point about religion is made from the opposing perspective: here there is a suspicion expressed that the British were trying to convert the Indians en masse to Christianity, when this is indeed the prescription put forward in the earlier article as a solution to the subcontinent's ills. Finally, when considering linguistic devices used, words such as "martyr" and "leader" in this second account are very indicative of the different way in which those who undertook the rebellion were viewed on the different sides of the fence.

The facilitator should allow a free-flowing discussion where possible for ten minutes or so, pulling out some of the above observations if necessary.

Following this stage of the exercise and a discussion about the points it raises, students should have established a basic grasp of the mechanism, purpose, and utility of CDA for reading beyond the immediately apparent text and drawing out deeper meanings from the narrative.

Stage 2. Analysis

The second stage of the exercise is the main part of the overall process and is split into two components. The first component concerns critically analyzing a text (or texts and/or other inputs) in small groups (ideally the same groups as for the previous stage) using a prescribed heuristic (see below); the second component concerns writing a strategic report based on the findings, again using some guidelines.

In this particular example, there is one text used, and it is constituted by an official statement issued by the Russian Ministry of Foreign Affairs (MFA) to mark the conclusion of 2016, posted on the Internet from its embassy in the United States. When looking at the world from a Western perspective, a consideration of how the Russian state views the world and its foreign policy priorities is particularly interesting and challenging. As Churchill famously said, for many observers Russia is "a riddle wrapped in a mystery inside an enigma" (Churchill 1939). In other words, trying to decipher Russia's strategic thinking (or indeed that of any number of states) from the outside is not an easy task. More importantly, one of the main purposes of this exercise is to allow analysts a chance to challenge their potential cultural groupthink perspectives on the world and consider alternative views and hypotheses, ideally in a fiercely dispassionate and objective way. Any number of texts or inputs could be used for this exercise, but one that is likely to offer a perspective different from that of the majority of the students is a good idea.

The text presented here (see appendix 8D) is a truncated version of the full 2016 Russian MFA statement.

The facilitator should hand out copies of the statement to all students but ask them to remain in their groups. The facilitator should then explain the analytical heuristic to be used, as follows:

Exercise: Russia's Foreign Policy? Analytical heuristic.
Russia's contemporary foreign policy stances, as derived from the Moscow MFA's statement, "Key foreign policy outcomes for 2016."

Analyze the Text

* How can the underlying ideology of Russia's foreign policy be described?
* Who are the "us" and the "them"?
* Provide some examples of positive-self and negative-other presentation.
* Provide some examples of rhetorical and lexical devices and style used in this statement.
* Which points of detail could be researched further?

Box 8.1

Example Rhetorical Devices

- Positive and negative descriptors and language
- Methods of identification of self and other (us and them)

- Euphemisms, similes, and metaphors
- Certainty and uncertainty of language
- Assertion of "givens" and "facts."

Before commencing the exercise, the plenary group as a whole will hold a brief discussion with the instructor to clarify any terms used in the exercise that may be unclear and to make sure that everyone understands what they need to do. For example, it should be explained that many texts will identify a subject and an object and set them as "us" and "them." In the example concerning 1857 India, for example, the British were the "us" in the first article but the "them" in the second. A standard rhetorical device is then to imbue the "us" with positive characteristics and the "them" with negative characteristics as a way of showing whose policy approach is right and whose is wrong.

Another key factor is that concerning the assertion of "givens" and "facts." As discussed earlier, we are considering this exercise in the midst of a feverish level of speculation about the validity of media in the political realm and its relationship to those in power. In both political rhetoric and in some sections of the media—situations very different to academic writing—it is the case that facts and understandings can be asserted and accepted by a willing audience without them having any particular evidential basis or validity when scrutinized. One of the Western accusations leveled at the Russian state currently is that they will present "alternative facts" (to use the words of a recent media counselor to the US president) to explain foreign policy and military activities in the international sphere, whether they are in Ukraine, Syria, or elsewhere. The job of the advanced intelligence analysts is to treat all assertions and theories with doubt in the first instance, until they can present some solid evidence on which such assertions may be based. However, spotting what is widely understood and what is not, which Schudson (1990: 118) described as "what everyone knows," is not always easy and can be missed when subjected to the work of skillful orators. For this exercise, spotting where assertions have been made, and then analyzing them using secondary sources and references, is a key part of the process.

Once the instructor is satisfied that the majority of students understand the task in hand and are ready to commence the analysis, a suitable amount of time is then allocated to allow the groups to analyze the text and record their results in accordance with the above heuristic.

At the end of this analytical phase of the exercise, some degree of discussion of the findings can be conducted, either in groups or in plenary, although care must be taken not to "give the answers away" for the next phase. The instructor can lead the discussion by asking what the groups found against certain questions in the heuristic. For example, one of the questions was about identifying "givens" in the text. In the statement, the MFA says that there "is no alternative" to the Minsk Agreements of 2015 for solving the Ukrainian crisis. This is stated in very definitive language as a "given," but would everyone agree with that, and on what basis does Russia feel that this is an unshakeable position? Wider analysis by the students would usefully look at the Minsk Agreements in terms of who were the signatories, what they established, and whether they are the one and only agreed way forward in the crisis among the international community. Depending on what was found, the students would need to consider how they communicated this particular element of their analysis.

Similarly, the first paragraph of the statement provides a nice example of "positive-us" and "negative-them" narrative. The "them" are not explicitly identified but are clearly the Americans (and possibly their allies), as reference to a "unipolar world" suggests. The impression given in the drafting of the narrative is that the Russians are part of a broad international front which accepts the sanctity of sovereignty and cooperation, while the Americans and their allies are more interested in selfish Realist interests. Consideration of this factor allows the student to place themselves in the Russian state's mindset and worldview and consider what perspective this offers on world affairs.

Once the instructor is satisfied that sufficient analysis and discussion has been had, the final stage of the process can happen.

Final Stage—Dissemination

In this final stage of the process, the groups of students are asked to collectively produce a short mock policy paper on Russia's foreign policy at the end of 2016, as derived from their official statement under analysis. A model for this paper frequently used by the author is the British Joint Intelligence Committee (JIC) model, which has the following characteristics:

- The top of the paper comprises a set of "key judgments," which are essentially the headline judgments for busy readers, and which could stand alone as the core elements of the paper.
- The body of the paper expands on these key judgments in a little more detail for those that have time to read through the whole paper.
- The paper does *not* provide the policymakers with explicit recommendations for what their policy should be, but it provides an objective and dispassionate analysis of what the intelligence suggests and the analyst's assessment thereof, without any grace or favor to current political agendas.
- Careful language is used throughout which tries to present the analysis in an objective way, which supports any judgments and assertions with appropriate evidence and logic; and which appropriately conveys any levels of uncertainty in the judgments in such a way that the policymaker has a clear idea of what the intelligence does and does not show.

The spirit of these guidelines is that they call, in essence, for something that would be very resistant to a critical discourse analysis, if conducted skillfully. A properly drafted strategic intelligence assessment should scrupulously avoid any ambiguity in its communication of what the intelligence shows, and convey relative levels of certainty over judgments very clearly to the policymaker. (Descriptive words and phrases such as "possibly," "verified" or "unverified," "evidence suggests that," and so on will be very useful.) Having a developed understanding of CDA can help the analysts ensure they avoid the pitfalls in their own dissemination of intelligence as far as possible.

In most cases, in the interest of time it is appropriate for the groups just to produce a bulleted set of key points supporting their analysis rather than to draft a whole paper. These can then be presented in turn to plenary and compared and discussed. In some cases it might be interesting to post some or all of these short papers on a website or a collaborative wiki, or indeed to conduct the whole exercise using groups based in different locations and comparing their results. The author has also used a similar task over a long period as the basis for a full term paper. Some degree of competition could also be introduced if appropriate, such as scoring the final papers and announcing a "winner." All of these factors will need to be tailored to the particular program and set of students at hand and to the objectives of the program.

Before commencing the report-writing stage of the exercise, the instructor may wish to provide an example of how the above JIC-style factors are brought to bear in the drafting. (Again, care must be taken here not to make it too easy for the students.) One example could be the factor concerning the Minsk Agreement discussed above. Here, the assessment is that the official Russian position on Ukraine is that the Minsk Agreements provide the only viable diplomatic way forward for the crisis, and all other avenues are inappropriate. Further investigation reveals that the agreements were signed between Russia, Ukraine, France, and Germany, and have generally failed to quell the violence or move the crisis beyond its rather stalled and violent status quo, at the time of writing. A key judgment may be that on Ukraine, Russia favors the Minsk Agreements as they allow them to suggest that they are working diplomatically to resolve crises with a broad international coalition that—significantly—does not include the United States or indeed the EU as a single unit, but that the reality is that the agreements appear to be failing to deliver any viable way forward from the current stalemate. Note can be taken in that particular example of the tentative judgment made, and the careful language used such as "appear to be" and so forth.

Debriefing

Objectives and Description
The aim of this simulation is twofold: to provide students with a different method of practicing critical thinking and reading on a real-world situation and to think

about how this experience shapes communication of intelligence to policymakers in the clearest and most objective way. At the end of the exercise—either immediately or subsequently after some reflection—it will be useful for students to consider how well it has enhanced their understanding of critical thinking and policy communication.

It is important to note that, as with any exercise of this nature, CDA should not be taken too proscriptively necessarily as a mandated technique or process. The debriefing should stress that it is merely one approach of many that provides students with a structured mechanism for exercising their critical thinking skills and for focusing on the importance of language in analysis and dissemination.

Conclusions

As CDA shows us, words often carry multiple or ambiguous meanings. The business of the intelligence analyst is, in many ways, the business of language and words, both in terms of what they might mean when intercepted and how they should be used to give a clear steer to the policymakers. In this sense, the word "exercise" has two meanings here. At one level, this chapter provides a sort of experiential analytical and writing exercise that current or aspiring intelligence analysts can use to try out the assessment of real policy issues in a safe learning environment. At the same time, CDA provides a useful mechanism for analysts to exercise their minds and critical capabilities, much as they would exercise their bodies in the gymnasium.

The modern intelligence analyst cannot exercise the mind too much. As discussed in this chapter, it could be argued that the contemporary era of postmodern discourse in an era of galloping information revolution is one in which the solid assessment of intelligence challenges, and the communication of that assessment effectively to policymakers, is as important now as it has ever been in history. Advanced analysts need advanced skills, and CDA may be one mechanism that can help to achieve that aim.

Appendix 8A

Initial Text: York and Clark

Question From Text: *What things about York made the Indians admire him?*

Text: *Although York was Clark's slave, he was a well-respected member of the expedition, using his strength and power to help the group survive in the wilderness. In fact, Lewis and Clark were able to build good relations with many Native American tribes because the people were so curious about York. They were amazed by York's black skin, size and strength. In 1811, Clark gave York his freedom.*

(Cited in Case 2005: 145)

Appendix 8B

First Comparative Text: The Indian Mutiny, or First War of Independence

The Sepoy Rebellion

London Quarterly Review, No. XVII, October 1857

Looking at the disasters which have befallen us, we may both console ourselves that they were not merited from the people, and at the same time feel that they are not unmerited from the God of our nation. Judging ourselves by Hindu standards, the people owed us nothing but gratitude. We have ruled them better than they ever were ruled; given them for the first time repose, security, and freedom; and brought into their country improvements which no other Asiatic race have yet received. But judging ourselves by Christian standards, we must not wonder that chastisements have overtaken us. If our women have been disgraced, how many of those of India have our officers and troops dishonoured? Have we not on that soil permitted wholesale murders of widows and of old men, under pretext of religion and though we interposed, at last, on behalf of the former, the ghaut murders of the Ganges—that Ganges which ran red at Cawnpore with English blood—still continue. Have we not introduced licensed drinking-houses, to debauch the people, for profit? Have we not fed on the odious opium revenue? Have we not trafficked in prostitution and the obscenest idolatry by our temple subsidies? Have we not steadfastly befriended Heathenism and Mohammedism, and yielded to Christianity the commonest liberties only inch by inch, as it was necessitated by public opinion? Have we not shut out, as far as possible, the name and fear of God from school?. . . .

Nothing but a social earthquake could break up that system of consolidated wrongs which we call India. The curse of its native rule was the twofold curse of idolatry and oppression; it has groaned for ages under the tyranny of "gods many and lords many." And now that we are about more thoroughly to supersede the rapacious and cruel rule of its chiefs, it will behove us to put to shame its foolish and obscene "divinities" by the exhibition of a purer worship. If we take the country and its people for our beloved Queen, shall we not put both it and them under the protection of the same true God? It is only as we are faithful henceforth to the spirit of our own institutions, civil and religious, that we may profit by this dreadful lesson, and hope to see the slow but steady light of prosperity advance above the plains and heights of Hindustan.

Appendix 8C

Second Comparative Text: The Indian Mutiny, or First War of Independence

India Today, 10 May 2016

India's first war of independence: all you need to know on its 159th anniversary.

India's first war of independence, better known as the Indian Rebellion of 1857, began on this day, May 10 in the year 1857. The first martyr of the revolt was Mangal Pandey and the war was the result of accumulation of many factors over time.

The rebellion of 1857 is considered the first blow that came to shatter the British rule in India. Some of the other rebellions and leaders included Rani Lakshmibai, Kunwar Singh, Bahadur Shah, Nana Saheb, Tatia Tope and Begum Hazrat Mahal.

Today, on the 159th anniversary of the starting of the Indian Rebellion of 1857, here is all you wish to know about the rebellion:

Causes of the revolt:

- There was discrimination among the British and Indian soldiers. It has been believed that the behavior of British soldiers toward Indian soldiers was quite rude.
- By January 1857, rumours had been taking rounds that the English cartridges were greased with animal fat. This was further sparked when during a fight, a low-caste sepoy taunted a high-caste sepoy for "losing his caste" after biting the cartridge as they were greased with the fat of pigs and cows.
- There had also been rumours that the British were trying to destroy the religions of the Indian people.
- One of the other reasons was the introduction of a new land revenue system which snatched the land from cultivators.

Reasons of its failure:

- Some epicentres of the revolt were Kanpur, Lucknow, Aligarh, Agra, Arrah, Delhi, and Jhansi.
- Due to all the epicentres being far from each other, there was a communication gap between the leaders of different parts of India.
- Due to the rebellion having no central leadership, it got limited to some parts of India only.
- Rebels did not have enough weapons and finance whereas British people had advanced weapons and enough finance.

Appendix 8D

Final Stage Text: Dissemination
MFA of Russia, Moscow
Key Foreign Policy Outcomes for 2016

The outgoing year 2016 was a difficult one for world politics and international relations.

The international situation remained tense. Acute contradictions between states and associations of states with regard to fundamental issues of the world order remained unchanged. Blood was shed in entire regions, where statehood and the legitimate basis of the government have been undermined by external interventions or foreign support to local extremist and radical forces. The terrorist threat in the belt of instability ranging from North Africa to South Asia's borders has taken on a systemic dimension. The entire world has to pay a high price for the attempts of a limited number of countries to retain their global "leadership" at all costs.

The vast majority of the international community clearly saw the ephemeral nature of a unipolar hegemony and the flaws of unilateral approaches. The demand for a constructive international agenda seeking to establish equal cooperation has increased.

Alongside other responsible nations, Russia has worked hard to prevent the further degradation of international relations, fraught with uncontrolled collapse and descent into full-blown confrontation. It confirmed and consolidated its status as a guarantor of global stability, a centre of attraction and support for those who are committed to the primacy of international law, healthy traditions and values, and who are ready and willing to use this as a basis to build clear and fair collective approaches to resolving the important problems of our time.

. . . Russia's vision of a changing world is reflected in a revised Foreign Policy Concept, approved by the Russian President on November 30, 2016.

The document contains reinforced provisions regarding the need to step up the fight against terrorism and to create, for this purpose, a broad international front based on a solid legal foundation. Considerable attention was given to various aspects of forming a polycentric world order, and working within such forward-looking international forums as the SCO, BRICS, RIC, the G20, promoting the EAEC and strengthening its external relations, including with ASEAN, in order to create a broad Eurasian economic space. Also, the Concept confirms the inviolability of the fundamental basis of Russia's foreign policy, its independence, pragmatism, multi-vector nature and its willingness to promote equal and mutually beneficial cooperation with all interested countries and groups of states.

. . . The developments in and around Ukraine have remained one of the dangerous factors that have a direct influence on Russia's security and interests.

Armed provocations, responsibility for which rests with Kiev, according to reports by the OSCE Special Monitoring Mission, combined with Ukraine's policy of subverting negotiations and the fulfilment of adopted decisions, made it impossible to achieve progress in carrying out the Package of Measures for the Implementation of the Minsk Agreements of February 12, 2015. Meanwhile, there is no alternative to these agreements, as a foundation for settling Ukraine's domestic crisis. This idea was emphasised more than once during the work of the Contact Group, regular dialogue between the foreign ministries and foreign policy assistants of the leaders of the Normandy Four, meetings with representatives of the US administration and the four-party summit in October 2016.

. . . Dialogue with the United States was complicated by an aggressive US policy of systemic containment of Russia, which included the build-up of sanctions pressure, the deployment of Ballistic Missile Defence (BMD) components and provocative military activities on Russia's western borders and in the Black Sea. The well-orchestrated campaign to accuse Russia of interference in the presidential election in the United States was designed to whip up anti-Russia sentiments.

In response to these actions, Russia worked consistently to convince its American partners to normalize dialogue based on equality and mutual respect for each other's interests. It also pointed out the need to settle old problems in bilateral relations, such as the abduction of Russian citizens by US security services in other countries and violations of the rights of adopted Russian children in the United States.

Russian-US interaction continued in the areas of Russian interests and international security, including the settlement of the Syrian crisis, the Treaty on Further Reduction and Limitation of Strategic Offensive Arms (2010) and dozens of other bilateral agreements. The United States had to admit the failure of its attempts to isolate Russia on the international stage: the presidents of Russia and the United States met twice and their foreign ministers met 14 times, including twice in Moscow.

When Donald Trump won the presidential election, Vladimir Putin sent a message of congratulations saying that he hopes to work together to lift Russian-US relations out of the current crisis.

References

Austin J (1962) *How to Do Things with Words*. Wotton-under-Edge. Clarendon Press.

Barthes R (1972) *Mythologies* (trans: Lavers A). New York: Hill and Wang.

Bruner JS and Postman L (1949) "On the Perception of Incongruity: A Paradigm." *Journal of Personality* 18: 206–223.

Buzan B, Waever O, and de Wilde J (1998) *Security: A New Framework for Analysis*. Boulder, CA: Lynne Rienner.

Case R (2005) "How to Conduct a Critical Discourse Analysis of a Text: A Guide for Teachers." *The CATESOL Journal* 17(1): 145–155.

Churchill W (1939) "The Russian Enigma." BBC broadcast, October 1, 1939. From http://www.churchill-society-london.org.uk/RusnEnig.html, accessed February 8, 2017.

Edelman M (1998) "Language, Myths and Rhetoric." *Society* 35(2): 131–139.

Fairclough N (1989) *Language and Power*. Harlow: Pearson.

Gastil J (1992) "Undemocratic Discourse: A Review of Theory and Research on Political Discourse." *Discourse and Society* 3(4): 469–500.

Hallin DC (1984) "The Media, the War in Vietnam, and Political Support: A Critique of the Thesis of an Oppositional Media." *The Journal of Politics* 46: 2–24.

Hirshberg MS (1993) "Consistency and Change in American Perceptions of China." *Political Behavior* 15(3): 247–263.

Hopkins MF (2007) "Continuing Debate and New Approaches in Cold War History." *The Historical Journal* 50(4): 913–934.

Jackson R (2005) *Writing the War on Terrorism: Language, Politics and Counter-Terrorism*. Manchester: Manchester University Press.

Jervis R (1968) "Hypotheses on Misperception." *World Politics* 20(3): 454–479.

Johnson LK (2008) "Glimpses into the Gems of American Intelligence: The *President's Daily Brief* and the National Intelligence Estimate." *Intelligence and National Security* 23(3): 333–370.

Kreps SE (2008) "Shifting Currents: Changes in National Intelligence Estimates on the Iran Nuclear Threat." *Intelligence and National Security* 23(5): 608–628.

Lowenthal MM (2006) *Foreword.* In Moore DT, *Critical Thinking and Intelligence Analysis.* Occasional Paper 14, Washington DC: Joint Military Intelligence College.

Malešević S (2010) *The Sociology of War and Violence.* Cambridge: Cambridge University Press.

May E (ed. 1986) *Knowing One's Enemies: Intelligence Assessment before the Two World Wars.* Princeton: Princeton University Press.

Moore DT (2006) *Critical Thinking and Intelligence Analysis.* Occasional Paper 14, Washington DC: Joint Military Intelligence College.

Richards J (2010) *The Art and Science of Intelligence Analysis.* Oxford: Oxford University Press.

Schudson M (1990) "Ronald Reagan Misremembered." In Middleton D and Edwards D (eds.) *Collective Remembering.* London: Sage.

Shlaim A (1976) "Failures in National Intelligence Estimates: The Case of the Yom Kippur War." *World Politics* 28(3): 348–380.

Song W (2015) "Securitization of the "China Threat" Discourse: A Poststructuralist Account." *The China Review* 15(1): 145–169.

Sorel G (1908) *Réflexions sur la violence. Paris, Marcel Rivière et Cie.* English edition: Sorel G (1961) *Reflections on Violence* (trans: Hulme TE and Roth J). New York: Collier Books.

Young RJ (1986) "French Military Intelligence and Nazi Germany, 1938–1939." In May E (ed) *Knowing One's Enemies.* Princeton: Princeton University Press.

9

Speak of the Devil

Simulating Competitive Analysis in the Classroom

Stephen Coulthart

Competitive analysis has its share of supporters and critics among national security intelligence practitioners and officials. Among supporters it is viewed as an important remedy for intelligence failures, large and small (Jervis 2015; Report of the Senate Select Committee on Intelligence 2005, 407). These supporters point to the successful implementation of competitive analysis, especially in Israeli intelligence (Zenko 2015, 61–64; Shalev 2010, 213–216). They believe that using conflict in the analytical process can help analysts explore alternative hypotheses and avoid groupthink. In 2004, this view was reflected in the Intelligence Reform and Terrorism Prevention Act, which calls for red teaming, a competitive analysis technique.

There are also competitive analysis critics who argue that it has little to contribute to national security intelligence and may even make intelligence products *worse*. One author writes, "despite the theoretical appeal of competitive analysis by outsiders, its application to strategic intelligence would fail . . . outsiders called in to refute or negate intelligence estimates would only muddle the process" (Stack 1997, 463). Others point to the pragmatic concern that intelligence analysts and policymakers rarely have the time for time-intensive competitive analysis techniques (Russell 2010, 383). Still others, while hopeful about the value of competitive analysis, are concerned with how it may be used to politicize intelligence (Mitchell 2006). This latter view informs the objectives and goals of this simulation and how competitive analysis techniques can be manipulated to reduce or even negate its value in intelligence analysis.

What Is Competitive Analysis?

Competitive analysis is a method of "structured analysis," which uses techniques to externalize analysts' thought processes in a transparent and systematic fashion (Pherson and Heuer 2014, 232). Succinctly defined, competitive analysis a method of structured analysis that uses techniques to pit "analysts against each other in debating contests designed ostensibly to produce a superior intelligence product from the same pool of raw data" (Mitchell 2006, 145). Competitive analysis is defined by a few traits:

- It is a group process. Competitive analysis requires at least more than one analyst to make debate and discussion possible.
- Competitive analysis requires structure in the form of rules; without this, analysts are engaging in an informal discussion.
- It requires competition and/or dissent between analysts. Dissent may be authentic or simulated solely for the purposes of the analytic exercise.

There are several types of competitive analysis techniques.[1] Devil's advocacy is designed to "counteract pressures toward homogeneity and conformity in small groups and thus enhance deliberations" (George and Stern 2002, 485). To use it, analysts appoint an individual or a group to act as devil's advocate and provide structured critique. The critiques are usually provided through multiple rounds of interaction between devil's advocates and the group being critiqued. With each round the critiqued group attempts to refute and/or incorporate the feedback of the devil's advocate. As a result, the final analysis should be developed so that it can rebut the "best possible case for an alternative explanation" (US Government 2009, 17).

Team A/team B differs from devil's advocacy in one key way. Whereas devil's advocacy's "purpose is to challenge a single dominant mind-set," team A/team B "recognizes that there may be competing and possibly equally strong mind-sets held on an issue that need to be clarified" (US Government 2009, 19). In other words, devil's advocacy challenges the dominant viewpoint while team A/team B brings together two strongly held viewpoints. Originally developed to improve executive-level decision making, multiple advocacy is similar to team A/team B in that it also seeks to manage and leverage dissent, but instead of two perspectives it takes into account multiple perspectives (George 1972). Another defining characteristic is that the process is overseen by a "custodian" who structures interactions.

Red teaming is a technique that helps analysts put themselves in the mind of an adversary to challenge operational planning and analysis. It is especially useful when analysts are simulating foreign adversaries. However, as discussed further below, accurately modeling thinking processes is difficult when the adversary is culturally distant to the red team members (Johnston 2005, 81–84). It is worth noting that red teaming may also be used as a technique to imagine an adversary's beliefs and intentions without challenging operational plans or analysis at all. For example, analysts might use red teaming to predict how a foreign dictator would respond to unrest in his country. Strictly speaking, this use of the technique is not a form of competitive analysis because it does not involve challenge or dissent of pre-existing plans or analysis.[2]

Competitive analysis techniques differ in form, but all have a core function: to address the problem of undue group conformity—that is, when groups have reached consensus too early in the analytical process. Among analysts and scholars of intelligence and foreign policy decision making, the problem is more commonly known as "groupthink." Formally defined, it is the "tendency for cohesive groups to become concerned about group solidarity and fail to evaluate their decisions and assumptions" (Park 1990, 229). The groupthink concept was developed by Irving Janis in a landmark study of foreign policy decision making (Janis 1972). A key condition for groupthink is the extent to which group members have a cohesive identity; the more cohesive, the more likely to have undue consensus, or groupthink, in decision making. Janis also identified "structural faults" as a key condition. These include factors such as insulation of the group, homogeneity, and lack of impartial leadership. Context is also an important condition. In provocative contexts, where complexity of the decision is high and moral dilemmas exist, groupthink is more likely (Janis 1972).

It is important to note that some of Janis's theory of groupthink has been challenged on empirical grounds by subsequent research. Some conditions, such as group cohesiveness, have not always been found to be indicative of groupthink.[3] Still, it is undeniable that certain group processes can lead to symptoms Janis identified as groupthink, such as an overestimation in the validity of groups' judgments, closemindedness, and self-censorship.

Competitive analysis should help sharpen national intelligence products; however, it has been used to politicize intelligence. The first high-profile misuse of competitive analysis occurred in the 1970s in an episode known as the "1975 Team B estimate." A team A/team B exercise was convened by President Gerald Ford to challenge the CIA's estimates of Soviet military capabilities and intentions. Team B was composed of policy hawks, who were unwavering in their belief that the Soviet Union possessed greater capabilities than contemporary CIA estimates suggested. Knowing the strong partisan bent of team B, the team A CIA analysts grew defensive. The process was further hampered when team B reportedly leaked its judgments to journalists (Mitchell 2006, 149). In subsequent years, a few commentators have concluded team B's warnings about Soviet capabilities were incorrect (Prados 1993; Mitchell 2006, 148–150).

The controversy of the 1975 Team B exercise did not preclude its use again in the US intelligence community. Perhaps the most recent and impactful misuse of team A/team B occurred in the aftermath of the 9/11 terrorist attacks. Secretary of Defense Donald Rumsfeld and other officials created a team B within the Pentagon called the Policy Counter Terrorism Evaluation Group (PCTEG) to evaluate intelligence on Iraq—in particular, links between Saddam Hussein and al Qaeda. In effect, PCTEG conducted its analysis "deductively, not inductively" and sought to prove their suspicions rather than critically test them (Mitchell 2006, 153). In other words, the group engaged in systematic and intentional confirmation bias to form a link between al Qaeda operatives and the Hussein regime. Not surprisingly the result of the PCTEG's effort was intelligence that supported US military intervention in Iraq.

The misuse of team A/team B has overshadowed the utility of competitive analysis in the US intelligence community despite several notable examples where it was used constructively. For example, in the weeks and months before the raid on Osama bin Laden's compound in Abbottabad, CIA director John Brennan ordered what was in effect a devil's advocacy exercise. The devil's advocates were drawn from the National Counterterrorism Center and two CIA analysts who were drawn from other units, all outside of the task force hunting Bin Laden. These uses might be indicative of training efforts to familiarize analysts with competitive analysis beginning more than a decade ago (Marrin 2003, 619).

There is some research evidence that competitive analysis techniques can improve decision making and analytical processes.[4] Devil's advocacy, in particular, has been evaluated by several studies. The author summarized the results of research evidence on the technique and found that in almost 75 percent of studies it improved the analytical process compared to other group decision-making methods (Coulthart 2017). The results of these studies suggest that devil's advocacy can strengthen analysis and possibly improve the validity of judgments. For other techniques, such as red teaming and team A/team B, there is too little evidence to draw inferences about their effectiveness.

The Assumptions and Conditions for Constructive Competitive Analysis

The politicization of the 1975 Team B and PCTEG illustrates how ill intent among government officials and analysts can lead to what Mitchell (2006, 146–147) calls a "team B coup":

> [Team B coups] resemble a political coup, the sudden seizure of power through unconventional means such as force or deception. In formal deliberative settings such as academic debate, remedies for such behavior are available, as when expert judges assess penalties against speakers who flout contest round conventions. However, similar remedies are lacking in the more loosely structured and less tightly regulated competitive intelligence analysis setting, a fact that makes the process prone to abuse.

Mitchell's discussion of team B coups explains how malevolent actors can subvert not only team A/team B analysis but competitive analysis more generally. To make this point Mitchell uses rhetoricians Douglas Ehninger and Wayne Brockriede's six directives as the basis for constructive competitive analysis (Mitchell 2006, 146). Synthesizing these rules into the following three assumptions creates a foundation for effective competitive analysis.

Assumption 1: Cooperative Spirit

Ehninger and Brockriede state that all participants should act in good faith to present and assess the value of their arguments. At its root, then, competitive analysis assumes a cooperative state of mind among participants. In practice, this means an intellectual openness and commitment to trying to understand the issue at hand and the positions of the opposition while developing the strongest possible analysis. While participants in the process have their own mental models or *Weltanschauung*, this does preclude intellectual openness and a devotion to seeking truth or other perspectives (Heuer 1999, 1–6). It is worth noting that PCTEG and the 1975 Team B did not fail because the outsiders were partisans. Rather these events were failures because of the unwillingness of team B members to see the process as a cooperative venture to develop rigorous analysis.

Assumption 2: Healthy Competition

A cooperative focus does not preclude vigorous competition but the level of vigor in the process will depend on whether dissent is authentic, meaning the participant truly believes in the points they are arguing, or if the dissent is being employed solely for the purposes of the exercise. The impact of using nonauthentic dissent, especially an institutionalized devil's advocate, is that it may lead to a "crying wolf" problem; the devil's advocate will lose credibility over time for repeated challenges to the analytic bottom line (Betts 1978, 80). Some research evidence backs this point: in one experiment, devil's advocacy teams using authentic dissent—that is, those who argued for a position they truly believed in—were more effective in stimulating critical thinking in the nonauthentic dissenting devil's advocates (Nemeth et al. 2001).

Diversity of viewpoints also plays an important role in competitive analysis because bringing multiple perspectives to bear is useful for considering alternative hypotheses and claims. The importance of diversity of viewpoints is most apparent in red teaming of cultures dissimilar to those of those conducting the analysis. For example, one scholar participating in a red teaming exercise at the Department of Defense observed the limitations of the technique when there is limited subject matter expertise of an adversary. He concluded that the resulting red teaming analysis reflected "an adversary whose behavior and decision making resembled those of educated, white, middle class Americans" (Johnston 2005, 82). In other words, the red team provided no new information on the adversary. Another issue with competition is the equality of resources available to participants. George and Stern (2006) provide a list of resources needed for fair competition in multiple advocacy, items that are applicable in all competitive analysis, such as "competence relevant to the policy issues, information relevant to the policy issues, and analytical support (e.g., staff, technical skills, informational infrastructure)" (George and Stern 2002, 492).

Assumption 3: Commitment to Fair Play

A final assumption is a commitment to fair play. Ehninger and Brockriede's directives call for a decision to be made about the veracity of the arguments made by the participants. In most competitive analysis techniques, there is no authority to assess the validity of the analysis with the exception of multiple advocacy's custodian who oversees the process. Regardless, Ehninger and Brockriede's directives speak to a larger point about adherence to following an agreed upon set of procedures. Failing to follow procedures may damage the legitimacy of using competitive analysis, such as when the 1975 Team B members leaked alarmist information about the Soviet threat to the press.

Basic Data

Instructional Objectives

The primary objectives are for students to learn how to use devil's advocacy in intelligence analysis tasks. Students will also gain an appreciation for how the violation of key assumptions of competitive analysis undermine its value.

Debriefing Format

The debriefing will involve a structured discussion of the simulation results followed by the review of a case study, the 1975 Team B exercise.

Target Audience

Graduate students and entry-level intelligence analysts.

Playing Time

The simulation takes approximately five to six hours. It can be conducted in one continuous session or drawn out over several shorter sessions. The round-based structure also allows the simulation to be run in online courses as well. Additionally, the simulation can be run in a "lite" or shortened format. Facilitators can reduce the amount of playing time by simplifying the analytic task and/or reducing the number of rounds. The key to running a shortened version is to make sure that the analysis is still subverted to demonstrate how competitive analysis can be damaged (see "Round 3: Subvert the Competitive Analysis," below).

Debriefing Time

Instructors should set aside approximately an hour and a half for debriefing.

Number of Players Required

The ideal number of players is 10–15. Players will be divided into a devil's advocacy team and one or more non-devil's advocacy teams. Alternatively, instructors can appoint more devil's advocacy teams.

Computers and Facilities

Each student should have a laptop and an Internet connection so that they can gather sources for their analysis. Students should ideally be instructed beforehand on collecting open source data and assessing the credibility of sources.

Facilitators Guide

Pre-simulation Briefing

Instructors should begin the simulation by telling the class there will be four rounds of analysis and that the most persuasive team (as judged by the instructor) will receive a prize. Sample prizes include bonus points or tangible incentives such as a gift card. The purpose of the prizes is to increase competition between the teams.

Tasks for the exercise should be estimative in nature and focus on a specific national or homeland security threat. For example: "what will be ISIS's capability to inspire mass casualty attacks in the United States and Europe over the next decade?" In formulating the analytic question, the instructor should take into account the time available for the exercise. If less time is available, then the instructor should make the question as unambiguous as possible to reduce the amount of time students will need to debate definitional issues. However, if more time is available for the simulation, the instructor can increase realism by providing a vague analytic question. Such ambiguous tasks are a hallmark of real-life intelligence analysis.

Descriptions of the Steps

Round 1: Set Up the Teams and Conduct the Initial Analysis (75–90 Minutes)

Each team will be presented with the analytic task and use structured brainstorming to analyze it in the first round. Teams will be provided with a sheet on how to use the technique, and they will then conduct open source research and prepare a three-minute briefing to the class using a bottom-line, up-front style. It is recommended that facilitators use the instructions on pages 27 and 29 of *A Tradecraft Primer: Structured Analytic Techniques for Improving Intelligence Analysis* (US Government 2009). Ideally, students should use a three-slide PowerPoint deck that includes the following: (1) two to three key judgments; (2) their substantiation for their judgments; and (3) key sources. It is extremely important that all teams take detailed notes on the other teams' briefings as they will need this information in the next round. Students should also be encouraged to ask their classmates clarifying questions. (Note: Depending on available time and prior student knowledge, instructors can integrate other structured analytic techniques, such as analysis of competing hypotheses or argument mapping.)

Round 2: Appoint the Devil's Advocacy (DA) Team and Begin Critiquing (75–90 Minutes)

The instructor will select a single team to act as a devil's advocacy (DA) team and send them to a separate room (separating teams is necessary for reasons that become clear in Round 3). Instructors will provide the handout of the DA rationale and instruction sheet. Again, it is recommended that facilitators use *A Tradecraft Primer: Structured Analytic Techniques for Improving Intelligence Analysis* (US Government 2009), specifically pages 17 through 18, to create the student instructions. The instructor will then ask the DA team to follow the instructions and critique the analysis of the other team(s) from the previous round. The DA team will construct a one- to three-slide brief critiquing the argument, evidence, and assumptions of the other teams. During this round the non-DA teams will attempt to improve their briefing and analysis. If students are familiar with alternative competing hypotheses or other techniques, they can further refine their analysis. Once both the DA and non-DA teams are ready, each will send a representative to the other teams to conduct a three-minute briefing. Again, both groups should take careful notes of the other teams' key judgments. As a way to motivate teams, the instructor can remind teams that they are competing for a prize.

Round 3: Subvert the Competitive Analysis (75–90 Minutes)

Instructors should explain to the DA team that the previous round was disappointing and that they should be more alarmist and exaggerate the threat. Another option is to tell the DA team that they can win the prize by stressing how dangerous the threat is. Instructors can be as creative as they wish, but the goal should be to force the DA team to violate any or all of the three assumptions of competitive analysis: cooperative spirit, healthy competition, and fair play.

Instructors should not let non-DA teams know that they have altered the DA team's approach. However, the instructor can make sure the non-DA teams notice the change in the DA team's approach. The non-DA team should continue refining their product on the basis of the previous round. A representative from the DA team will present the alarmist critique of the non-DA teams from previous round. The non-DA teams will rebrief to the DA team. As with previous rounds, students should be engaged and taking notes during their classmates' briefings.

Round 4: Polarization and Writing the Analysis (75–90 Minutes)

In the final round, the DA team continues what is now, hopefully, a strong and probably unfair critique of the non-DA teams Round 3 analysis. There is no need for a briefing for Round 4, but each team should spend the balance of the time drafting a short, one- to two-page final analytic memo. Instructors may also elect to add additional rounds to draw out the effect of subverting the devil's advocate.

An optional memo template is provided in the annex. The purpose of the memo is to give students an opportunity to see the process of competitive analysis from initial brainstorming to final report. Alternatively, instructors can assign students to write a short reflection paper that can be used during the debriefing.

Debriefing

Objectives and Description

The debriefing focuses on three objectives. First, it should help students understand how consensus methods of intelligence analysis, such as structured brainstorming, differ from competitive analysis. Students should also notice how the assumptions between the two methods differ. Sample questions include:

- Was there an analytic consensus within the teams in the first round? If not, how did you manage it?
- Was there an analytic consensus between teams in the second round? Why or why not?

Second, the debriefing should cover the effect of devil's advocacy on the analytic process. In particular, instructors should emphasize how critiquing can lead to more rigorous questioning of assumptions and evidence as well as the importance of following the assumptions of competitive analysis. Some sample questions that address these issues include:

- For the DA group, was it easy to change from a consensus mindset in Round 1 to a critical mindset for the remaining rounds?
- For the non-DA groups, did the critique affect your analysis? Were there any "blind spots" that you missed (e.g., missing evidence or weak assumptions)?

Third, the debriefing should cover the effect of subverted devil's advocacy in the third and fourth rounds. It is suggested that instructors assign readings on the misuse of competitive analysis in national security intelligence. Mitchell's (2006) article on the 1975 Team B coup is an excellent reading to set up the discussion and show the practical implications of subverted competitive analysis. Example questions include:

- For the non-DA groups, how did it feel after the DA team had been subverted in Round 3? Did you still pay attention to their critique? Why or why not?
- For the DA group, did you find it difficult to violate the assumptions of competitive analysis? How would you say violating the assumptions affected your critique of the other groups?

Conclusion

There is significant evidence that competitive analysis techniques, such as devil's advocacy, team A/team B, and red teaming, have the potential to improve intelligence. In theory, these techniques should cut down on the amount of groupthink and improve intelligence analysis. A significant body of research evidence suggests this is true of devil's advocacy. However, there is a well-known history in US national security intelligence of high-level decision makers subverting competitive analysis techniques to support their chosen policies. This manipulation occurs through the violation of the basic assumptions of competitive analysis: cooperative spirit, healthy competition, and fair play. The aim of this simulation is to address the benefits as well as limitations of competitive analysis for future and current analysts.

Appendix 9A

Insert Descriptive Title of Memo Here
[The title is best done at the end. Try to come up with a title that is descriptive of the memo's contents.]

Key Judgments

- Main point #1 succinctly explained in a couple of sentences
- Main point # 2 succinctly explained in a couple of sentences
- Main point [. . .] succinctly explained in a couple of sentences.

[This is the summary of the piece. About 10 percent of the words in the memo should be used for the key judgments. Make sure to do this last. Where appropriate use words of estimative probability and analytic confidence.]

Background

[This should be no more than a 20% of the memo. It should include background information that answer key questions, such as the basic who, what, why, where, and when of the topic. This section can also address important technical terms or concepts so that they need not be dealt with in the following section. When needed use footnotes. Sources should be formatted according to a style guide.]

Substantiation

[The section that follows the background section will contain your analysis, and will generally be the longest part of the paper (c. 70% of the memo). This section is often called "substantiation" because it substantiates the assertions originally made in the introduction. Avoid using bullet points and be sure to right in the bottom up-front style (BLUF) with topic sentences at the beginning of each paragraph.]

Notes

The author would like to thank Alex Claver for comments on an earlier draft of this chapter.

1 Other scholars deem some competitive analysis techniques that fall outside of the definition provided here. For example, Russell (2010) identifies scenario planning (also known as alternative futures analysis) as a competitive analysis technique. Since this technique does not typically involve challenge or debate between analysts, it is not discussed or included in the list here. See Richard L. Russell, "Competitive Analysis: Techniques for Better Gauging Enemy Political Intentions and Military Capabilities," in *The Oxford Handbook of National Security Intelligence*, ed. Loch K. Johnson (Oxford: Oxford University Press, 2010), 375–388.

2 For example, in the US government's *A Tradecraft Primer*, red teaming is listed as an "imaginative technique" alongside structured brainstorming, not a challenge or competitive analysis technique.

3 For a slightly dated but useful critique of groupthink literature, see Won-Woo Park, "A Review of Research on Groupthink," *Journal of Behavioral Decision Making* 3, no. 4 (1990): 229–245.

4 For a discussion of the evidence on the power of dissent, see Charlan Nemeth, *In Defense of Troublemakers: The Power of Dissent in Life and Business* (New York: Hachette Books, 2018).

References

Betts, Richard K. "Analysis, War, and Decision: Why Intelligence Failures Are Inevitable." *World Politics* 31, no. 1 (1978): 61–89.

Coulthart, Stephen J. "An Evidence-Based Evaluation of 12 Core Structured Analytic Techniques." *International Journal of Intelligence and Counterintelligence* 30, no. 2 (2017): 368–391.

George, Alexander L. "The Case for Multiple Advocacy in Making Foreign Policy." *American Political Science Review* 66, no. 3 (1972): 751–785.

George, Alexander L. and Eric K. Stern. "Harnessing Conflict in Foreign Policy Making: From Devil's to Multiple Advocacy." *Presidential Studies Quarterly* 32, no. 3 (2002): 484–508.

Heuer, Richards J. *Psychology of Intelligence Analysis.* Washington, DC: Center for the Study of Intelligence Analysis, 1999.

Janis, Irving L. *Victims of Groupthink: A Psychological Study of Foreign-Policy Decisions and Fiascoes.* New York: Houghton-Mifflin, 1972.

Jervis, Robert. *Perception and Misperception in International Politics.* Princeton: Princeton University Press, 2015.

Johnston, Rob. *Analytic Culture in the US Intelligence Community: An Ethnographic Study.* Washington, DC: Center for the Study of Intelligence, 2005.

Marrin, Stephen. "CIA's Kent School: Improving Training for New Analysts." *International Journal of Intelligence and Counterintelligence* 16, no. 4 (2003): 609–637.

Mitchell, Gordon R. "Team B Intelligence Coups." *Quarterly Journal of Speech* 92, no. 2 (2006): 144–173.

Nemeth, Charlan. *In Defense of Troublemakers: The Power of Dissent in Life and Business.* New York: Hachette Books, 2018.

Nemeth, Charlan, Keith Brown, and John Rogers. "Devil's Advocate versus Authentic Dissent: Stimulating Quantity and Quality." *European Journal of Social Psychology* 31, no. 6 (2001): 707–720.

Park, Won-Woo. "A Review of Research on Groupthink." *Journal of Behavioral Decision Making* 3, no. 4 (1990): 229–245.

Pherson, Randolph and Richards Heuer Jr. "Structured Analytic Techniques: A New Approach to Analysis." In *Analyzing Intelligence: Origins, Obstacles, and Innovations*, edited by Roger Z. George and James B. Bruce, 231–248. Washington, DC: Georgetown University Press, 2014.

Prados, John. "Team B: The Trillion Dollar Experiment." *Bulletin of the Atomic Scientists* 49, no. 3 (1993): 23–31.

Report of the Senate Select Committee on Intelligence. WMD Commission Report. March 31, 2005.

Russell, Richard L. "Competitive Analysis: Techniques for Better Gauging Enemy Political Intentions and Military Capabilities." In *The Oxford Handbook of National Security Intelligence*, edited by Loch K. Johnson, 375–388. Oxford: Oxford University Press, 2010.

US Government. *A Tradecraft Primer: Structured Analytic Techniques for Improving Intelligence Analysis.* March 2009.

Shalev, Aryeh. *Israel's Intelligence Assessment before the Yom Kippur War: Disentangling Deception and Distraction.* Brighton: Sussex Academic Press, 2010.

Stack, Kevin P. "A Negative View of Competitive Analysis." *International Journal of Intelligence and Counterintelligence* 10, no. 4 (1997): 456–464.

Zenko, Michael. *Red Team: How to Succeed by Thinking Like the Enemy.* New York: Basic Books, 2015.

10

Spymaster
An Introduction to Collection Management (A Simulation)
Kristan J. Wheaton

While linguists may struggle to translate intercepted transmissions and photographic interpreters may pore over images of suspected weapons caches, the management of the assets used to collect this raw information is usually left to more senior intelligence professionals. This role, collection management, is often misunderstood by entry-level intelligence professionals as a result.

Failure to understand the challenges of collection management, however, can lead to frustration on the part of the entry-level professional. This is particularly true if it means that entry-level professional's intelligence unit will not be able to support operations due to a lack of collection. It is, therefore, common to see a block of instruction mixed into whatever training the entry-level professional might receive that touches on the role of the collection manager in the overall intelligence process. This class or series of classes, often taught as a lecture and wedged, as it inevitably is, between much more interesting and relevant course material directly related to the professional's job, is often ineffective.

The goal of Spymaster is to introduce a game-based learning, cooperative approach to teaching the basics of collection management. This simulation is by no means a replacement for more formal instruction in collection management. It does, however, make instruction at the entry-level more hands-on, experiential, and as a result, more effective.

Basic Data

Instructional objectives: The primary objective for this simulation is to give students and entry-level intelligence professionals some experience balancing the different kinds of equities that real-world collection managers routinely have to balance.

Simulation objectives: Participants work as small teams of collection managers deciding which requests for information to attempt to fill before they become "overcome by events." Each team seeks to maximize the number of points gained for various pieces of information (each with its own "information value") while also trying to keep the collection assets under the team's control from being "burned." The value of information, the march of time, the ease with which some assets are burned, the relative difficulty of collecting some forms of information, and the role of chance in intelligence operations will force the players to make a number of difficult decisions.

Debriefing format: Debriefing is led by the instructor and guided by key questions (see appendix C—Debriefing Materials).

Target audience: Undergraduate and graduate students in intelligence studies programs or in introductory or advanced courses about intelligence. This simulation would also work well with entry-level intelligence professionals in the national security community and, with some minor modifications, in the law enforcement and business areas as well.

Playing time: Typically about 50 minutes for teaching the game, playing the game one to three times, and debriefing.

Debriefing time: Approximately 5–15 minutes.

Number of players required: The simulation can be played solitaire but works best with four players (one for each "INT"—SIGINT, GEOINT, HUMINT, AND OSINT). Spymaster is a "cooperative" game (like Forbidden Island or Pandemic), where all the players either win together or lose together. The simulation as part of classroom instruction works well with any number of players from 1 to 30, but would require multiple copies of the playing cards (see appendix B—Spymaster Cards). The simulation has not been tested with groups larger than 30, but such large groups would likely be unwieldy and lead to a diminished learning experience.

Participation materials included: See appendix A—Instruction and appendix B—Spymaster Cards.

Debriefing materials included: See appendix C—Debriefing Materials.

Computer/Internet: Not required.

Other materials/equipment required: This simulation typically takes place in a single classroom and works best if students have access to a table or a large desk. In addition to the cards (see appendix B—Spymaster Cards), each team will need one six-sided die (or a dice rolling app on a smartphone).

Facilitator's Guide

Materials

Appendix A—Instructions
Appendix B—Spymaster cards

Pre-simulation Briefing

The simulation begins by dividing the class into groups of four and by giving each group one set of the complete set of Spymaster cards (see appendix B—Spymaster Cards). The groups of students self-select which INT they want to represent (one INT per student) and take the cards representing assets for that particular INT (all INTS have three assets except for OSINT, which has four). Odd numbers of students can be accommodated by assigning two INTs per student or having more than one student control a single INT. Obviously, the less this is done, the better.

The instructor should brief the students on the goal of the simulation (i.e., to gather as many of the information requirements cards as possible while losing the fewest number of collection assets along the way). In general, the best way to learn this game is to play it, and it is advised that the instructor keep the pre-simulation briefing as short as possible.

Conducting the Simulation

Once students have selected which INT they are to represent, the remaining cards should be laid out on the table according to the instructions (see appendix A—Instructions). The instructor should, following the instructions, run through the first turn with all of the groups. This can be done collectively rather than one at a time, but it is important that the instructor ensure that each of the groups plays the first turn correctly.

The game is conceptually simple and one turn, done properly, is usually enough for students to grasp the basic concepts and complete the remainder of the game on their own. The instructor should circulate among the groups of students to ensure that they are playing the game properly and to answer any questions that might come up. Likewise, the instructor should be on the lookout for good examples that will help reinforce certain learning objectives in the debrief. Finally, depending on the time available, students should be encouraged to play the game multiple times. The game plays much more quickly the second time around, and it is not uncommon for players to play two or three games in a one-hour block of instruction.

Debriefing the Simulation

The objective of this simulation is to familiarize the players with the balancing act that characterizes real-world collection management. As such, there are five main categories of questions to explore in the debrief:

1. *The value of information.* Each piece of information collected has a different value to an organization. Some information is clearly more valuable than others. In the game, this value is clearly marked on the cards. How does an intelligence professional know which piece of information is most valuable? How does the student's intel organization designate which pieces of information are potentially the most valuable to collect?
2. *The march of time.* Time plays two roles in the game. First, certain pieces of information need to be collected by a certain time in the game, otherwise they are of no use. What are some examples of this in real life? Second, how does the need to collect certain pieces of information by a certain time alter the overall collection strategy? How does this relate to the value of the information to be collected?
3. *The ease with which some assets are burned.* Different assets have a different likelihood of being uncovered or "burned." How did this impact the

collection strategy? How did this impact the team's interpersonal dynamic? Did players with more easily burned assets become more defensive about their use?

4. *The relative difficulty of collecting some forms of information.* Just as some pieces of information are more valuable than others, some pieces of information are better protected than others. When does the risk to collection assets outweigh the value of the information collected?

5. *The role of chance in collection operations.* All collection operations have some chance of failure. In this game, the base failure rate is one in six for the most well-resourced operations. Is this too high? What failure rate is "acceptable"? What failure rate is realistic?

Conclusion

Specifically designed to introduce newly hired intelligence professionals and intelligence studies students to the world of collection management, this simulation introduces a variety of important concepts including the value of information, the march of time, the ease with which some assets are burned, the relative difficulty of collecting some information, and the role of chance in intelligence collection operations.

Requiring only about an hour to conduct and debrief, the simulation can be played solitaire or in a full classroom setting. The game uses a relatively uncommon mechanic known as cooperative gameplay, such that the entire team either wins or loses the game together. That said, the different kinds of assets owned by the different players sets up the possibility for realistic inter-team conflict regarding the use of various assets. Furthermore, the game creates a number of situations analogous to those which intelligence professionals might realistically be faced with in the field.

Appendix A—*Instructions*, appendix B—*Spymaster Cards*, and appendix C—*Debriefing Materials* can be found on the companion website listed below. https://textbooks.rowman.com/art-of-intelligence-2

11

Distraction, Deception, and Deterrence

The Mysterious Tradecraft of the Great Pulcinella

Chris Jagger and Shaun Romeril

Mastering Deception

The mythical character Pulcinella can occasionally be spotted innocently sauntering between the ancient cobbled streets of Naples in southern Italy. His only hope to entertain? Dressed from head to toe in baggy white theatrical robes, his face is covered by a black Ogre-like mask. Pulcinella, as a Neapolitan may explain, has mastered his craft. A magician and street entertainer, he employs cunning charm and kaleidoscopic charisma to distract and deceive unbeknown and bedazzled victims for criminal gain. A self-preservationist living in a city made difficult through corruption, his personality has formed in response to his environment. Witty, charming, and cruel, his character attracts them all. The perfected thief, while complementing the elegance of your newly appointed attire, will covertly deny you of your most valuable possessions. Legend says he was born in the darkest street of Naples sometime during the 17th century. Others say he was the most capable criminal to have ever lived. He was a master of distraction and deception.

Like Pulcinella, criminals, terrorists, foreign states, and indeed other kinds of sophisticated adversaries may employ distraction and deception to shatter our attempt to understand them. When they do, they often succeed. To defend against tripping and becoming snared in their carefully placed traps, one must employ a great deal of critical thinking. One must ask the "What If?" question repeatedly. You must learn to think like a criminal.

The Challenge to the Analyst

The security community habitually describes the task of analyzing our adversaries as a puzzle-like game, or jigsaw building. The basic assumption underpinning this logic is that with well-honed skill in detection, we should be able to find the pieces, matching them to form a perfect picture. A complete puzzle can inform decisive action. Sadly, this playful analogy can often be too simplistic. Rather the art of analyzing sophisticated adversaries, such as those who fall into the national security arena, might be more accurately described as mosaic building.

The information collected is often fragmented, spread out over time, with many missing pieces. Those you can locate may have been planted for you, containing the sharp edges of deception. Certainly, the information is often uncertain as to its immediate utility. Clouded and colorful, your job is to piece the information together using a combination of carefully honed critical and creative thinking. Your aim is to build a picture open to multiple interpretations, to build hypotheses leading to numerous plans.

Assumptions

The investigative and intelligence resources of the authorities are limited. Our adversaries will employ measures to absorb these resources, keeping the operational focus away from their true activities.

Knowing this, adversaries may attempt to buy information from official sources to assess the threat from the authorities. Some will try to corrupt officials in positions of influence. Others may even deploy their own members to join law enforcement or become an informant for them.

In some instances, our adversaries will employ measures to deter us entirely from doing our job. This may involve intimidation tactics such as threats of violence, actual violence, and blackmail.

The effectiveness of their attempts to distract and deceive us will vary from group to group, but long-established, well-structured, and territorially based organizations will be best placed to deliver deception.

Lesson Method

Combining lecture, case studies, discussion, and debate with two simulation exercises, students will discover the range of weapons of distraction and deception open to adversaries.

Facilitator's Note

The lesson has been designed to provide handrails, not handcuffs, to its facilitation. You are encouraged to make the lesson your own by adding topical examples and facilitating discussions in your own personal style.

Primary Learning Outcomes

Students will consider the utility of these weapons in helping the adversary achieve their objective.

They will explore the challenges in identifying deception from the perspective of the investigator, intelligence collector, and in particular, the intelligence analyst.

Working in teams, students will learn how to form plans and take measures to lessen and where possible illuminate the impact of distraction and deception.

Practicing presentation, discussion, and debate, students will see the benefits of applying multiple minds to complex intelligence challenges. They will practice the art of communicating uncertainty and work toward forming confident and influential presentation styles.

Simulation Objectives

Two separate simulation exercises are employed during the lesson for the purpose of engaging students into an experiential mode of examining distraction and deception from alternative perspectives.

First, they will learn to "think like a criminal," then form a criminal masterplan to distract and deceive the pursuing authorities.

Second, they will create a law enforcement plan designed and tailored specially to defend against their target's attempts to distract and deceive them.

Each simulation is followed by presentation, discussion, and instructor-led facilitated debate.

Lesson Structure

Lesson time: 405 mins / 6.5 hours

Part 1—Developing a deceptive mind

- Step 1, 10 mins: Deception overview
- Step 2, 10 mins: Mini case study
- Step 3, 30 mins: 007 weapons of distraction, deception, and deterrence
- Step 4, 10 mins: Discussion—what else?
- Break

Part 2—Employing deception

- Step 5, 5 mins: Split group into teams
- Step 6, 30 mins: Assimilate and discuss storyline in teams
- Step 7, 90 mins: Simulation 1: Hatch a criminal plan to deceive the police
- Step 8, 20 mins: Present plans (x2 10 minutes)
- Step 9, 20 mins: Challenge plans, Team 1 vs. Team 2, then Team 2 vs. Team 1 (x2 10 minutes)
- Break

Part 3—Planning against deception

In two teams—

- Step 10, 30 mins: Counter measures: Building a fortress
- Step 11, 90 mins: Simulation 2: Hatch a police plan to mitigate against criminal deception
- Step 12, 20 mins: Present plans (x2 10 minutes)

- Step 13, 20 mins: Challenge plans, Team 1 vs. Team 2, then Team 2 vs. Team 1 (x2 10 minutes)
- Break

Part 4 — Conclusion

- Step 14, 20 mins: Summary led by facilitator

Part 1—Developing a Deceptive Mind

Step 1: Deception Overview—Lecture/Discussion   Here lies the facilitators' opportunity to provide an intellectual framework for the concept of deception. We would advise beginning with a simple brainstorming exercise. Representing their responses on the whiteboard in key words, one might ask the students, "What words spring to mind when you think of deception?" and "When do you think deception might be employed, and by whom?"

During the brainstorming, the facilitator might add a series of definitions and request short topical examples from the students:

Df1: "The act of deceiving someone"
Df2: "A thing that deceives"
Df3: "The act of propagating beliefs in things that are not true, or not the whole truth"

Step 2: Case Study (Fictional)   The facilitator may wish to draw on their own example here. However, we have provided the following case study that may be best delivered in combination with a map and a few photos of Kosovo.

"Following the 1999 war, by 2001 both NATO and the United Nations were working in close cooperation to provide security in Kosovo. A primary objective of the peacekeeping effort was to disrupt and arrests individuals who presented a threat to the safe and secure environment. NATO was chiefly concerned with extremists and terrorists, while the UN's mandate was to investigate organized crime. With significant overlap between each phenomenon, close cooperation between the UN and NATO was called on daily.

"In March 2002, NATO received an intelligence report, assessed as reliable, stating there was an immediate threat to all UN buildings in Pristina. A cross-working group of senior staff at both NATO and the UN were immediately called together to decide how to respond. It was decided that since this was only a single piece of intelligence, physical security should be raised at the main UN buildings but nothing more. Twenty-four hours later a second piece of intelligence was received, repeating the threat, but this time from a new source. Twenty-eight hours later a third piece was received, then a fourth and a fifth. Each piece of intelligence was assessed as reliable and believed to originate from different sources.

"Both NATO and the UN decided to place maximum security at all of their buildings in the capital area of Pristina. This included restriction on the movement of personnel (only essential travel outside of buildings was allowed). All intelligence capabilities owned by the UN and NATO were deployed to identify the specific threat. The impact on resources was massive, with all ongoing investigation halted and investigators redirected to the new threat."

In truth, this was false information, designed and fed into NATO and the UN with the intention of deceiving them, misdirecting their assets, and observing their responses.

Following the case study, the facilitator might invite students to discuss the following question: "How did they do it?" Write key words summarizing their answers on the whiteboard.

Answer: A single individual (working for a domestic terrorist group intent on overthrowing the newly appointed Kosovo government) approached both the UN and NATO over a period of months with the offer of passing information about an organized crime group in Pristina. On each occasion he insisted on his identity being protected and treated as a covert informant. He repeated this approach with different departments across the UN and NATO until he had five different avenues for passing over his information. At first, the information he passed was accurate. It was based on knowledge he'd acquired of a criminal group that his terrorist organization once had dealings with but no longer needed to cooperate with. Once he'd established trust and a reputation for reliability, he began to feed in false information and threats to the UN. His aim was to see how they responded and whether he could influence their actions.

Step 3: Weapons of Distraction, Deception, and Deterrence In pairs, students should next be asked to assimilate and then discuss each of the following weapons of distraction, deception, and deterrence.

The armory of the adversary may include the following.

1. SMOKE SCREEN *Example*: Adversaries may divert our attention to false inquiries. A terrorist group sets off a small improvised explosive device (IED) at a culturally or politically sensitive location. While no one was injured, damage was done, and the nature of the location will likely distract resources into a full investigation. While the security and intelligence agencies are focused investigating the IED, the terrorist group meet to plan and/or prepare for a significant attack in comfort that the focus of the investigative and intelligence will be elsewhere.

Other examples include false emergency calls and giving bomb warnings and the planting of dummy explosive devices.

For a terrorist group, such methods can often achieve at least two aims: to build or maintain an atmosphere of terror as well as tie down investigative and intelligence resources. This was effectively used by the Provisional IRA (PIRA) in England during the early 1990s.

2. THE MASQUERADE *Example*: An organized crime group suspects they are under surveillance. They are cognizant that capability to conduct investigations and intelligence operations are limited by cost and resource availability. An individual within the criminal group who they suspect is being watched is selected to distract the police. He arranges to meet with group of individuals who are unrelated to his criminal endeavors, but he does so in suspicious and intriguing circumstances. The meeting might be organized late at night and at a discreet location. Using numerous methods of transport to create further suspicion and dry up as many of the resources of those following him as possible (foot, car, public transport), he also employs crude counter surveillance. This further raises suspicion that he is to attend an important criminal meeting.

As a result, the police waste significant resources trying to identify who his fake conspirators are and their intentions.

3. REVERSE DOUBLE AGENTS *Example*: An individual working for the adversary applies to join the authorities but continues to work for the criminal entity. Alternatively, an individual already working for the authorities is recruited by the adversary. Similarly, a member of a criminal organization may try to have themselves hired by the police as an informant. These methods are employed so the adversary can gain insights of the level of knowledge of the authorities through their tasking to collect intelligence as well as using the corrupt individual to plant false information.

4. FALSE RECONNAISSANCE *Example*: A terrorist group tries to persuade the authorities that they are actively targeting a person/building/event by conducting obvious hostile reconnaissance against them. The aim is to create a perception that an attack is imminent and therefore distract resources and focus.

5. CYBER SECURITY *Example*: Organized crime groups have been known to employ hackers to acquire valuable information about the maturing of police investigations into their activities. Such information can provide significant opportunities for the criminal group to evade further detection, corrupt evidence, and intimidate witnesses.

In some instances, hackers have been used to deface law enforcement websites. This may be done to embarrass and erode public confidence in the police.

There have been cases where criminal groups have hacked into the private email accounts of police officers in search of compromising information in an attempt to blackmail them.

6. PUBLIC RECORD AND OPERATIONAL RESEARCH *Example*: Terrorists will actively scrutinize publicly available documents to identify potential human sources, key investigating staff, and investigative/intelligence tactics. They will use this information to seek out opportunities to conduct deception and to intimidate witnesses. In the 1980s, PIRA used public libraries along with government staffing records and reference books such as *Who's Who* to identify and locate prominent figures for assassination.

They would also carry out operational research to attack the security agencies while responding to an incident (e.g., the PIRA would study how both the police and military responded to a bomb threat in a specific location). In this example, the authorities would create several security perimeters around the suspected location of the bomb. One of those perimeters would contain a geographically fixed control station for the police, military, ambulance, fire brigade, and so on. Having observed this, in a future bomb threat the PIRA would then have a secondary bomb planted at the predicted location of the control station.

Note: This technique has also been used by making false police emergency calls (e.g., a terrorist group calls in a false bomb threat to observe how the police respond).

7. SOURCE MANIPULATION *Example*: The opposition has identified a possible source (either human or technical) and feeds false intelligence into this source with the intention of generating mislead activity and diverting attention. This could, for example, include a criminal having pre-organized and scripted conversations on the telephone with other members of the criminal gang designed on the assumption that they are being monitored by the authorities.

This may also be used as a method of exposing an informant within a crime group's own network. For example, they pass false information to the member of the group they suspect to be a police informant, suggesting there is a credible and immediate threat to an individual's life. In such cases the police must respond immediately to protect that individual, even if it means exposing their investigation to the criminal group.

Step 4: Deception, What Else? To gauge students' thoughts, facilitate a short brainstorming session spurred by the following question:

"What other methods of deception can you think of, and how might they be used?"

Part 2—Employing Deception

The next part of the lesson is built around a simulation exercise designed to encourage students to put deceptive weapons to work from the perspective of a criminal group.

Step 5: Create Teams Divide the group into teams of four (or thereabouts). Give each time a private space from which to work. The following roles should be adopted by team members:

- The Leader
  This role has the purpose of leading group discussions, keeping time, and ensuring that each and every team member is participating equally.
- Recorder
  This role has the purpose of visualizing the teams' ideas on the whiteboard in mind mapping format.
- The deceiver
  This role has the purpose of pushing forward each of the weapons of deception and encouraging the team to seek out opportunities to use them.
- The Presenter

This role has the purpose of presenting the final results of the teams' discussion to the main group.

Equipment needed: A conference-style setup with a single table, whiteboard, and flip chart is desirable.

Step 6: Storyline   Provide each of the team with a printout of the story below. Ask them to spend 20 minutes reading the story individually and then 10 minutes discussing it as a group and creating a timeline of key events. The discussion is to ensure that each member of the team has interpreted the story in the same way.

THE STORY   April 2017: A criminal group known as the Folkestone Braggers, located in Kent in the southeast of England, are intent on expanding their criminal enterprise from the local distribution of cannabis to the importation of cocaine. The Folkestone Braggers, comprising eight individuals, two of whom are blood tied through family connections, have been in criminal operation for five years, since early 2012.

June 2017: John Richmond of the Folkestone Braggers was arrested for smoking cannabis in a public place. This was the first time that John had been arrested and questioned by the police. The amount in his possession was considered by the police to be for personal use only. While in police custody, he was asked where he purchased the drugs from. He refused to answer the question. Following unsuccessful police questioning, he was released with a caution.

July 2017: Ian Richmond, the group leader of the Folkestone Braggers, decides that he wants to test out an importation method by smuggling cocaine in spare car parts shipped in from Europe to the UK via sea. Ian has heard that competing smuggling groups have used this method successfully, bringing the drugs from France to England via the Dover seaport. Ian is concerned, however, that the police and customs officers at working at the port may already know about this method of smuggling.

Ian registers a company specializing in the import and export of car parts from Europe.

August 2017: The police in Kent have received intelligence that a criminal group known as the Folkestone Braggers are intent on starting a new smuggling operation to bring cocaine into the UK. At present, the police don't know how the Folkestone Braggers are going to do this. The police know the identity of three members of the group, although they have no evidence at present to arrest them. Those members are known as Chris Jagger, Rubén Arcos, and Shaun Romeril.

Further intelligence is received confirming the group's intent to import cocaine, so Kent Police's organized crime department launch a full-scale investigation into the Folkestone Braggers.

September 2017: Ian Richmond has made contact with a French organized crime group who are prepared to sell him cocaine. He is to meet with them in

November for the first time at a restaurant in Paris where he will organize buying the drugs and then using his own team to traffic the consignment into the UK.

October 2017: Ian Richmond and Chris Jagger travel to Paris in an empty white lorry. They take the ferry from Dover.

November 2017: Ian Richmond and Chris Jagger meet with criminal associates in France and establish a deal to purchase a large consignment of drugs.

December 2017: The Folkestone Braggers bring the cocaine from their secure storage unit in France to the UK. The drugs are hidden inside car parts. They evade detection at the border and are successful in selling the cocaine on to a distribution network within a week.

January 2017: Having successfully established a new network and secure method for bringing the cocaine into the UK, Ian Richmond decides to increase the volume and frequency of importations.

Step 7: Hatch a Criminal Masterplan Using the story above, each team should now be challenged to hatch a criminal master plan to deceive the police, with the aim of keeping them off the Folkestone Braggers' scent. Each team should try to use each of the weapons of deception while building their plan.

Step 8: Present Plan Each team should now be invited to return from their private break out areas to the main class room.

The teams are then given 10 minutes to present their plans to the rest of the group, carefully explaining how each of the weapons of deception that they have selected would assist them in keeping the police off their scent.

Step 9: Challenge Plans Once both teams have presented their plans, opposing teams are offered the opportunity to challenge each other's plans for vulnerability and risk.

Part 3—Planning against Deception

Step 10: Counter Measures: Building a Fortress To defend against the risk of an adversary using distraction, deception, and deterrence against our operations, the police, intelligence, and security community implement many precautionary elements to their activities. In groups, the following should be assimilated and discussed.

1. VETTING Background research conducted on employees with the aim of identifying possible areas of vulnerability that may be exploited by the adversary. If a vulnerability is discovered, the hiring entity will have to decide whether they are willing to accept any linked risks. For example, an applicant may be in significant financial debt. In this case, the hiring entity would need to decide if that debt could make the applicant open to bribery.

2. CYBER SECURITY AND IT MONITORING The police, intelligence, and security community employ high levels of cyber security. Employees are trained to be vigilant at all times when operating in cyberspace.

Employees who work with sensitive or classified government information are often regulated by strict information security handling procedures. If an employee accesses an intelligence report, a record is made. The employee is forced to give an explanation as to why they are accessing the information, and that reason must correlate with certain standards (e.g., they must be properly justified in reading the report).

IT monitoring of employees often takes place in organizations that investigate organized crime and terrorism. Such monitoring can help lead to the identification of corrupt employees.

3. INFORMANT HANDLING PROCESSES Rigorous procedures exist in the informant handling domain to, as best as possible, ensure that the informant's motivations are understood by the government entity handling them. Informants are often developed slowly and carefully, and the information they pass over is constantly tested and challenged for its reliability.

4. CRITICAL THINKING To spot distraction and deception in particular, intelligence analysts must always employ high levels of critical thinking when assessing and analyzing intelligence reports. They should be seeking to answer the "What if we're on the wrong track?" question at all times. They must be cognizant of and identify groupthink, confirmation bias, mirror imaging, and perception bias, always searching for alternative explanations and building lateral hypotheses.

Step 11: Hatch a Police Plan Returning to their teams, students should now form a police plan to mitigate and preempt the possibility of the Folkestone Braggers deploying deceptive weapons against their investigation. Each team should build their plan on the basis of the examples offered by their opposing team in the criminal master plan presentation in Step 8.

Step 12: Present Plans Each team should now be invited to return from their private breakout areas to the main class room.

The teams are then given 10 minutes to present their plans to the rest of the group, carefully explaining how they will help the police to defend against the weapons of deception offered by their opposing group.

Step 13: Challenge Plans Once both teams have presented their plans, opposing teams are offered the opportunity to challenge each other's plans for vulnerability and risk.

Part 4—Conclusion

In the final part of the lesson, the facilitator should sum up the observations and outcomes of each of the groups' presentations. The facilitator might end the lesson with a final group discussion, building on the question.

Step 14: Summary Discussion "So what to me, my team, and my organization?" If you were an intelligence analyst working for Kent Police, what recommendation would you make to defend against the possibility of a criminal group like the Folkestone Braggers employing deception against you.

For an adversary to effectively conduct distraction, deception, and deterrence activities against the security and intelligence community, they will usually need to be exceptionally disciplined, sophisticated, organized, and centrally controlled. Badly delivered attempts can reduce the effectiveness of the criminal group and cause them to become nervous or suspicious and even confuse their own members. Poorly conducted attempts at distraction, deception, and deterrence can in some cases even provide opportunities for the law enforcement and intelligence community. For example, the attempt may actually bring a criminal to the attention of the police who was otherwise unknown!

12

Strategic Visioning

Processes to Facilitate Decision Making within Complex Social Systems

Sheila R. Ronis and Richard J. Chasdi

As part of a strategic management process, every organization should develop a strategic vision to provide a general direction of where their organization wants to be in about a ten-year period. Some organizations go out more than 20 years, and some even more, but usually, a vision statement will describe a period in about a decade, something about where the world is going in that time frame and the role that the organization will play in that future. Full-scale visioning processes can take several weeks or even months of expert research to create and execute. But an abbreviated visioning process can approximate a full process, when time and resources are limited. This chapter describes a process that can be used to develop such a vision while also preparing an organization to embark upon a strategic management process, as well.

Basic Data

Instructional Objectives

There are three major instructional objectives when teaching an organization or a group of graduate students in a strategy course how to go through a process such as that outlined in this chapter:

1. Develop a strategic vision for an organization of any size in business or government, or for a group of students
2. Experience how a vision is developed
3. Enable the participants to experience a future and how the strategic vision "fits" into that future.

Target Audience

The target audience for this exercise can be a group of planners or policymakers in an organization, company, or government agency or department. The process can also be used in a classroom with students who are learning to develop strategic visions within the context of a strategic management course.

Playing Time

The strategic visioning exercise described in this paper can usually be completed within a two- to four-hour time slot—or can be spread out over one or two classes if it is being used within a strategic management course depending on the length of the class.

Debriefing Time

Because there is no "game" as such, there is no need to debrief the process, though it helps to show the agenda and explain the process.

Number of Players Required

These processes can be developed using any number of people. Traditional class sizes of 20–30 students are ideal in an educational setting, but the lead author of this article has facilitated this process using as few as 3–10 people or as many as 60–80 in a planning unit of an agency or department of government or within a company setting.

Requirements Such as Computers and Facilities

The only requirement that is essential is drawing paper and markers that can be seen in a group environment. This process does not require sophisticated electronics, though sometimes it is helpful to project the agenda of the exercise using PowerPoint slides.

Facilitators Guide

Pre-simulation Briefing

The process should begin by briefing the group on an agenda of all the steps in the strategic visioning process. Then, the broader group is divided up into groups of four to six for the remainder of the steps. Groups should be seated at work tables with large poster paper and markers available on each table to "draw" the system and its components.

Descriptions of the Steps with an Estimation of the Time Required for Each Step

When that happens, organizations can use the short process to approximate the larger version so that some benefits can be gained. The following steps describe the process, as illustrated in figure 12.1.

Step 1. Define the System

The short process begins by asking each participant to state his or her top three assumptions about the current "system." The system is usually defined as that

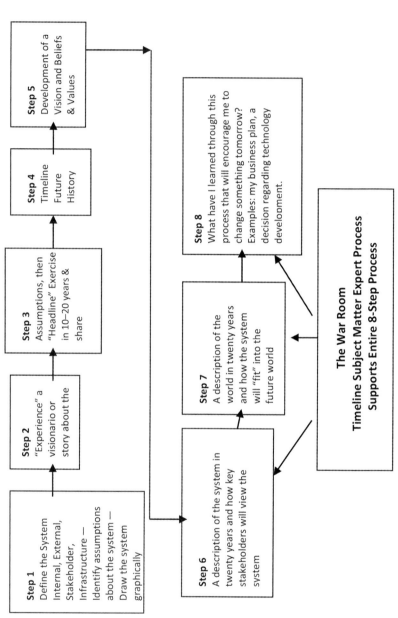

FIGURE 12.1 Timeline Subject Matter Expert Process

organization or suborganization for which the process is being developed. The current "system" is then defined in its entirety. This includes the external environment, or the forces on the system such as political, economic, sociological, technological, or environmental; the internal environment, such as people and organizational culture, resource allocation, processes to accomplish work; and the stakeholder environment including groups with a stake in the organization, such as employees, suppliers customers, communities where the organization resides, and so forth. It is essential that the definition capture the identity of the system as it currently exists, not how it could be in the future. Normally, it is helpful to have the participants draw their system out and identify the external, internal, and stakeholder environments on the paper. This exercise works best when a group of participants is broken up into groups of four to six.

External Environment

The external environment consists of those conditions in which the system operates. It includes the major political, military, governmental, economic, sociological, cultural, religious, technological, and competitive forces in the world.

The more effectively an organization understands these forces, the more likely they can anticipate the changes that will affect them. The identification and elaboration of these elements constitutes an effective external environmental scan. A scan is a process to identify important elements of the world or the organization and learn about them.

Stakeholder Environment

The stakeholder environment includes those groups or individuals who have a stake in the organization. The most important stakeholder for a business is the customer. Equally important is the employee. Without either stakeholder, there is no company. Regardless of the organization, there are customers who can be identified. They represent the users of the output from the organization, inside or outside. For example, in a consumer business, the buying public is the customer. Inside a manufacturing environment, there are multiple customers. They can range from the next person who receives the output of a process to a dealer network that receives a product for distribution to the ultimate buyer of the product.

Other major stakeholders of organizations include suppliers, communities that benefit from the organization and its work, governments that are affected by or must regulate the organization, unions that represent a workforce, competitors who are affected by the organization, and other strategic "partners." A major stakeholder in most corporations include stockholders and the financial, investment communities. In government organizations, the stakeholders will include elected officials, such as Congress and the White House as well as the people of the United States in this country, on whose behalf they are working.

The more global an organization is, the more complex its stakeholder environment. Governments around the world become stakeholders, and their laws and regulations are essential to understand. It is one of the areas of overlap between the stakeholder and external environments. Every organization needs to understand its stakeholders and at any given point in time, how to communicate effectively with them.

Internal Environment

It is also important to regularly explore the internal environment of the organization. This includes the people of the organization and how well they work together, as a team, to accomplish the work of the organization. Is the organization structured effectively and efficiently to accomplish work, or is the structure a barrier? What are the functions of the organization? How well do they work together? What is the organization's overall process capability? Is it measurable? What about process integration, that is, how does the process of one function interface with the process of another?

A crucial element of the internal environment is the culture of the organization. How would it be characterized? Is it a positive force for change in the organization or a barrier to change? Are there formal, written statements of beliefs and values? What does the company stand for?

How are decisions made? What is the resource allocation process? How does the organization invest in its leadership for future generations? What is the infrastructure which supports the entire organization? What are the organization's unique core competencies that separate it from others?

Identification of all these elements and the answering of all these questions, constitutes the internal environmental scan. In addition, it is typical for an organization to regularly ask its employees a variety of confidential questions to ensure regular feedback.

The System Draw

After the environments have been scanned and the elements have been identified, it is useful to graphically draw the overall system and how the elements relate to one another. This is helpful, especially at the macro level.

The environmental scans and the system draw constitute defining the system.

Step 2. Experience a Vision

The next step in the visioning process is the presentation of an example of a vision. Ordinarily, this can be in written form to acquaint those developing the vision, or it can be described in oral form with or without visuals. What is most important is that those individuals who are developing a vision understand how comprehensive one can be. It frequently is helpful to go far into the future, to describe the vision. This enables the individuals to break out of their thought patterns, think "out of the box," and accept nontraditional ideas. Ordinarily, a story is written, set in the future that includes the organization involved in the visioning process.

Step 3. The Headline Exercise

After experiencing the example, individuals are then asked to write a story about the organization for a year, about 20 years into the future. Examples of headlines referring to their organization are provided, and they can write the story behind the headline or they can make up their own headline in that time frame and write that story. This enables the individuals to create a future in their own minds. It also is a simple way to help people think creatively. This activity works well when people are grouped into twos or threes.

Individuals then share their stories with one another.

Step 4. Timeline Exercise

After the headline exercise is completed, groups are asked to put together a timeline from the present out to 20 years or so, and asked to choose two or three areas that they will explore into the future along a timeline. The groups try to think through how an area might evolve over the time period, and what assumptions could occur year by year, though usually groups think through the areas in five-year intervals. This helps the groups think through plausible ways a future might unfold.

The timelines are then shared with the groups.

Step 5. Development of a Vision, Beliefs, and Values

The groups are then asked to develop a set of assumptions that they have made about the year, 20 years out. These assumptions are then used by the groups to develop a vision statement. Normally, the facilitator develops a "straw man" statement which the groups then try to use as a starting point, and several versions are developed until a consensus is developed. A statement of beliefs and values are also usually developed.

Step 6. Description of the System in 20 Years

A description of what the system will look like in 20 years is now developed and how key stakeholders will view the organization in 20 years.

Step 7. Description of the World in 20 Years

A description of the state of the world in 20 years and how the "system" fits into the future world is then developed. Usually vision statements are descriptions of what an organizations *wants* to look like in 20 years: an ideal state.

Step 8. What Have I Learned?

The visioning process is not meant to be a prediction or a forecast, but a learning process for those engaged in it, to more effectively focus the organization and point it in the right direction in a proactive way. Decision makers should ask themselves, "What have I learned through this process that will encourage me to change something tomorrow?" Examples include business plans, technology plans, and so forth.

Debriefing

Step 8 could be considered the debriefing process for the exercise. In a group setting, lessons learned are usually shared within the groups, and then the groups share their lessons learned with all the participants.

Conclusion

This exercise can be adapted in many ways to assist organizations in developing visions of the future and be better prepared. It can be scaled for use by any "system" level from the individual or family to the organizational, institutional, government, or national level.

Author's Note

The preceding is based on a chapter in *Timelines into the Future: Strategic Visioning Methods for Government, Business and Other Organizations*. Reprinted with permission of the publisher.

Appendix 12A

Examples

Working with the college of engineering of a major research university in the Midwest of the United States in the late 1990s, the following examples were developed to define the assumptions about the current system.

Assumptions about the Current System

- National rankings are important
- Functions of the university remain teaching, research and service
- Resource allocation to the college of engineering will remain about the same
- Reputation comes from research and graduate students
- Research contributes to the value of the undergraduate experience
- Partnerships with industry are very important
- We need to be comprehensive in disciplines.

Going Out to the Future

The group was then read a story, an example of a scenario in the year 2085. This was used to begin to get the groups in a different mindset that would be out of their usual planning time frame.

The following assumptions were identified as those in the year 2085:

- Mankind is going into space
- There will be more global cooperation
- There will be many fundamental breakthroughs
- Our "biology" will prevail
- There has been no massive war or annihilation
- New technologies have to be invented
- No encounters with alien people

- No other biological life forms
- People have bought into this as a future
- One small perturbation in any given year could give a completely different outcome
- Terra forming ruled illegal.

Coming Back from the Future — Headline Exercise

After going well into the future in the year 2085, the groups come back from the future to a more familiar time frame—the year 2020. Each group is asked to write a headline for their virtual magazine and a story behind the headline for the 2020 timed frame. The following are the stories that were written with a Generic University (GU) name written to ensure privacy.

GU Outreach Education Revenues
Surpass On-Campus Dollars

In the past two decades, GU, under the leadership of the College of Engineering, College of Business, and College of Education, have paralleled industry expansion into India and China, since now these two countries represent 50 percent of the world's population. The industry segments of transportation, environment, energy, and social system support now employ 30 percent of the US workforce and 20 percent of the workforce in China and India. GU partnerships with industry around key technologies have grown with this industry expansion in both research and outreach education.

Our revenues from workforce education activities in the United States, China, and India now employ 3,000 GU faculty and staff. Four-way interactive partnership models exist such that industry funding can move faculty expertise without country or institutional barriers.

This consortium has just succeeded in becoming the prime contractor for the new Lunar Base Technology University to open in 2025, funded by the UN Global Foundation.

FAA Certifies Fully Automated Airline

The administration of the FAA announced yesterday the certification of the Boeing 949 airliner which will be the first to operate without an aircrew. It remains to be seen whether the traveling public will access this development.

The supervision and control systems of the new airliner are based on artificial intelligence technology developed by the FAA Center of Excellence at the Ohio State University. The system includes four independent and redundant systems, each of which is capable of flying and landing the aircraft on its own. Technology for fully automated landing of the aircraft was first tested in Britain 40 years ago.

The Gore Commission of 1996 called for a reduction in aviation accidents by 80 percent leading to the establishment of the FAA Centers of Excellence including the one at GU responsible for this development. The Commission report motivated the move toward automated systems.

The administration pointed to the statistical reduction in aviation accidents that followed from the automation of cargo flights about ten years ago. He also emphasized the prevalence of pilot error in findings by the NTSB on the probable causes of accidents.

Nevertheless, development of the 949 has faced intense opposition from aircrew unions and politicians and others in the community who feel human oversight is essential when lives are at risk.

Assumptions about 2020

For the purposes of this process, the system was defined as "Generic University College of Engineering."

The following assumptions were identified during the process of writing the stories:

- Lay the groundwork in 2000
- Ranking is a way we value ourselves
- Still in business
- Stay as graduate and undergraduate institution
- Being a public university will continue
- The physical nature of the college will persist
- Relatively stable supply of undergraduates
- We will remain a part of a system of many public universities
- Departments won't be the same
- Diversity sensitivity is important
- Universities will need to cooperate.

13

The Climb Challenge

A Game Focused on the Logistics Build for an ROI-Based Early Warning Alert and Scenario Analysis System for an Organization

Nanette J. Bulger

C hallenges to companies are vast today given the global nature of competition and markets. Dynamics vary depending on regional business "ecosystems or business environments," which we define in figure 13.3, and it is, therefore, a challenge to any organization looking to service a market and compete within those markets because of the difference in regional needs and requirements. As a result, it is critical to have a real-time alert system and a process for monitoring and analyzing changes within that alert system. You must be able to measure predictions on an ongoing basis within your organizational planning processes and run applicable scenario analysis exercises. We call this the *ROI-Based Early Warning Alert and Scenario Analysis System*, and this is the subject of our game.

Scenario systems, litmus test options, and supporting alert systems help us monitor dynamics in the market that may provide opportunities or may alert us of dynamic shifts and risk within a "business ecosystem." We will define risk in greater depth in a moment. We will also define what a "business ecosystem is, how we define drivers within the ecosystem, and how they feed our scenario-based system as we explain the steps of the game.

So, What Is a Scenario-Based System?

Let's first address the definition of a scenario analysis system and outline what is required to ensure implementation and sustainability within the organization before we discuss the game itself at any great length. Making decisions in dynamic markets is not a static exercise and the use of scenarios helps your company develop a competitive advantage. According to Paul de Ruijter, "Taking into account various possible futures based on one or more models enables an organization to decrease the reaction time needed when a new development actually occurs" (Ruijter, 2014, p. 57).

Global markets are effected by a number of influencers we call "drivers," and, conversely, those drivers have measured influence on markets. Additionally, the importance of various drivers may change, increasing or decreasing in importance over time and often directly proportional to other related factors. For example, an election of a new government may bring new regulations. New regulations may bring about an inability for a specific demographic population to purchase your product. As a result, these are all drivers that, in combination or individually, create a specific scenario called a "what if" scenario. Understanding these drivers and the influencers of these drivers, which in turn affects the market, helps you to understand, monitor, and anticipate global situations on an ongoing basis. A formal and frequently held set of "what if" scenarios and the accompanying strategic discussions based on the dynamics manifested via these driver sets is the basis for ongoing early warning and a scenario analysis monitoring system. These drivers are used to test a specific hypothesis or multiple scenarios. An early warning–based scenario analysis system, however, is only as good as the processes and inputs that take place within the system and the measurable impacts that result from the system. Interestingly, scenario analysis and early warning system builds are often taught separately despite the fact that they coexist and that good early warning monitoring is essential for ongoing scenario analysis. Teaching the mechanics of this process to the participant is the foundation of our game.

While it will be important to have a somewhat in depth description of scenarios, let us first discuss what is needed to implement a sustainable early warning and scenario analysis process, which is how the game is constructed. In order to implement and sustain such a system, there are four critical and necessary elements that need to be addressed as you are building the scenario analysis sustainable program. When we have a real-time system that alerts and monitors dynamics in the markets and helps us to determine the impact on our organization on an ongoing basis, we have a true alert monitoring and scenario-based decision process and system.

The Four Critical Phase Areas Required to Implement an Early Warning Alert and Scenario Analysis System

There are four critical areas (phases) of an ROI-based ongoing scenario-based system. These four critical areas are necessary if your program is to launch effectively and survive as a sustainable, viable process over time. Often, processes fail because they have not focused on all of these critical areas and have not taken into account all of the elements of "people, process, and tools" that are required for success. The game outlined in this chapter will take the participant through all four critical areas in the form of the phases and enabling steps as outlined in figure 13.1. The four critical areas (phases) that are required for a scenario-based strategy system are as follows:

1. *Discovery Phase One—Build a collaborative integrated organizational system* based on integrated intelligence methodology (Bulger, 2016, p. 4).
2. *Design Phase Two—Build a robust driver-based monitoring system* that alerts of market shifts.

3. *Develop Phase Three—Design and build "cascading" tools* that are metric-based for use in implementing and building impact analysis. This means that the information sets and resulting outputs are based on the complexity required at different levels of the organizations and that are less detailed and more impact and recommendation focused the higher up the target audience sits. It does not mean that the decision is less complex but rather the deliverable is less detailed while being based on the complex detailed analysis and deliverables that are constructed at lower levels. (For executive audiences, the detail is usually referred to as a source or in an appendix.)

4. *Deploy Phase Four—Build a scenario system process that integrates into the planning cycles or cadence of the company.* Most forget to do this. Some will argue the necessity of it. Understand that success is reliant not only on having the right answers but on conveying them in a manner that is digestible for the organization. How many great analysts have failed because they were "in sync with the market" and "out of sync with the organization"? Both are important!

Before we get into the game, let's address some additional basic background questions. What is risk, and what is a scenario analysis system?

A scenario analysis system is, simply put, a system of vigilantly understanding market dynamics, the drivers of those dynamics and the process of litmus testing combinations of those drivers to alert an organization of impending and unforeseen crisis, future events, risk, and opportunities for competitive advantage. It should consist of a formal process that is integrated into the business planning cadence of the company and used to support decisions and monitor dynamics. We will speak about business planning cadence and what it is in this chapter. If all is designed correctly, ROI is a natural outcome of scenario analysis. In other words, we make the right decisions at the right time with the right team because we have a disciplined real-time capability that helps us anticipate results that lead to success.

A formal system will enable the development of collaborative initiatives that drive and influence key executive decisions. It means you bring experts together, support topics with solid intelligence and insights, and develop "what if" scenarios based on proven market drivers and their probability of occurring. The team learns the elements of the company's strategy including mission, vision, and strategic direction. This is critical to understanding of the scenarios later on and in how to build the driver-based ecosystem and other tools required to track and maintain strategic direction. As a result, it is equally important to understand key decision makers and key expertise that add validity and value to your impact analysis. The more open the discussion is and the more robust the supporting efforts are, the less apt decisionmakers are to fall into groupthink. "The danger of groupthink is still present, even scientists can be wrong" (Ruijter, 2014, p. 56). As a result, driver-based scenarios pose options and reduce the temptation for this phenomenon. Driver-based scenarios are developed to flush out any risk that might pose a threat to our competitive edge and to help us anticipate the results of future moves. So what is risk?

Risk Defined

There are several types of risk. There is catastrophic risk and there is what we define as progressive risk. "Catastrophic risk" (Grossi, 2005) happens as a result of an extreme dynamic change/shift in the ecosystem. For instance, the 2011 tsunami in Japan disrupted corporate logistics and supply chains for a number of companies. Companies had to shift strategy and processes to protect the manufacturers of their products around the world. Other common examples include political situations, wars, and disease. "Progressive" risk is our definition of something that could happen in the short term or near future or as a result of a buildup of events and issues. An example of progressive risk might be a pricing change by a competitor or other such dynamic shift(s) that we must be ready for if we are to be in anticipatory mode rather than in reaction mode. Within our ecosystem, we should be measuring the drivers that affect these dynamic changes on an ongoing basis and ensuring that we are reviewing the correct ones over time in order to see how they may affect our competitive advantage in the market and our subsequent strategy.

Challenges Abound! Game On!

Now that we have covered some background, let's address the true essence of this chapter: the game. The purpose of the game is to teach the reader how to set up an early warning–supported scenario analysis system within their organization. In this chapter, we will not go into explaining the details related to the critical thinking needed to formulate strategy based on scenarios but rather the process for setting up the program. There are many books written on that subject, but they fall short of instructing the reader in preferred practices for making good strategy a reality via the build of a sustainable program. The purpose of this game is to do just that, and to teach the reader how to logistically set up the program and useful tools that will help in the creation of an end-to-end scenario analysis system that, by default, results in the implementation of the organization's ongoing alert efforts. By "start to finish" or "end to end" we mean a sustainable scenario program that will exist throughout the fiscal year, create real-time insights, and be renewable and updatable for the years to follow. Given all of these parameters, the vast complexities and roadblocks, and what essentially appears as an insurmountable challenge when building such a system, we carefully constructed the game to ensure that all four critical areas (phases) are covered and considered in full.

Why build this as a game? The best way to master complex issues is through experiential learning. Hence, we have created the Climb Challenge,[1] a series of games addressing a variety of program issues and obstacles to competitive advantage. The Climb Challenge works for a number of different types of issues and challenges and is industry and discipline agnostic. For this case, however, we are focused on using Climb Challenge program methodologies to develop a program for the development of a driver-based scenario analysis system.

The Essence of the Climb Challenge

Why do we call it the Climb Challenge? The Climb Challenge mountain theme is a powerful metaphor for overcoming unforeseeable obstacles that through perseverance and strategic thinking result in conquering (summiting in victory) an issue and gaining success; reaching the height of perfection. The goal of any game is to make it an experiential learning activity that is by default, fun. Each team encounters obstacles along the way that mimic real-life situations and detailed required steps need to overcome those challenges. We "gear up" each extreme team and send them out into the "cold" with one goal: to reach the summit of achievement by working together, collaborating, developing tools of necessity along the way, and ultimately, resulting in success, which in this case is to build the ROI-based ongoing scenario-based system.

The Detailed Steps of the Climb Challenge

As we discussed earlier, an ROI-based ongoing scenario-based system is made up of four critical areas (phases) including building a collaborative integrated intelligence system, a robust driver-based monitoring system, a set of tools, and a set of touchpoints and process build that coincides with the planning cadence of the organization.

The importance of this game is to simulate the participant's engagement as a workforce employee hired to develop an organizational function and skill set for integrated insights, intelligence, and analytics decision support capabilities. In the course of building a true competitive intelligence (CI) function in actual work settings, this individual or team is most often required to build viable programs and processes to support their efforts. One of those programs is and should be to build monitoring systems, real-time alerts, and scenario analysis processes which should culminate in a driver-based scenario analysis system, hence the reasoning for choosing this all-important topic of constructing such a capability for this chapter.

There are a number of steps that are required in the complex process of setting up such a capability and a number of deliverables that are required during the scenario build process. As a result, we have included them in the game. Now let's outline the four critical areas (phases) again and the six carefully crafted steps that we will master in order to build the driver-based scenario analysis process for the organization.

As stated earlier and illustrated in figure 13.1, the six steps of the game are clustered under four phases that include discovery, design, development, and deployment. Phase Four, which is called "Deploy," is the actual build of the scenario analysis system, but the preceding phases ensure that we have built the right foundation for the program sustainability. You will note in figure 13.1 that each phase requires a debriefing to the other teams after each individual step. Note that below we have illustrated more detail including debriefing timing and instructional tools and outputs. Later we will show you the actual game using the mountain climbing Climb Challenge theme.

The above steps ensure that all of the necessary factors are addressed in order to create the system. Often, scenario and strategy sessions are "one-offs" and include a select few "experts." Deliverables are often not standard, there is no real-time monitoring to support discussions, and there is little follow-through. Our simple game addresses these factors, albeit at the high level. Now, let's walk through each step in the game that will result in a scenario-based strategy system for our organization.

Discovery Phase One—Step One—Understanding Organizational Hierarchies

The Discovery Phase One consists of an individual step, as indicated in figure 13.1, and that is to understand the organization. If we are talking about scenario-based strategy, why do we care about organizational hierarchies? The reason is that scenarios and the resulting strategies are developed by teams, typically within the company or directed by the organization. They are usually engaged in some sort of "planning or strategy process" and, of course, need to use information about the markets that help them make decisions. It is important for each participant in the game to achieve an understanding of the way the organization develops its strategy, who is involved in that development, and who the key decision makers are. These decision makers are critical to aiding you and your team in achieving credibility by creating opportunities for you to insert robust collaboratively created insights into the strategic process They help to "blaze the trail" for your function and insights delivery processes and add insight and perspective to your analysis.

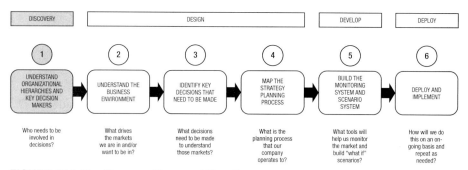

FIGURE 13.1 The Discovery Phase and Step One

Source: Nanette J. Bulger

So, who are these decision makers that you should be engaging with? Who makes the decisions and who should be making the decisions? Many believe that a "seat at the CEO table" is the only way to gain credibility; an unspoken but preconceived notion is that the CEO is the only one who makes decisions in the company and that the only place to truly have influence is in that executive's office. Surprisingly, in a number of cases the CEO is often the person asking for data rather than intelligence and relies heavily on trusted supporters for strategic positioning. So hear me when I say that the key to building robust scenarios is having the right people be a part of the process, and that doesn't just mean the CEO. There are a number of decision makers and supporters within the organization and at a number of levels in the organization who may contribute at various levels of the hierarchy.

So what should you do? Seek out and identify influencers throughout the organization. Business unit presidents, controllers, Mergers & Acquisition directors and vice presidents and a number of senior directors are often key and respected influencers.

- To start, find "paths of least resistance" by building synergies and building impact analysis tools in partnership with critical adjacent expert influencers who are willing to work with you as a starting point. Less convincing is needed and success with this subset of decision makers often gets attention and soon others want "in on the game."
- Second, resist the perception that strategic thinking begins and ends with the formal up-front, early in the year, strategic planning process (Bulger, 2016). Strategic thinking doesn't just happen during the strategic planning process. Strategic thinking takes place regardless of whether you are at the front of the strategic planning cycle or in the yearly execution phases, as in marketing and sales. Do you ever wonder why many strategic plans are shelved and never used? It occurs for precisely this reason. Every strategy consultant wants to help you with strategy and long-range planning that supports your front end outlooks and plans but leaves you with no "strategy for implementation or real-time monitoring and anticipatory systems" across the rest of the year during the operational implementation stage because they consider this "tactical." Try telling a sales person or a marketing person that all they do is tactical operations work. Given the lack of consideration for all of this, it is nearly impossible to set up a true scenario analysis ongoing system or to test and monitor the ongoing initiatives or end results of your predictions and actions; hence many programs falter.
- Third, the essence of building a true comprehensive scenario analysis system means that we must also consider constructing our process as an ongoing initiative that exists across all planning cycles.

In Phase One, Step One, there are two basic parts, Part One and Part Two, that have to be addressed. These include understanding decision makers and understanding key stakeholders. Note that at times, a resource may be both (i.e., a CFO may help you with your financial intelligence analysis [Bulger, 2016, p. 75] but may also be a benefactor of the impact analysis you do and may use it to do financial forecasting). Let's now describe both parts of Step One.

Phase One Discovery Phase—Step One—Part One: Understanding Organizational Hierarchies—Remember what we said earlier. The best decisions are made through robust but tempered analysis and resulting findings based on sound supporting insights provided through a network of experts. The challenge requires expertise in data gathering followed by sound analytics in conjunction with the ability to engage a number of experts across a vast global community, all while delivering convincing ROI-based results that capture the attention of the highest-ranking decision makers in organizations. Much of the data gathering for this exercise is changing industry as we speak, given all of the new tools and technology available in industry today. That subject will be covered in subsequent papers. Although some efforts differ depending on organizational types and setting, similar steps and senior level expertise is required to be successful. In Step One—Part One, the first output is to outline the organization and determine what type of organization it is (i.e., a pyramid, a matrix, or other type of organization).

Phase One Discovery Phase—Step One—Part Two:—Understanding Key Decision Makers—Understanding key decision makers means understanding those who are ultimately responsible for the strategic direction of the company. The responsibility rests squarely on their shoulders. Understanding these stakeholders aids you in the development of your deliverables (Bulger, 2016, pp. 68–71), the key intelligence topics and the blind spots that may exist in the organization. You will be required to build your processes to include many of these influencers, but you need to know who they are first.

- This step is where you will outline the key decision makers and communication pathways between individuals. At this juncture you are also learning who possesses insights or access to insights that should be integrated into the overall process.
- Identify a network that will develop the insights and analysis that will feed the system on an ongoing basis. Ultimately, design your insights organization that will enable global implementation and sustainment of the work through insight collection, analysis and collaboration. Build relationships and collaborative deliverables. The best way to sell an idea is to have support for the idea, particularly from critical functions within the organization to which you are trying to sell the idea. But selling is not the only reason you engage others. They have a perspective on a situation that you may not have and so they can offer a varying point of view based on experience, interfaces, and expertise. For these two reasons, engage with others. For instance, if you are performing a financial side-by-side analysis, try partnering with the finance department.
- Build a relationship battle map to determine who to work with on a variety of impact analysis and go out and build those relationship s and collaborative deliverables (Bulger, *The Evolving Role of Intelligence: Migrating from Traditional Competitive Intelligence to Integrated Intelligence*, 2016, pp. 10–11).
- Debrief the other teams on the current organizational set up and challenges. Identify paths of least resistance, critical partnerships and key stakeholders. The output of Phase One, Step Two, Part Two is to develop a simple battle map (Bulger, *Data Visualization Workshop*, 2017) that identifies the key stakeholders and the relationship between stakeholders. This mapping enlightens us on *how they make decisions and what decisions they need to make.*

Integrating successful decision tools into the process via key company internal partnerships enables the recognition of intelligence as a key component in robust decision making and the natural development of an early warning capability. You will need to show what is possible, not wait for an invitation for involvement in organizational decision making.

Phase One, Step One, Parts One and Two Logistical Steps

a. Build the organizational charts
b. Identify key decision makers and map them with a battle map
c. Identify key expertise partners via "paths of least resistance
d. Debrief the game participants.

Phase One, Step One, Parts One and Two Outputs

a. Organizational chart
b. Battle map of key decision makers and possible expertise partners.

Design Phase Two—Step Two—Understanding the Business Environment

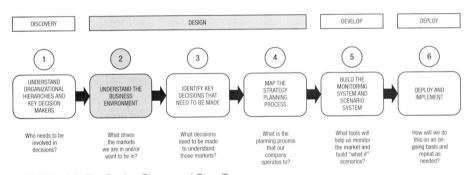

FIGURE 13.2 The Design Phase and Step Two

Source: Nanette J. Bulger

The second critical phase required to build a scenario analysis decision system is to build a concrete driver-based monitoring system which provides the basis for the capturing of changes in market dynamics on an ongoing basis. Often experts talk about developing early warning but have no set integrated process, identified intelligence touchpoints into that process or, most importantly, a driver-based system in place that identifies critical weighted metrics and driver sets that indicate or trigger changes. A good driver-based monitoring program systematically identifies maps and measures all indicators in a market ecosystem or business environment as detailed in Figure 13.3 (Bulger, 2016) and qualitatively or quantitatively weights them according to importance and then builds scenarios based on these drivers sets, litmus testing them in ongoing scenario analysis exercises. In general, drivers are defined as the following;

- Things that "encourage/enable/force a dynamic shift" in the business environment.
- They are the foundational elements behind predictive analytics.
- They can range from a number of elements and be radically different depending on where I sit in the world market and are the basis for assumption based modeling and predictive analytics.

(Bulger, *Predictive Analytics*, 2015)

The importance of measuring drivers that alert of risk and possible changes in the environment is essentially the basis of the early warning program. Drivers exist in all major areas of a business environment or business ecosystem. Figure 13.3 outlines a typical business environment or business ecosystem. Arguably, every organization has some form of an ecosystem in which they compete. Understanding what drives the dynamics related to these factors is the basis for scenario analysis and subsequently, early warning. Without this basic step, you will have neither a sound scenario analysis system nor a robust early warning system. It is essential to develop a process to monitor and use changes in the environment to

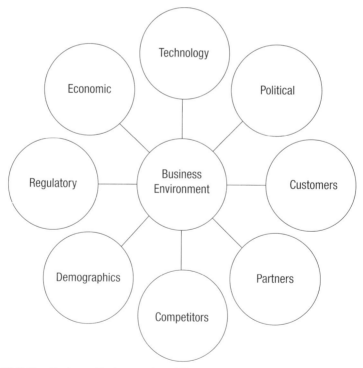

FIGURE 13.3 The Business Environment and Ecosystem

Source: Nanette J. Bulger

keep a pulse on where the market is and what drives it. As a result, Phase Two—Step Two requires that the participants in the game build an ecosystem for their organization in the markets in which they compete and want to compete. Using figure 13.3 as a guide and figure 13.4 as a template, the participants will outline the drivers under each category that exist in their target markets.

As you are identifying and outlining the ecosystem, use the Ecosystem Driver Assessment Chart in figure 13.4 to capture your information. You will use this chart in a future step to prioritize your drivers. After you have determined what drives market in a particular region, list all of the drivers in the columns in this chart under the headings "Eco System Driver Category" and "Sub Driver." As an example, in figure 13.4, political issues are prevalent in the market we are studying (they often are in all markets). We acknowledge that a political "change in leadership" could change policy. You may surmise that policy is very important to your company because regulation changes may affect your market. Therefore, a political election is a critical driver that you should monitor. We will get into how much and how many drivers we should monitor in Phase Four, Step Six.

Do not fill in the other columns yet because you do not have enough information to do so accurately, although you may have some idea. It will be important to understand now what key decisions need to be made.

A	B	C	D	E	F	G
Eco System Driver Category	Sub-Driver (if needed)	Numbered Driver or Sub-Driver	Level of importance or prioritization [1-4] High=1, Low=4	Urgency [1-4] High=1, Low=4	General Market Impact at present [1-4] High=1, Low=4	Frequency of Update
Political	**Country Election**	1				

FIGURE 13.4 The Ecosystem Driver Assessment Chart

Source: Nanette J. Bulger

Step Two Logistical Steps

a. Map the business environment
b. Identify drivers in each ecosystem driver category
c. Debrief the game participants.

Step Two Outputs

a. Ecosystem Driver Assessment Chart.

Design Phase Two—Step Three—Understanding Key Decisions That Need to Be Made Critical Element Two—A Driver-Based Monitoring System

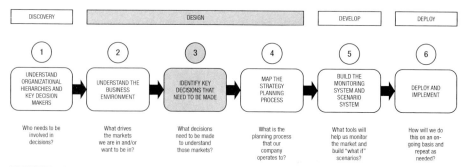

FIGURE 13.5 The Design Phase Two and Step Three

Source: Nanette J. Bulger

Before we proceed any further with the population of the Ecosystem Driver Assessment Chart, we will address what questions need to be answered about the target markets. It is important that this step take place at this juncture. Now that you have identified key stakeholders and influencers within the organization that you built in Phase One—Step One, Parts One and Two, and you have outlined the ecosystem and all of the accompanying drivers within the ecosystem in Phase Two—Step Two, you now have enough information to address key intelligence queries and topics and to discern what questions are relevant to strategic positioning. Trying to understand key intelligence questions (topics) or KIQs (KITs) before you yourself understand the business ecosystem may lead you to accepting, as fact, that decision makers always know what questions need to be made and are the most critical and that is not always the case. Note that we are saying, "decisions that need to be made." We are saying this because we want you to look beyond what the executives are saying and asking for and review the ecosystem you have just prepared to see if there are any gaps in thought process or areas where a decision maker has overlooked something critical or something that could signal a crisis of some sort.

Understand what critical questions executives have and be inquisitive about what is driving markets but never rest on the fact that executive always know what decisions need to be made. They are smart people, no doubt and they are in the positions they are because they likely earned that seat. That said, even the smartest most astute leaders may miss things that happen in the market and so it is your job to fully understand what is driving a market and build an alert system to help them see those areas they may have missed.

Those questions and critical decisions you outline in Phase Two—Step Three as indicated in Figure 13.5, are questions that become the topics of your scenario analysis activities and are those questions on which you will weight your driver sets in your ecosystem exercise. These topics and the associated driver sets in the ecosystem should be re-addressed for validity at least every six months as they can change depending on strategic direction and market dynamics.

It is this combining internally centric and externally centric views and perspective that gives credence to your assumptions and subsequent scenario discussions.

- What are the questions the organization has?
- Are they the right questions?
- Are they leading us to the right answers and the right decisions that need to be made?
- How do we know what to monitor?

So, there are two major parts to Step Three as follows:

1. Review all of your management's strategic questions.

   - Do they support strategic direction?
   - Does the strategic direction seem viable?

2. Construct what we call a driver integration map (Bulger, 2017). We have outlined one of these maps in figure 13.6. Note that at this point, you have outlined the business ecosystem in which you exist and all of the associated drivers with each focus area of the ecosystem. You have also identified and vetted all of your key decisions that need to be made and the key questions uses to answer them. Often key questions have subquestions that need to be answers in order to build up to the top level critical questions. Using driver integration maps to structure this is a good way to identify not only the key subquestions but now all of the drivers and metrics needed to answer and monitor those decisions. These maps will help you sensibly construct the breakdown of the driver sets, prioritize drivers, identify combinations of drivers, and identify subdrivers. Once you do this, you will be able to select the most significant drivers, determine the urgency of them happening and develop an ongoing monitoring system which will be addressed following this activity.

In figure 13.6 we will illustrate the breakdown. The critical decision pertains to what market we should aspire to have a competitive advantage in. One of the key questions that needs answering to come to a decision is as follows: "Should we be focused on X market?" Next, we may want to break the answer down by different market segments as they answer may be different depending on the structure of our company and focus market areas or the various regions of the globe that are effected by different drivers. We then set out to determine what drives the market and what measures or metrics we will use to measure and monitor the market. Note in this illustration that the drivers and metrics may exist at varying levels. It is these drivers and combination of drivers that you will monitor as part of your early warning program.

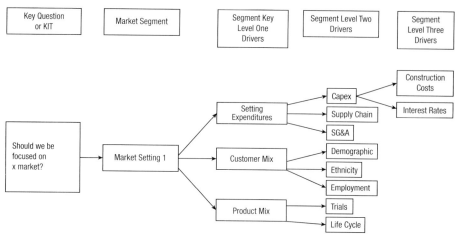

FIGURE 13.6 Driver Integration Map

Source: Nanette J. Bulger

3. After you have completed the driver integration mapping exercise, you will now have identified a set of cascading drivers that you are able to use to populate your Driver Weighting Diagram shown in figure 13.7 by taking the following steps outlined below.

A	B	C	D	E	F	G
Eco System Driver Category	Sub-Driver (if needed)	Numbered Driver or Sub-Driver	Level of importance or prioritization [1-4] High=1, Low=4	Urgency [1-4] High=1, Low=4	General Market Impact at present [1-4] High=1, Low=4	Frequency of Update
Political	**Country Election**	1	1	4	4	**Yearly**

FIGURE 13.7 Weighting the Drivers

Source: Nanette J. Bulger

i. *Identify and list all of the drivers and subdrivers in Column A and Column B.* At this point, there may be many of them. Do not panic. We will be winnowing down the list of those we will monitor, however we will keep the full list for review on a yearly basis.

ii. *Sequentially number them in Column C* so that they are easily identified. This is merely for identification purposes and nothing more. We will use this numbering later on in a set of deliverables, as you will see.

iii. Weight the drivers for *importance and impact* and prioritize the drivers accordingly in *Column D*. We use a qualitative 1–4 scoring capability to weight the importance of drivers but you may consider other methodologies and weighting processes if you so desire. Just ensure that process is clearly defined.

iv. Take the top ten drivers in each Ecosystem Driver Category and rate them for *urgency in Column E*: (1) Is it occurring now, (2) six months from now, (3) one year from now, or (4) more than one year from now.

v. Then rate them for *probable impact in Column F*. Some will prove to be rather insignificant and others more important using a scoring of 1–4. How do you determine this?

1. Certainly four parameters are as follows;

   a. likelihood of happening in the near future
   b. likelihood of it having a future impact
   c. number of related drivers or subdrivers to it that are obvious
   d. predicted level of direct impact it would have on your strategy going forward. Often these measured are made via statistical analysis; however, we will be covering only the basic mechanics and thought process behind this for the purpose of this chapter.

vi. Finally, determine a *frequency of update in Column G*. Some drivers will have to be updated on a weekly basis. It may be sufficient to update others on a yearly basis. Will it be updated yearly, biannually, quarterly, monthly, or daily? Note this as it forms the basis of your monitoring and early warning system.

2. You are now ready to build your dashboard that you will keep updated on an ongoing basis as part of early warning. We recommend only addressing the top 10–20 drivers outlined in the template you create in figure 13.7 and that you have determined are of top priority and tend to be more urgent than others. Figure 13.8 is an example of a dashboard. This is a one-page dashboard that contains all necessary sourcing, impact analysis, and identification of drivers. As you can see, this creates an automatic monitoring system. These dashboards are important because they serve a number of purposes. The first one is to monitor the drivers in the environment so that you know what to look for in the environment in terms of changes. The second purpose serves as a tool for delivering impact analysis about the market. This can be used and delivered to a number of operational disciplines including, but not limited to, the executive management. Keep it simple, one page, and to the point. Include a short summarization of impact on the dashboard as indicated in Figure 13.8.

   We recommend that the dashboard be reviewed, at minimum, each month for updates. If dynamics in the market change, you will want to be able to move drivers on and off the list accordingly.

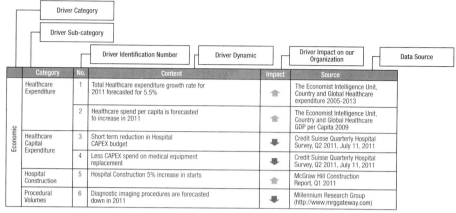

FIGURE 13.8 Sample Driver Dashboard

Source: Nanette J. Bulger

Design Phase Two—Step Four—Map the Strategy Process Critical Element Four—The Global Scenario Process Built in to the Planning Cadence of the Company

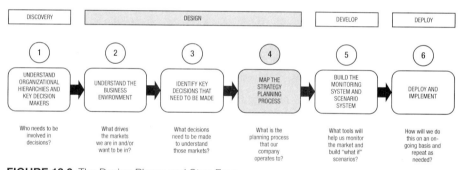

FIGURE 13.9 The Design Phase and Step Four

Source: Nanette J. Bulger

Now lets's turn our attention to the process which makes all of this come together and is often left completely out of any scenario analysis process creation or overlooked for its importance. Consider this. Every company needs a strategy. If they do not have at least the minimum in place, they are usually out of business before too long or just plain lucky. Every "Goliath" has met his or her "David" sooner or later and so, without a vision for where you are and where you are going, you are forging ahead blindly. So it is safe to say that every company strategizes about something whether they have a formal strategic planning process or not and every company has a business planning cadence which we define as the way the company thinks and how they plan. This includes how they conduct their business, develop innovations, go to market with products, and generate sustainable revenue.

This is the strategic planning or business cadence process outlined in figure 13.10. It is made up of five events that occur in a company. For the purpose of this discussion, it is only important to know that there are five major events, and they may take place over the course of an entire fiscal year or may be abbreviated depending on the company business models. It is important to note that some organizations may abbreviate some of these steps and we are only spending time here on this subject because this is where you will build and insert your scenario analysis processes into what we call the planning process, or sometimes, the business cadence. By doing this in a disciplined manner, we create an ongoing scenario process and early warning system by default that works in concert with the companies planning activities.

Lead and encourage members of the organization to work together to develop scenarios, to monitor various scenarios and conduct scenario session ongoing throughout the planning process. Since an organizational planning process is already often comprised of sporadic roundtables and strategy approval sessions with key decision makers and KOL (key opinion leaders), it is an opportune process in which to insert this formal litmus test, ongoing scenario analysis capability.

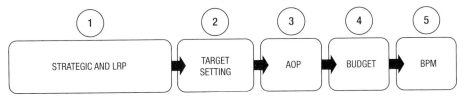

FIGURE 13.10 The Business Planning Cycle and Business Cadence

Source: Nanette J. Bulger

So how do we mesh early warning, scenario analysis with planning cycles? Remember the business ecosystem we outlined in detail earlier in this chapter in figure 13.3 and the driver sets and dashboards we created in figures 13.7 and 13.8, respectively? All of this information and our knowledge of the business cadence enable the creation of a very powerful visualization and alert system for executive management called the Bulger-Sweeney Urgency Quadrant (Bulger, Sweeney, 2012). This visualization in covered in detail in my Predictive Analytics and Structured Analytics Classes with Bulger Institute and The Ticani Institute. This visualization will become the basis for our discussions during scenario sessions and serve as the basis for our first early warning output. By positioning your prioritized drivers on the quadrant based on the impact weighting and timing of impact that you outlined in the table in figure 13.9, we have now integrated strategic planning and impact drivers and produced an alert system that is one page, can be updated on an ongoing basis, can be used for scenario analysis sessions, and creates the basis for an early warning alert system. Figure 13.13 illustrates a sample of what you now need to create from all of the outputs you have developed to this point.

Development Phase Three—Step Five—Build the Monitoring System with Metric-Based Deliverables

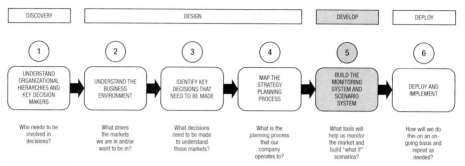

FIGURE 13.11 The Development Phase and Step Five

Source: Nanette J. Bulger

Now that we have covered the four critical areas required as a foundation for the development of a true monitoring and scenario-based system, we will walk through the process on how to implement such a program into our organization via the planning process and sustain it over time. In figure 13.10, we outlined the general planning process over the course of an organization's fiscal year and now we are ready to insert our real-time Bulger-Sweeney Urgency Quadrants (Bulger, Sweeney, 2012) and/or dashboards into the process. Note that by updating these on an ongoing basis, the organization gains real-time access to insights and market dynamics on an ongoing basis in an easy, visualized format. This serves to improve our "time to insights" and is one of the metrics we will use to validate our program. This will be covered later in this chapter. The resulting output is ongoing one-page updates for management and an evolving early warning program with ongoing scenario sessions that are supported by updated deliverables about the dynamics in the market. While there are a number of other factors and areas that could be covered in the course of this writing, but we have dedicated one chapter in this book for this purpose.

Note further that, during each scenario session, the "urgency quadrants" and/or the dashboards will be used as discussion tools. There are indeed other output deliverables, but we are only addressing a few in the course of writing this chapter. During the actual sessions, we will use combinations of the drivers to litmus test specific assumptions and determine "what if" scenarios based on shifts in the driver dynamics. See Figure 13.12 for an example "What If" scenario template. From this, we will be able to make predictions about what events will occur and what outcomes may result and determine the effects on our business. This is the essence of scenario analysis. Repeating this process on a frequency basis forms the basis for robust early warning, collaboration, and knowledge build about markets.

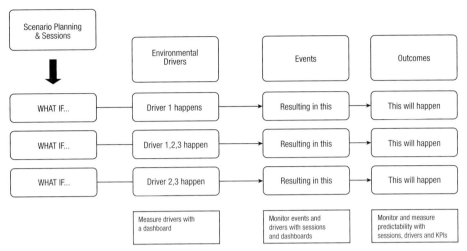

FIGURE 13.12 "What If" Scenario Template

Source: Nanette J. Bulger

Deployment Phase Four—Step Six—Deploy and Implement

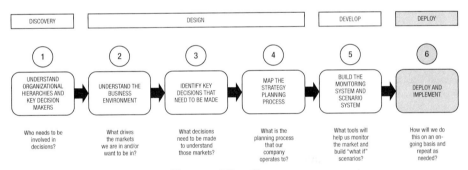

FIGURE 13.13 The Deployment Phase and Step Six

Source: Nanette J. Bulger

The final step in the game, as detailed in figure 13.13, is we deploy the program and implement our deliverables. We understand the organization, the key influencers and stakeholders, the ecosystem, how the organization plans. We have development management type visualizations and analytics. Now we need to ensure the program is sustainable and ongoing. There are two important initiatives to develop in this step.

The first step is to develop a planning schedule and frequency of updates. The next step is likely the easiest to create and provides a framework on which you build your program. Building a calendar across the fiscal year and the planning cadence, allows you to do the following insert the timing of deliverables, the scheduling of sessions and a plan for updates. The important thing is that in includes a fiscal timeline and highlights events including your deliverable visualizations and your ongoing scenario sessions. Use your creativity in developing your calendar! The overall benefits are as follows:

- A good support and alert tool for management.
- A collaboration tool in that you may then work with various departments to understanding their strategic needs and how you might build a level of effort to serve their decision needs.
- An anticipatory tool to determine when certain events and subsequent impacts and dynamics will happen in the market.

The second step is to create a set of metrics by which you may easily measure ROI or return on investment. Refer again to Figure 13.8. All of your impact deliverables and the associated scenario analysis system should measure at least the three metrics posed herein.

- Accuracy over time: When you are monitoring dynamics in the market on an ongoing basis and you are developing impact analysis outputs, you are able to measure the accuracy of your assumptions and predications over time.
- Time to insights: When you are monitoring dynamics and developing deliverables with frequency of updated related to the type of driver it is and then conducting ongoing sessions based on a planned calendar, your deliverables will begin to manifest a knowledge build and will be updated on an ongoing basis, giving the latest results available.
- Business optimization: When we develop outputs based on disciplined collection, analysis, discussion and scenario analysis, we have more available insights and results and need to rely less on consultant programs to understand the market (i.e., vendor management cost avoidance is one easy way to measure a ROI in terms of cost).

Logistics for Running the Actual Mock End-to-End Scenario System Game Called the Climb Challenge

As a final subject of discussion in this chapter, we will present the logistics for the actual Climb Challenge. As we mentioned at the beginning of this chapter, the Climb Challenge works for a number of different types of issues and challenges and across industry and discipline, but this one, in particular, is focused on building a scenario analysis system for your organization.

The Climb Challenge for a Scenario-Based Strategy System is broken up into six distinct steps across the four phases that result in the creation of an ongoing monitoring and scenario system for an organization. This is how the game works.

Game Logistics and Steps Overview

1. The participants are clustered into teams usually of five to eight members, depending on the number of total participants.

2. Each team is given a multinational organizational company and an accompanying scenario (it could be an NGO, government group, or private multinational) and a number of disparate research deliverables and elements about that organization and the market. The facilitator of the game may choose the companies and put together the company data pack.

3. Each team is required to sift through significant data to build an analysis. In order to make the problem realistic and in the context of the challenges an insights, analytics and intelligence professional would face, we include some elements that may not be relevant so they have to sift through the data. The participant is required to choose the relevant pieces of information. In the case of this game, every team may or may not be given the same multinational situation and company. That is up to the instructor.

4. The game is broken up into six steps and clustered into four phases including the discovery phase, the design phase, the development phase and the deployment phase as we detailed earlier in figure 13.1. All of these are, by default, conducive to the development of a maturity model and best practice migration road map for a scenario analysis strategy system build. Each Phase requires a debriefing to the other competing teams after each step.

At the basic level, in order to build the scenario-based system, each team has to think about and construct how they would do the following:

- Utilize all of the organizations resources to develop insights that will be used during scenario "what if" analysis.
- Build a vision of the business environment or ecosystem and the critical drivers of that ecosystem.
- Have a methodology for litmus testing assumptions via the building of driver-based templates and dashboards on an ongoing basis via a series of scenario sessions.
- Build an ongoing and sustainable alert monitoring system supported by a calendar and scheduling of events and updates.

Then each team is required to build the essential logistics of an ongoing monitoring, early warning and scenario analysis system utilizing the above. Tactically, each team learns that building the system requires them to do the following:

- Build a business environment and business ecosystem and associated delivery tool such as a dashboard or other structured visualization.
- Learn how to construct a function to support the organization, given that all organizations are unique in some aspects and given that change is hard.
  - An effective mapping of the organizational structure and relational battle map outlining key stakeholders and decision makers. You need to create a provision for the development of collaborative insights so you will have to break down silos and bring insights together. You need to build an organization that can do these things.

- Support the system with ROI-based metrics that illustrated how you are affecting the bottom line. Best practice means you are both efficient and effective in your programs. Effective means basically that you are contributing to the bottom line revenues directly and can measure that. As a result, you have the challenge of putting metrics around whatever you do.
- Develop a planning calendar and alert system indicating various touch-points across the fiscal calendar which they needed to map out how the company plans for the future outlook and long-range planning.
- Most importantly, learn how and why early warning is a natural outcome of this methodology and a simple example of how you might commence the development of an EWS for your company.

Required Outputs of the Game

During the game, the participants are asked to prepare and present different strategic support tools (there are many, but we have addressed only dashboards and urgency quadrants in this chapter), which have been designed to provide quick snapshots of the various aspects of the market they were operating in. Thus, the assessment tools outlined in figures 13.3, 13.4, 13.6, 13.7, and 13.8 aim to provide the environment overview that an insights, analytics, and intelligence professional needs in order to identify and concentrate on the most important informational areas and to build anticipatory scenarios for analysis across the planning cycles.

As a further analysis in the case, the participants are then asked to produce an organizational roadmap, chart a potential planning structure, and illustrate the integrated intelligence function (Bulger, *The Evolving Role of Intelligence: Migrating from Traditional Competitive Intelligence to Integrated Intelligence*, 2016) of the company based on its structure and intelligence needs. Moreover, the participants must develop an output delivery calendar which would include the entire planning process of the company, the intelligence deliverables package, the frequency of distribution, and update of each deliverable. This provides the foundation for an early warning program and the driver sets that are developed, monitored and updated on an ongoing basis to support ongoing scenario analysis. Because all of this is built into the planning cadence of the company, it helps to develop faster turn on decisions, less churn and duplication and ability to spend time doing things that create ROI rather than leave the company in reactionary mode. All of this can be measured in terms of effect on the bottom line or ROI.

Deliverables

a. A one-page executive briefing in the form of a State of the Market report
b. An Urgency Quadrant
c. Scenario Matrix with drivers
d. Driver dashboard used during scenario sessions and for ongoing monitoring

e. Calendar of Events including a map of deliverables and scenario sessions and why they are indicted as such
f. A proposed organization that is presented to the executive team with ROI metrics to support the need and value add of the organization
g. A set of metrics and how you are going to measure them over time as well as what benefit they afford the organization.

Awards

The resulting presentation and deliverables are rated and graded. The top team (five participants) that does an outstanding job during its team exercise and submits the most comprehensive final assignment projects is given "High Honors"—the highest Climb Challenge recognition. The second-highest award is "Honorable Mention" and is given to the second-highest-ranking team of five participants.

All of the above is presented during a final debrief where judging will take place by an expert team of professionals.

The awarding process this selection committee as follows:

1. A selection committee identifies the winners in terms of highest honors and honorable mention.
2. Participants then present their findings in learning labs at two major global conferences and are awarded a small scholarship for their achievements.
3. The work is then published and the student is given the opportunity to use the scenario they came up with in their job search as an example of creation and implementation.

Summary and Debrief

There are a number of elements to the game. During debrief, you will want to challenge your students by asking some of the following questions:

- Address, with the class, how they might set up their organization to focus on the development of a good program and why it was critical to do so. What did they see as critical things to look for within the organization that helped them decide how to set up the supporting function?
- Did the drivers that they chose help them in constructing and building an early warning system as a result?
- What other one-page summaries and structured analytics could have been used with executive management in addition to the Urgency Quadrant to explain what is happening in the ecosystem?
- How could this process be implemented tomorrow with in an organization? What risks are inherent in the implementation of this full process? How would you mitigate them?

As a result of participation in the game, the participants learn not only how to collaborate as a unit but to create an actual program that would be required of them in an organization. The final package (Bulger, 2017) serves not only as a learning experience but as a package and display of skill sets that the participant may use in throughout their career.

Note

[1] The CLIMB Challenge is a 2015 trademarked name by Nanette J. Bulger and Crystal Pieschel. Nanette J. Bulger owns the entire process; however, Crystal Pieschel and Nanette J. Bulger own the trademarked name together.

References

Bulger, N. J. (2016). The Evolving Role of Intelligence: Migrating from Traditional Competitive Intelligence to Integrated Intelligence. *The International Journal of Intelligence, Security, and Public Affairs, 18*:1, 4.

Grossi, P. (2005). *Catastrophe Modeling: A New Approach to Managing Risk*. New York: Springer Science+Business Media Inc.

Ruijter, P. D. (2014). *Scenario Based Strategy*. Surrey: Gower Publishing Limited.

14

Practitioner Perspective

Competitive Simulations in Support of a Product Launch in the Biopharmaceutical Industry

Alfred Reszka and Daniel Pascheles

Competitive simulations, also known as "war games" in some industries, are an excellent way in which a CI professional can bring value to his/her company. The essence of a competitive simulation is to act out the possible scenarios in a given commercial (or other) setting in order to predict competitor strategies and tactics and stress-testing internal plans. In this chapter, we approach competitive simulations from the company (nonconsultant/vendor) perspective. Although our perspective comes from conducting competitive simulations in the biotechnology/pharmaceutical (BioPharma) industry, we made every attempt to make this chapter relevant, regardless of your industry.

Key decisions that one must make from the company perspective include deciding whether or not to conduct a competitive simulation. Once it is determined that a simulation would be beneficial, it is important to time it in such a fashion that allows time for preparation, execution, post-simulation analysis, as well as sufficient time to change strategies in case weaknesses are unveiled. To this extent, one must know in advance what the intended outcomes are, what steps are necessary to achieve those outcomes, what information will be required upfront in order to level-set with participants, and what deliverables will be required in order to drive the necessary strategic changes or pivots.

The first and most important step in deciding to engage in a competitive simulation is to ask the question of whether or not to have one in the first place. Considerations on whether or not to drive toward a "go" decision for the simulation address the very things that they can help you and your company decide. Near- to mid-term uncertainty in a commercial or other setting—situations where there are multiple possible outcomes driven by different possibilities—make for ideal competitive simulation "go" decisions. Drivers of uncertainty can include the launch of a new product (yours or your competitor's), meaningful product enhancements, or situations where one feels that an existing strategy isn't delivering or cannot deliver sufficiently moving forward. In the commercial setting, this may include situations where one or more (limited to a few) key competitors are all vying to win in the same market. In such a case, it is important to separate strategy from tactics. While it is not the purpose to detail the differences between strategy and tactics, a few guidelines are in order. Strategy is a higher-purpose outline that guides tactics (where do we play, what do we leverage, what is our rollout plan). Hambrick and Fredrickson[1] developed the five-diamond strategy method, which is an easy to understand and execute model for strategy development. Tactics in the commercial setting come a bit closer to the sales force and their interactions with clients. One way to think of the differences between strategy and tactics is to think of what the marketing team is trying to accomplish (strategy) and how they want the field sales force to execute (tactics).

Once one has a strategy and set of aligned tactics in hand, the competitive simulation is a powerful means of pressure-testing the plan and identifying weaknesses and new opportunities. The next step is to identify the key players in your organization that must participate in order for the simulation to have the highest probability of success. The answer to "who should participate?" will differ based on the nature of your organization. Large multinationals may want to include the global marketing team, its support function members and collaborative partners (market research, market access, research and development, manufacturing, etc.), and local marketing teams situated in the countries that will leverage the learnings. Local market participation is key when factoring in local customs and differences that influence how one engages in business in each market. Smaller, single-market (or limited market) companies may benefit from having members of the sales team participate as well. In any and all cases, it is very important to have senior management buy-in and participation. Again, there will be differences based on company size and situation, but in all cases, the one or few individuals that hold decision-making power and authority are critical members to have participate in the event. These participants may not be suitable to participate on competing company teams in order to avoid the possibility that (a) the team will end up following whatever they put forward during the simulation, (b) lower-ranking participants may feel uncomfortable in participating fully knowing that "the boss" is in the room, and (c) the boss should be there to provide purpose and learn the collective thinking of the teams. For these reasons, we often have senior management float between teams throughout the exercise and also serve as judges when teams readout their findings.

After assembling one's internal teams, the next step is to decide who will assemble the required parts of the competitive simulation and who will guide the teams through the simulation itself. If there is funding for hiring an external consultant or vendor, this typically is the easiest method. An external provider also is the likely best choice if one's company has little or no experience with competitive simulations. Assuming, for example, that there is funding and a need for an outside party to conduct the simulation, a few factors must be taken into account. While it is important that simulation providers develop expertise in one's area of commercial focus, we prefer to hire consultants that already have extensive experience. In other words, they can develop and hone their expertise elsewhere (i.e., for other companies) before we consider them for helping us with our projects. Of course, less experienced providers may be necessary in cases where the market is relatively new (i.e., nobody has extensive experience), or they may also be willing to come in at a lower budget. Price also becomes a factor in deciding what one asks the external provide to provide. Broadly speaking, external consultants can provide at least three different components that are required for a successful simulation.

The first major requirement is a backgrounder that level-sets all participants on the facts and intelligence going into the simulation. This can be assembled from internal documents (if one is willing to share these with an outside party), secondary intelligence sources, and primary competitive intelligence. The backgrounder package can be assembled by (a) you, (b) the external party that will conduct the exercise, or (c) by a second third-party provider. The second major requirement is staff that are fully capable in facilitating the discussion, as well as scribes that can capture the learnings during the simulation. Depending on the number of competitive teams participating in the simulation, one will need to replicate this for each team. For discussion facilitators, it is important that they be fully versed in the commercial space of interest, as well as your product and those of your competitors. They must have excellent communication skills, highly organized thinking skills, and preferably plenty of years of experience facilitating competitive simulations. The third major component relates to what happens after the simulation is complete. One may be satisfied to have the vendor provide the scribe notes and a summary deck describing the key takeaways from the event. One may also wish for a consulting vendor to start the real work after the last day of the simulation: interpreting the findings, developing insights, and making recommendations for changes and updates to the strategy. In all cases relating to the pre-work, simulation, and analysis, one can decide to do the work internally or bring in outside help. The decisions that are made in these regards dictate the type of consulting team that is hired. In our experience, CI firms are great at assembling the pre-simulation backgrounder and some are good at conducting the simulation itself. In limited cases, the same providers also can do an excellent job with post-simulation analyses and recommendations. On the other hand, strategy consultants do an excellent job with post-work analysis and consulting, and they can be equally effective in facilitating the workshop. However, they may fall short in the upfront preparation of the backgrounder. This is particularly true when primary CI is required to assemble the background document. In some cases, one might have sufficient intelligence already in hand, in which case a consulting firm can comb through it and assemble an effective background package. In other cases where research is required, the best win-win approach is to have a primary CI firm prepare the backgrounder, and they may also conduct the simulation (or not). A strategy consultant can step in to run the simulation, or they may also come in to help with the final analysis. In cases where the internal team is fully capable of interpreting the findings from the simulation, it may be better to consider hiring a CI vendor for the upfront work and the simulation. There are no hard and fast rules, and experiences from simulations can always be leveraged the next time around. Within our organization, we have used each approach noted above based on the product (or pipeline asset) and the particulars around the knowledge base and participating team members.

There are cheaper means of conducting competitive simulations, and these can be considered. The first is to leverage a "cookie cutter" approach, which we do not employ in our industry for a number of reasons. The second is to go it alone and design and execute a simulation using mostly or exclusively internal resources. We do not recommend the second approach if there is insufficient experience with competitive simulations in your organization. On the other hand, one's organization may wish to develop internal capabilities if competitive simulations are integrated deeply and frequently in the business plan. A good means of achieving this is to begin with the assistance of external CI firms or consultants and internalize the process after the first one or two simulations have been successfully completed. With regard to the cookie cutter approach, there may be limited situations where this can fully and effectively meet the business need. We operate in complex environments and markets, and so we require a degree of customization that most accurately reflects our business environment. Moreover, when we ask our internal clients and senior leaders to participate in such an exercise, we need a high probability that we can deliver.

Once one has committed to engaging in a competitive simulation, timing becomes a factor, depending on what event one is planning for. In the event that one's company is planning to launch a new product, timing needs to allow for the possibility that the simulation will reveal flaws in the launch strategy. For BioPharma, nine months (plus or minus a month or two) prior to launch is ideal, provided that the initial launch plan already is in place. Timing is predicated on the relatively slow timelines for product development and regulatory approval in this industry. In more dynamic industries, such as technologies, the timing might come much closer to launch in order to best understand the competitive situation. Regardless of the industry, an initial launch plan needs to be fleshed out and run through the model. In certain circumstances, a second post-launch simulation may be warranted to course correct or to capitalize on a better understanding of the market and the moves that competitors have made in order to maintain market share. In all cases, one must consider other internal events that could interfere with full participation of the simulation teams and leadership. In cases where conflicts have arisen, we often are put in a position to postpone, which may be fine if one has a sufficient buffer of time before launch. In cases where the request is to push forward the simulation day, one runs the risk that preparation is rushed, which in turn can jeopardize the outcome of the event. For this reason, it is best to plan carefully in consideration of all scheduling variables in order to maximize the probability of success.

Assuming that the decision to conduct a competitive simulation is made and that timing is optimized, it is best to begin by determining what the desired outcomes are. One of the most common triggers is related to the launch of a new product. In these cases, we may have multiple companies conducting simulations in order to model the launch (launching company and its competitors). By this, it is important to recognize that while you may be modeling your competition, they too may be modeling you. In the case of a company bringing a new product to market, the main goal is to anticipate how competitors will respond to a launch and detect possible weaknesses to the launch plan. In the case of a competitor bringing a new product to market, a common goal is to test the launch counterstrategy in one or more contexts. The primary objective would be to identify the best launch plan for the competitor and identify weaknesses that can be exploited in one's own marketing strategy. This may be sufficient if there are only two competitors in the future market. In the case that other players are also participating in the market, it also is advisable to model their reactions to the launch (against the new entrant and against your product). In either case, the main intent is to identify competitor strategies and tactics that are designed to take market share from your product. It is for this reason that participants in a competitive simulation are asked to step away from their customary roles and try to immerse themselves into the thinking and mindset of the competitor with a real intent to win. Quite often vendors will provide apparel and other materials that represent the competitor and assist with the immersion process. The ability to step away and truly think and strategize like the competitor is key to the success of devising their launch (or counter-launch) strategy. Once this is accomplished, it is best to return to the existing marketing plan, and to your own company identity, in order to identify weaknesses and opportunities that had not been revealed or validated prior to the simulation. This can be leveraged to create market scenarios, as well as markers that can provide evidence of success and risks.

There are additional benefits to conducting a competitive simulation that go beyond refining the market plan. In most cases, simulations can be leveraged in order to increase internal awareness, level-setting and alignment around the future market scenarios. It also can create a pep rally–like environment to generate energy and enthusiasm for the launch. This can lead to a better sense of unity within newly formed marketing teams that can radiate to enhance collaboration and alignment around shared goals. Learnings from simulations also have the potential to affect more than the market plan. One of the most important outcomes is informing the forecast, which has important financial implications but also can influence supply chain, manufacturing and distribution planning. Insights in many cases can inform future plans for market research, and in certain circumstances may affect research and development plans for product enhancements or new products.

So what are the steps in preparing for and conducting a competitive simulation? The first thing that we recommend is to have a launch strategy and associated tactics in place. This is not to say that one cannot use a simulation in order to develop the first strategy document, but it can be difficult to model competitor responses to one's own strategy when one does not already know what they might do during the launch process. In considering the strategy and possible competitor actions (the obvious choices), it is important to separate these actions into two different categories: constants and variables. Constants are known factors that are highly unlikely to change depending on how the market evolves. An example of this in the pharma space is generic pricing in the US market, which follows a predictable path that one can anticipate based on numerous prior examples. Variables are the key factors that one wants to model during a simulation. Variables can include, but are not limited to, messaging around product attributes, counter-messaging around competitor product weaknesses, promotional spend, payer strategies, sequencing for market rollout, and services and other offerings that can accompany each competing product. In short, variables are the things that one can change with an expectation that changing might have an influence over market perception and uptake. All of these (and more) are elements that interact with the strategy and tactics that one is intending to pressure-test during the simulation.

The second key step relates to the simulation participants and venue. Beginning with the latter, we have found that an off-site location, such as a hotel with conference facilities, is best. This can minimize distractions from the workplace and temptations to slip out to visit the office. More important, one needs the right people with the right background in order to conduct the best simulation. Beyond the senior sponsors that can lend a sense of legitimacy to the event, it is important to select participants that can offer a variety of perspectives. Generally speaking, this means including more than just members of the marketing and sales teams. Some of the best participants come from other groups within your organization, including market research, market access and pricing, forecasting, manufacturing, research and development, corporate strategy, regulatory and investor relations, among others. With participation from a diverse group of individuals pulled from several functions, this creates a need for level-setting before the simulation begins. The best way to get you to that state is through development of an informative, and yet pithy, backgrounder.

What to Include in the Backgrounders

1. Simulation scope definition
2. Competitive objectives
3. Identified competitor products and their profiles
4. Competitive timelines for new products and product improvements
5. Market geographies
6. Marketing materials from competitors
7. Competitor corporate objectives
8. Revenue forecasts
9. Available market research
10. Payer profiles (for BioPharma)
11. Regulator positions (for BioPharma)
12. Society materials (for BioPharma)
13. Standards of practice (for BioPharma)
14. Clinical data for your product and those of your competitors (for BioPharma).

The background document needs to cover all of the bases using the least amount of words in order to increase the odds that participants will actually read the document. Included content can be any of the following: a backgrounder on your product and the current strategy for launch, intelligence on the competitor products and strategies, including product profile, marketing messages, existing market research and samples of competitor branding. It is also important to understand the competing company, its vision and goals, as the strategies that they have put into place. Key here is to understand how the competitor product(s) of interest align to the success of the company goals. Having such a backgrounder also allows for quicker reference during the simulation when critical information is required to align the discussion. Ideally, a backgrounder is made available one to two weeks prior to the simulation in order to give participants time to review and digest its contents. Even with the best backgrounder in place, it is also important to dedicate the first 30–60 minutes of the simulation to covering the material in case some haven't yet read it (a common occurrence) or in order to ensure that there is no ambiguity in the storyline.

Execution of the simulation is relatively simple and best described in the steps outlined below. These steps are offered as an example, and there are numerous variations that can be employed to tailor the workshop to your individual circumstances.

Executing the Simulation

1. Level-set on assumptions—cover the backgrounder and seek opportunities to clarify
2. Tee up the problems to be addressed—what are we trying to achieve?
3. Discuss the framework for the simulation—participants like to have a sense of where things are going
4. Assemble as teams to devise the best competitor strategies against our product being launched—this is us thinking and behaving like "them"
5. Teams should include diverse membership to maximize opportunities to see different views
6. It is critical to encourage every member to actively participate
7. Senior leaders/sponsors may not be assigned to any specific team, which offers them the opportunity to float from team to team and avoids the possibility for team bias in favor of that leader's opinions
8. Share out and pressure-test identified competitor strategies

   a. This is often done as a reassembled large group
   b. Members from opposing teams can ask questions to challenge thinking and pressure-test learnings

9. Reassemble a second time into competitor teams to refine the strategy based on responses from other teams (may not be necessary, depending on outcome from prior step)
10. Share out the second findings as before
11. Rank order and score the competitor strategies
12. Reassemble as "Us" into a single large team and brainstorm how to adjust or pivot in order to counter the competitor strategies that have been prioritized
13. Subteams can be formed to tackle individual issues revealed about the competitors and their products
14. Recommend specific actions or changes to the strategy that could position your product optimally
15. Senior sponsors judge and score the recommendations
16. Post-simulation deliverables:

    a. Simulation summary of findings
    b. Listing of key blind spots

c. Key opportunities identified
d. Missing elements or opportunities for additional development, lifecycle management
e. Red ocean/blue ocean scenarios
f. Revised strategy document
g. Allow consultants about two weeks to generate a draft summary and allow time for revision before dissemination.

For some, the end of the simulation workshop is the end of the project, but for others, it could be the beginning of some of the most important work on the strategy. In some cases, this is because the workshop revealed shortcomings or unexpected opportunities that were not effectively factored prior to the exercise. In other cases, key evidence was lacking at the time of the workshop, in which case different scenarios were developed to account for the possibilities. In this situation, one needs to build into the strategy contingency plans that dictate a forward path, depending on the evolving situation. The arrival of required data then enable an opportunity to fully flesh out the actual scenario and map it against the predicted impact on the existing plan and contingencies. It is better to have this planned in advance, so that there are no delays or hiccups in execution. Regardless of the reason for returning to the strategy, it is important to engage in a process whereby revisions and additions to the strategy document are cross-referenced against the findings of the workshop. In the event that substantial changes are made, it may be prudent to run a mini-workshop with the same participants to ensure that nothing is missed. As one approaches and enters into the launch plan, it is also necessary to be vigilant in monitoring for signals that could reveal whether the simulated outcome(s) are materializing. As noted above, it may also be prudent to conduct a follow-up simulation months after the product launch, especially if new realities are manifesting that were insufficiently addressed in the original workshop.

In summary, competitive simulations are a powerful means of testing market and other strategies. The quality of the outcomes from a competitive simulation depend on the effort that one puts into the effort before, during, and after the actual simulation event. Although there are many steps required to successfully benefit from a competitive simulation, three are critical and must be done well. First is the pre-workshop backgrounder packet. Assembling these is relatively straightforward, but it also is either time consuming or can increase expenses. Since this document is used to level-set on understanding the situation and the risks, the effort or expenses are worthwhile in order to ensure that all participants are aligned going into the exercise. Second is senior sponsorship. Without this, one runs the risk that the right people are not attracted to participate or that the outcomes of the exercise are not effectively utilized. As noted above, a good senior sponsor has decision-making power and lends credibility to the simulation (but is careful not to create bias toward their pre-existing ideas). Third is the post-workshop effort to generate fully fleshed out insights and translate these into more effective strategies. Focus should be on key takeaways and their implications vis-à-vis the strategy going into the exercise. The overall value that a competitive simulation can bring to winning strategies is high. Provided that one executes the plan well, the return on investment can be extraordinary.

Practical Guide to Plan and Execute a Competitive Simulation

1. Start with the end in mind by deciding what the strategic output will be for the workshop:

    a. Optimizing your product launch
    b. Pressure-testing a counterstrategy to your competitor's launch
    c. Any other initiative where you need to model a competitor's behavior in order to better plan your strategy

2. Choose a date and length for the workshop, as well as the venue:

    a. Two days is ideal when participants have sufficient time to allow for an in-depth workshop
    b. One may only have time for a one-day workshop, but less time, while not unheard of, may diminish the return on investment

3. Select your participants:

    a. Begin with selecting senior sponsors and leaders
    b. Diversify your participant base by involving personnel from a variety of relevant functions within your organization
    c. Best efforts will involve multiple stakeholders with different views on the same issues
    d. The total number of participants will depend on the number of competitors and scenarios that you wish to model (between 7 and 15 participants per company/scenario is typical)
    e. A simulation generally will not involve fewer than 20 or more than 50 participants:

        i.   Too few will lack the varied inputs that are needed
        ii. Too many will dilute focus and the quality of interactions.

4. Craft the agenda for the workshop (see example agenda at the end of this outline):

    a. Ideally, there will be two to four breakout sessions that run simultaneously with each modeling the behavior of a given competitor or scenario:

        i.   Breakout sessions address a discrete set of questions and strategy elements
        ii.   Teams readout their findings after each round to the larger collective audience
        iii. There can be two or three rounds of discussion, with each digging deeper into the mindset of the competitor
        iv.   The goal for each breakout group is to enable the participants to think like the competitor and indeed to behave like the competitor truly wants to win in the marketplace

      v. Assign a team leader for each breakout group:

         1. Task this individual with facilitating the discussion, keeping focus and adhering to timelines

         2. Identify and brief each leader well in advance of the workshop to ensure alignment.

  b. Reassemble as one team, returning to represent your company, to explore implications:

      i. The collective team discusses key learnings from each of the individual breakout teams

      ii. The collective team ideates about effective measures and strategies that can counter the measures and strategies ideated about the competitor's likely plans

      iii. Develop a list of action items (typically three or more) and assign leaders for each that can take responsibility for translating each into action

      iv. Create a plan for continued analysis and understanding that can translate into additional strategic options after the workshop has completed.

5. Before the simulation workshop requirements:

  a. Develop a background packet with relevant competitive and competitor intelligence that can be used to level-set the team before the workshop

  b. Assemble a related presentation deck to be reviewed at the beginning of the workshop to emphasize key elements where all participants must have knowledge

  c. Select a venue for the workshop that pulls participants out of their office mindset and minimizes distractions that can otherwise interfere with focus.

6. On the day of the workshop:

  a. Have the senior sponsor address the participants regarding the purpose of the workshop and its importance to the company's success, as well as the expectations for all participants to participate fully and without distraction

  b. Ask participants to exhibit behaviors that minimize loss of focus:

      i. No cell phone use or texting

      ii. No computer use or emailing

      iii. If any of the above must be done, request that attendees step out of the workshop so as to not distract other participants.

  c. Present the deck that level-sets all participants on the known facts about the competitor and their assets, as well as any relevant plans of your company that will be impacted if the competitor succeeds

  d. Review the agenda (see sample one-day agenda below)

  e. Execute on the agenda and ensure that focus is maintained

    f. Direct breakout participants to their locations or rooms where working materials are provided:

      i. Large paper pad on easel for documenting ideas
      ii. Wall space for attaching completed worksheets
      iii. Computer and projector for preparing slides to be presented to the larger audience after the breakout session is complete
      iv. Optional images of the competitor, apparel with competitor company logos or other token items that help the participants shed their work persona and more fully immerse into the mindset of the competition
      v. Printed backgrounder with relevant reference material on the competitor and their product(s).

    g. After each round of breakout session, have participants readout their findings to the larger collective audience for feedback and discussion
    h. After the final breakout session is completed, reassemble all participants and ask them to return to their normal mindset as members of your own company to discuss implications and next steps
    i. As a collective, develop a plan with assigned responsibilities and timelines that convert the learnings into tangible and impactful actions
    j. Convene an (optional) executive panel that:

      i. Reviews the competitor learnings
      ii. Considers your action plan to counter the competitor
      iii. Asks questions and pressure-test your logic
      iv. Votes for the best team effort.

7. After the workshop:

    a. Create an executive deck that captures the learnings and actin plan developed in the workshop
    b. Continue to refine the action plan and strategies arising from the workshop
    c. Socialize the executive presentation deck to inform and ensure alignment around the plan.

8. Best practices:

    a. Start planning approximately three months ahead of the workshop
    b. Ask relevant participants to block time on their calendar for the selected dates of the workshop
    c. Send welcome letter with logistics two to four weeks prior to the workshop if travel is required for the participants
    d. A well-constructed backgrounder should be shared with participants seven to 10 days prior to the event
    e. Off-site venues that are well away from the office can minimize distractions
    f. Senior sponsors should not be team participants:

      i. In order to allow the teams to ideate more independently
      ii. To allow them to float between groups to observe in a neutral fashion
      iii. To reduce bias should there be a judging panel that rates the outputs from each breakout team.

TABLE 14.1	Sample One-Day Workshop Agenda (Pharmaceutical Example)

Time	Topic—New Competitor Launch in Healthcare Space	Responsible
9:00–9:15	**Welcome, Introductions and Objectives** • Welcome and Background • Workshop process overview	Sponsor & Facilitators
9:15–10:15	**Introduction** • Review clinical program findings • Discuss key challenges and identify market implications	Sponsor & Facilitators
10:15–11:15	**Breakout Group Exercise #1:** • Review competitive materials • Create competitor launch plan for differentiation and success	2–3 Groups
11:15–12:00	**Exercise #1 Group Presentations and Discussion**	Each Group Presents
12:00–13:00	*Lunch*	ALL
13:00–14:00	**Breakout Group Exercise #2:** • Refine competitor plan for success • Discuss implications from competitive immersion for product clinical trial strategy/vulnerabilities • Identify action items for each of the possible scenarios • Discuss potential adaptation/future direction of current life cycle plan	2–3 Groups
14:00–14:45	**Exercise #2 Group Presentations and Discussion**	Each Group Presents
14:45–15:00	*Break*	
15:00–16:30	**Bringing Everything Together & Developing Our Counterstrategy**	ALL
16:30–17:00	**Next Steps and Closing**	ALL

Note

[1] Hambrick, D. C. and J. W. Fredrickson, "Are You Sure You Have a Strategy," *Academy of Management Executive* 15, no. 4 (2001): 48–59.

About the Editors and Contributors

Rubén Arcos, PhD, is a Lecturer and Researcher in Communication Sciences and Director of the Graduate Programme of Specialist in Strategic Communication, Hybrid Threats, and Security at Rey Juan Carlos University in Madrid. He is founding co-director of IntelHub, a joint initiative between the American Public University System, the University of Leicester in the UK, and Rey Juan Carlos University in Spain. He is a freelance contributor to *Jane's Intelligence Review* and deputy editor of the *International Journal of Intelligence, Security, and Public Affairs*. He has served for almost ten years as instructor and coordinator of the first ever Master's degree in Intelligence Analysis in Spain. He is a member of the research group *Ciberimaginario*. He was appointed national member of NATO Task Group SAS-114 on "Assessment and Communication of Uncertainty in Intelligence to Support Decision-Making." His research is focused on intelligence analysis and production and strategic communication, and his research has been published in *Intelligence and National Security, International Journal of Intelligence and Counterintelligence, Public Relations Review, Technology Analysis and Strategic Management*, and the *European Centre of Excellence for Countering Hybrid Threats*, among others. His latest book is *Intelligence Communication in the Digital Era: Transforming Security, Defence and Business* (co-edited with Randolph H. Pherson).

William J. Lahneman is a Professor of Security Studies and International Affairs at Embry-Riddle Aeronautical University in Daytona Beach, Florida, and a Senior Research Scholar at the Center for International and Security Studies at Maryland (CISSM) at the University of Maryland's School of Public Policy. He holds a PhD in International Relations from the Johns Hopkins University School of Advanced International Studies (SAIS), an MA in National Security Affairs from the Naval Postgraduate School, Monterey, California, and a BS from the United States Naval Academy, Annapolis, Maryland. A former commander in the US Navy, he was a Surface Warfare Officer with subspecialties in Nuclear Propulsion and Strategic Planning. He is a US Fulbright Scholar (Rey Juan Carlos University, Madrid, Spain, 2019). His publications include "IC Data Mining in the Post-Snowden Era" in the *International Journal of Intelligence and Counterintelligence* (2016); *The Art of Intelligence: Simulations, Exercises, and Games* (2014) (with co-editor Ruben Arcos); *From Mediation to Nation Building: Third Parties and the Management of Communal Conflict* (2013) (with co-editor Joseph Rudolph); and *Keeping U.S. Intelligence Effective: The Need for a Revolution in Intelligence Affairs* (2011).

Nanette J. Bulger is a globally recognized strategist, analytics expert, engineer, transformation consultant, author and lecturer. She has 38 years of global profit and non-profit experience with startup and multinational organizations. She has authored a number of advanced decision tools for business and spent five years leading the largest analytics global non-profit, SCIP. In 2017 she was appointed as the leading expert in analytics by the Beijing Innovation Center in China. She is currently Executive Director of SAIMAH, The Society of Artificial Intelligence in Medicine and Healthcare. She also independently consults and was appointed to the expert consulting community, LEADX3M in Cambridge, MA USA. A passionate driver of corporate social responsibility and the use of decision frameworks in support of CSR, she founded global WISA, Women in Insights, Strategy and Analytics and SCIP for a Better World.

Richard J. Chasdi is a Professorial Lecturer in the Department of Political Science at the George Washington University. He received a BA in Politics from Brandeis University (1981), an MA in Political Science from Boston College (1985), and a PhD in Political Science from Purdue University in 1995. Dr. Chasdi is a Fulbright specialist scholar (2017), who has written four books about terrorism and counterterrorism and several book chapters, refereed articles, and encyclopedia entries. His first book, *Serenade of Suffering: A Portrait of Middle East Terrorism, 1968–1993* (Lexington Books, 1999), was awarded *Choice* magazine's "Outstanding Academic Title" award in international relations in 2000.

Irena Chiru is Director for Research with "Mihai Viteazul" National Intelligence Academy, Bucharest, Romania. From this position, she coordinates and facilitates the development of international research programs as well as international conferences and symposia for the Academy. She coordinates research projects with EU and national funding as well as projects aimed at creating a competitive research infrastructure. Her role also includes the promotion of knowledge and understanding of key global issues impacting the international intelligence community. She holds a PhD in Sociology and has graduated a number of advanced training course in communication science and intelligence analysis. She is a Professor of Intelligence Studies, and is author and co-author of several books, chapters and articles focused on the interaction between intelligence

and communication. In the last six years she has been the promotor and organizer of the Intelligence in the Knowledge Society international conference, the main hub of intelligence studies in Central and Eastern Europe and a landmark event. This event brings together academics and practitioners from all around the world.

Stephen Coulthart is an Assistant Professor of Security Studies in the National Security Studies Institute at the University of Texas at El Paso. He earned a PhD in Public and International Affairs from the University of Pittsburgh. His research focuses on intelligence analysis and emerging national security technologies and has been published in *Intelligence and National Security, International Affairs*, and the *Journal of Conflict Resolution*, among others. He has provided training and analytical support to numerous governmental and nongovernmental entities in the United States and Europe.

Carolyn Halladay is a Senior Lecturer in the National Security Affairs Department of the Naval Postgraduate School. A historian and a lawyer, Dr. Halladay's academic focus is contemporary Central Europe and questions of culture and ethics in homeland security. She also researches and teaches in political extremism, civil-military relations, national security law, and the ethics of intelligence. She serves as the academic associate in the Center of Homeland Defense and Security at NPS.

Cristina Ivan is acting head of the National Institute for Intelligence Studies of the "Mihai Viteazul" National Intelligence Academy. She holds a PhD in Literary and Cultural Studies from the University of Bucharest, where she researched reflections of violent religious extremism in the British discursive space and cultural productions (2000–2010). Over the past ten years she has specialized in applied research of radicalization and violent extremism, propaganda, and disinformation. She has also worked in and coordinated various national and European-funded projects in her fields of interest. She is author of several books, studies, and papers in fields such as terrorism, radicalization, extremism, cultural studies on war narratives, and so forth.

Chris Jagger Following a career with the Metropolitan Police, National Criminal Intelligence Service, United Nations, NATO and the Serious Organised Crime Agency, Chris formed his own company called 2creatEffects. He now spends his time working as a writer, consultant, researcher, lecturer at Universidad Rey Juan Carlos, and workshop facilitator. He has a passion for helping build Dynamic habits of mind that allow individuals and teams to challenge the status quo and achieve innovation. In 2017 he published *Escorting the Monarch—We Lead Others Follow*, a history of a specialist mobile security police team.

Roger Mason is Vice President and Co-founder of LECMgt, based in Porter Ranch, California, USA. He is a consultant specializing in crisis management and wargame and simulation design. He is a published author and serves as a visiting instructor at the Inter-University Master's program in Intelligence Analysis in Spain. He has designed wargames and simulations for government, business, and national defense clients. (Author's Note: I wish to thank Joseph Miranda for his assistance and advice in the development of this game. Eric Harvey assisted with the play testing and graphic organization of the game. Their help and expertise were invaluable.)

Florina Cristiana Matei is a Lecturer at the Center for Civil-Military Relations (CCMR) of the United States Naval Postgraduate School. She researches, publishes, and teaches on a wide range of issues concerning civil-military relations, democratization, security sector reform (SSR), intelligence, countering/combating terrorism, organized crime, and street gangs. She earned a PhD from the Department of War Studies of King's College (University of London); an MA in International Security Affairs from NPS; and a BS in physics (Nuclear Interactions and Elementary Particles) from the University of Bucharest. She co-edited (with Thomas Bruneau) *The Routledge Handbook of Civil-Military Relations* (2012).

Daniel Pascheles is Chief Executive Officer and Partner of Molekule Consulting since 2017, a global CI and strategy consulting company in the healthcare space. Over the last 30 years he has built and led world-class global competitive intelligence and strategy groups for companies such as Merck & Co./MSD. As manager of large CI teams, he oversaw and led during his successful career in the biopharmaceutical industry hundreds of primary CI projects, competitive simulations, and strategic planning sessions. He studied Pharmacy at the Swiss Federal Institute of Technology (ETH) in Zurich, Switzerland, and received a PhD in Pharmaceutical Technology from the same university.

Randolph H. Pherson is CEO of Globalytica, LLC, and President of Pherson Associates, LLC. He teaches advanced analytic techniques and critical thinking skills to government and private sector analysts across the globe and has authored or co-authored ten books, including *Structured Analytic Techniques for Intelligence Analysis* and *Critical Thinking for Strategic Intelligence*. Mr. Pherson was a career CIA intelligence analyst and manager, last serving as National Intelligence Officer for Latin America. He is a recipient of the Distinguished Intelligence Medal and the Distinguished Career Intelligence Medal. He received his AB from Dartmouth College and MA in International Relations from Yale University.

Alfred Reszka, PhD, is Executive Director and Head of Strategic Business Intelligence at Merck & Co., Inc. He leads a team that collaborates with clients from research and development to marketing and manufacturing across a variety of business functions requiring scientific, medical, and business intelligence. Roles and responsibilities include strategic consulting, benchmarking, and strategy development. Areas of focus include corporate strategy, product surveillance, outcomes research, pricing and value, global and emerging markets, licensing, business development, and M&A.

Julian Richards is a Professor of Politics at the University of Buckingham and Co-director of the Centre for Security and Intelligence Studies (BUCSIS). Prior to academic life, he spent 17 years working for the British government at Government Communications Headquarters (GCHQ). He has written extensively on intelligence analysis techniques, international security policy, and counter terrorism.

After a 30-year career as a police officer, predominantly in the national security arena, **Shaun Romeril** has an extraordinary blend of operational leadership, intelligence development, and planning expertise. Previously in the army, he was operationally deployed in Northern Ireland and with the UN. Most of his police career involved counter terrorist (CT) Intelligence operations at New Scotland Yard, leading covert units in close liaison with the intelligence agencies. Shaun was also the program manager for the National Police CT Network Olympic plan and responsible for the its design and delivery during the highly successful London Olympic and Paralympic Games.

Sheila R. Ronis is President of The University Group, Inc., a management consulting firm and think tank specializing in strategic management, visioning, leadership, national security, and public policy. She is also an Adjunct Professor of Management at Walsh College, where she retired as Distinguished Professor of Management and Director of the Center for Complex and Strategic Decisions. In addition, she is an Associate with Argonne National Laboratory University of Chicago. Her BS is in Physics, Mathematics, and Education. Her MA and PhD are from the Ohio State University in Large Complex Social System Behavior. She and her colleague, Professor Leon S. Fuerth, support the federal government and global foresight communities.

Karen Saunders is Managing Director at Globalytica, LLC, where she also teaches analytic tradecraft and researches illicit trade networks, transnational crime, corruption, and terrorism. Her specializations include post-Soviet organized crime, illicit financial and commodity flows, threat finance, Central Asian terrorism, and human trafficking. She has taught courses on intelligence analysis at Marymount University and the University of South Florida, and international relations at American University in Washington, DC. She received a dual BA in International Relations and Russian Language from Tufts University, an MA in International Development from American University, and has completed PhD coursework at American University.

Kristan J. Wheaton is a Professor of Intelligence Studies at Mercyhurst College in Erie, Pennsylvania. His research interests include the use of games in teaching intelligence analysis and intelligence support to entrepreneurs. His games are currently used by both the Federal Bureau of Investigation and the

National Geospatial-Intelligence Agency to teach analysts how to recognize and overcome cognitive biases. He is a retired foreign area officer with the US Army. He is also the author of *The Warning Solution: Intelligent Analysis in the Age of Information Overload* and *How to Get a Job in Intelligence* and co-author of *Structured Analysis of Competing Hypotheses: Theory and Application* and *Wikis in Intelligence Analysis.* He holds a JD from the University of South Carolina, an MA (Russian and East European Studies) from Florida State University, and a BBA (Accounting) from the University of Notre Dame. He is the recipient of the CIA Seal Medallion and the State Department's Superior Honor Award and is a member of the South Carolina Bar.